Three Fires Unity

Three Fires Unity

The Anishnaabeg of the Lake Huron Borderlands

PHIL BELLFY

UNIVERSITY OF NEBRASKA PRESS

LINCOLN

Portions of this manuscript originally appeared in
*Lines Drawn upon the Water: First Nations and the
Great Lakes Borders and Borderlands*, edited by Karl S.
Hele (Waterloo, Ontario: Wilfred Laurier University
Press, 2008), 21–42.

Library of Congress Cataloging-in-Publication Data
Bellfy, Phil.
Three Fires unity: the Anishnaabeg of the Lake
Huron borderlands / Phil Bellfy.
p. cm.
"Winner of the 2010 North American Indian Prose
Award."
"Portions of this manuscript originally appeared
in Lines drawn upon the water: First Nations and
the Great Lakes borders and borderlands, edited by
Karl S. Hele (Waterloo, Ontario: Wilfred Laurier
University Press, 2008)"—T.p. verso.
Includes bibliographical references and index.
ISBN 978-0-8032-1348-7 (cloth: alk. paper)
ISBN 978-1-4962-1661-8 (paper: alk. paper)
1. Ojibwa Indians—Huron, Lake, Region (Mich. and
Ont.)—History. 2. Ottawa Indians—Huron, Lake,
Region (Mich. and Ont.)—History. 3. Potawatomi
Indians—Huron, Lake, Region (Mich. and Ont.)—
History. 4. Ojibwa Indians—Huron, Lake, Region
(Mich. and Ont.)—Social conditions. 5. Ottawa
Indians—Huron, Lake, Region (Mich. and Ont.)—
Social conditions. 6. Potawatomi Indians—Huron,
Lake, Region (Mich. and Ont.)—Social conditions.
7. Huron, Lake, Region (Mich. and Ont.)—History.
8. Huron, Lake, Region (Mich. and Ont.)—Ethnic
relations. I. Title.
E99.C6B426 2011
977.004'97333—dc22
2010046306

Set in Dante MT.

To the memory of Apiish Kaakoke, White Raven,
my Seventh Father

Contents

Illustrations

Preface

From the swirling waters of the rapids at Sault Ste. Marie to the St. Clair River delta that gives rise to Walpole Island, the Lake Huron borderlands are a treasure trove of history and culture. Native people have lived in this area since the glacial waters subsided and the Great Lakes took on their present configuration—about twenty-five hundred years ago. The rich fisheries and abundant wildlife induced them to stay in the region after having migrated west from their ancient homeland on the Great Salt Sea in the land of the rising sun far to the east—the land of Gitchee Gumee of Longfellow's *Hiawatha* fame.

The people of this area, collectively known as the "Anishnaabeg," are made up of the Ojibway (or Chippewa), Ottawa (or Odawa), and Potawatomi tribes. They have thrived for millennia in the rich land of the Lake Huron borderlands, but when the Europeans (more specifically the French and British) arrived in the early seventeenth century looking for land and resources, the Native peoples were forced to adapt to an era of war and conflict as they tried to defend their homeland against the invaders. A way of life, little changed for generations, was now altered forever in a radically short span of time. Regional disputes became more intense, often fueled by European conflicts and their cruel methods of war. Conflict over the fur trade and access to trapping territories exacerbated ancient rivalries, and warriors often found themselves hundreds of miles from home fighting enemies they barely knew, for reasons they may never have fully understood.

Yet throughout these European proxy wars, the Native people of the area fought valiantly to preserve control and occupancy of their homelands. It is odd, then, that even today the more dominant society of North America calls the actions of the Native warrior Pontiac and his tribal allies "Pontiac's Rebellion"; Native people themselves are more inclined to view him as one of the leaders who fought vigorously to defend his homeland against European invasion.

After the Europeans settled their differences with the various tribes under the Treaty of Ghent in 1814, the Native people of the area, once seen as a military threat, were now relegated to the role of abandoned "allies" and left to fend for themselves as they dealt with the new "American" government or the Canadian authorities, divided by a new line drawn through the heart of their homeland.

The new threats the Native peoples faced were no longer military ones as the days of Tecumseh and Pontiac had long been over. Instead the new threats were legal and diplomatic ones; guns and arrows gave way to pen and paper. But throughout this treaty-making period, one thing remained steadfast: the quiet determination of the Lake Huron borderlands Native people to continue to live in their home territory, enjoying the fruits of the land where the Creator had put them and where the bones of their ancestors were buried.

The overwhelming importance of such a goal meant that when the time came to negotiate treaties with the Europeans, Native people felt compelled to send their most capable negotiators, regardless of who lived on the American or Canadian side of the border. The result of this treaty-making process with the British and the Americans is an astonishing number of "cross-border" treaty-signers, individuals who signed treaties on behalf of all the borderlands Native people. This book tells the story of how the people of the upper Great Lakes, and the individuals who ably represented them at various treaty councils, made the best deals possible for their nation under very difficult circumstances. It begins with an exploration of the Lake Huron borderlands area, explaining its geological development and how the Native peoples came to settle there; describes the various Native groups who came to live in the area prior to European contact; and briefly traces the events of the contact years, detailing the numerous conflicts, wars, and eventual treaties that occurred.

This voyage of discovery ends with a look at the contemporary state of indigenous life in the Lake Huron borderlands and how the Native peoples have endured as a nation — a nation originally forged in the salt air of an ancient sea, tempered in the cool waters of the upper Great Lakes, and matured in the political fires of North American nation-building.

Acknowledgments

As do many academic books, this one started out as my dissertation, but the research and my involvement with the project have stretched out over twenty years. Throughout that time this project has taken a few turns and has been, of course, aided by many. First, my committee deserves special mention: George Cornell, Jim McClintock, and Victor Howard. Helen Tanner and Richard White also gave me sage advice. Margaret Cunniffe helped greatly through her editing skills over these many years. Margaret Pearce created the maps for this volume. I especially need to say *miigwetch* (thank you) to the People of the Three Fires, especially the Ogemaag of the area under study: Dave White, Dean Jacobs, Dean Sayers, Lyle Sayers, Aaron Payment, Joe McCoy, Jeff Parker, and Bucko Teeple. Of course, as this book has been a work in progress for the past two decades, numerous others have helped make it what it is today. I send all of them a heartfelt *chi-miigwetch* as well.

Introduction

The area was a significant part of an empire that embraced most of the known world, transformed from a land of warring, primitive, and almost entirely illiterate tribes into a united realm under an administration based on the rule of law. . . .

The early policy of employing friendly chieftains as client "kings" was never intended to be more than a temporary expedient. The process of absorbing the tribes into the normal framework of the provincial administration greatly encouraged the adoption of "civilized" ways. . . .

Based on considerations of manpower and expense, it was decided to hold only the part that was reasonably easy to control and that was profitable. . . .

Considerable trouble had occurred in the region before, but it paled into insignificance before the tremendous destruction wrought by a *barbaric conspiratio* when, in unnatural alliance, the tribes attacked simultaneously. The garrison fell, but it was not in fair fight.

— PETER SALWAY, from *The Frontier People of Roman Britain*

To anyone familiar with European imperialism since 1492, the above passage could be referring to virtually any part of the world except Europe. In point of fact, the author, Peter Salway, is describing the Roman invasions of Britain from 43 AD until the early fifth century when they finally left the island, at which point it fell into what Salway calls the "province of the Dark Age historian." The particular area Salway refers to was the borderland region between that era's British and Scottish peoples.

This book will attempt to shed some light on another, albeit more modern, "borderland" —that of the Lake Huron area of the upper Great Lakes region that spreads across both the United States and Canada. During this process, I hope to illuminate some of the "Dark-Age" qualities that characterize so much of the written history of the indigenous people from this area, in order to show how their lives were impacted by European contact and how the imposition of imperial hegemony was maintained over their homelands. More specifically, I will be examining the cultural, social, and political aspects of the Anishnaabeg who have lived in, and continue to live in, these Lake Huron borderlands in order to determine how the imposition of the Canada–U.S. international border running through their homeland affected them and continues to do so today.

In this book, I explore the treaties, wars, and policies of the relevant political entities, among other social forces that brought about this division. While division is an obvious theme, I also examine the strong links that have served to maintain unity among the Anishnaabeg over a period of nearly four hundred years of European contact. Common language and culture clearly promoted ties between these groups, but I also probe the unity achieved through their common political struggles. These struggles demonstrate, too, that the sovereignty of the Anishnaabeg has not only been maintained, from their own viewpoint, but has been recognized as well by the British and Americans.

My study is essentially chronological, beginning with an examination of the geologic forces that formed the distinct natural features of the Lake Huron borderlands. This environment contained a multitude of rich and bountiful natural resources that compelled the migrating Anishnaabeg to settle in the area. Not surprisingly, these same resources (especially fur) provided the impetus for European exploitation of the region as well.

Organization of Chapters
Chapter 1 explores the Lake Huron borderlands area and its geological development, describes the Anishnaabeg prior to contact with Europeans, and presents the orthography underlying

the various names that have come to be associated with these people. Some consideration is given to the Eurocentrism behind the "common" tribal designations and the confusion engendered by these designations.

Chapter 2 presents the beginnings of European contact circa 1600 when the French first visited the area seeking mineral wealth and decided to remain in order to exploit the area's enormous fur resources. The French era, which lasted until the first Treaty of Paris in 1763, represents the one postcontact period during which the Anishnaabeg enjoyed political autonomy and sovereignty over their Great Lakes homelands. The chapter also chronicles the successful defense of these homelands in the face of Iroquois and British hostilities and concludes with a discussion of the Anishnaabeg's defense of the Lake Huron borderlands under the Ottawa chief, Pontiac. (While Pontiac's "Conspiracy" has been misnamed and his "defeat" greatly exaggerated, this military engagement did signal the end of the French influence in the region and the ascendancy of the British.)

Chapter 3 explores the short-but-intense period of British hegemony over the whole of the Lake Huron borderlands. While the second Treaty of Paris in 1783 formally ended the American Revolutionary War, I have chosen to end chapter 3 with the signing of the 1795 Treaty of Greenville, which is the first major treaty between the Anishnaabeg and the new United States government.

Chapter 4 examines the period during which the Anishnaabeg, the British, and the Americans waged a tripartite struggle for control of the Lake Huron borderlands, as well as the important role that the issuance of "presents" played during this crucial period.

Chapter 5 discusses the period of the most profound changes to the Anishnaabeg way of life, engendered in large part by the loss of much of their traditional homeland to the governments of Canada and the United States. The chapter begins with a discussion of these land-cession treaties. Concomitant with the cession of land was the threat of removal. In the United States, removal meant forced resettlement in "Indian Territory" west of the Mississippi River; in Canada the Anishnaabeg were encouraged to emigrate to a "Canadian Oklahoma" on Manitoulin Island.[1] The pressures to emigrate, and Anishnaabeg initiatives in the face of these removal threats, are explored.

Chapter 5 also presents an analysis of over fifteen hundred names of treaty-signers, in addition to other names found in government documents of the period. The analysis uncovers a surprising number of individuals, who, as representatives of the Anishnaabeg, signed treaties with both the United States and Canadian governments. Other cross-border links between "American" and "Canadian" Anishnaabeg are presented as well. The variety and extent of these connections helped these indigenous peoples to maintain a degree of autonomy and sovereignty despite the numerous threats posed by Europeans coming in contact with them for the first time in their history.

Chapter 6, the final chapter, begins with a discussion of resource exploitation in the Lake Huron borderlands and how this exploitation changed — and continues to change — the Anishnaabeg way of life. The chapter concludes with an examination of how the Anishnaabeg have continued the struggle to maintain their identity, sovereignty, and homelands throughout the tumult of the twentieth century and in the face of two separate sets of federal "Indian" policies. Jay's Treaty and other cross-border Native issues are reexamined within this context as well.

Clarifying an Understanding of the Terminology Used

The clarification of terms used in this study is crucial to an understanding of the Anishnaabeg and the Lake Huron borderlands. Such terminology as "frontier," "boundary" (or "border"), and "borderlands" have multiple connotations and meanings in this particular context and, in the early years of European residency in the area, even became controversial for their lack of definition (this will be discussed in more detail later).

The word "frontier" can be defined in several ways: (1) a *commercial frontier*, represented by the fur trader, trapper, and hunter; (2) a *military frontier*, represented by a line of army posts; (3) a *cession frontier*, marked by the limit of land acquired from the indigenous population; (4) a *public land frontier*, marked by the limit of lands surveyed and opened for sale; and (5) a *population density frontier*, determined by the density of the European-American population.[2] While the first four terms are relevant here since they had the most profound effect on the indigenous populations of the Great Lakes area, a fifth term, the "population density frontier," needs closer scrutiny as it is probably the most widely held definition. This was the term used, and championed, by the U.S. Census Bureau when it declared the "frontier closed" in 1890.

In 1893 Frederick Jackson Turner expanded upon the term "frontier" when he delivered his now-famous lecture in Chicago, held simultaneously with the Columbian Exposition honoring the four-hundredth anniversary of Columbus's "discovery." In that address, later published and entitled *The Significance of the Frontier in American History*, Turner claimed that the term "frontier" "is an elastic one, and for [his] purposes does not need sharp definition."[3] The ambiguity of his "definition" has led to endless controversy over the concept of a "frontier" and its role in American history and has resulted in sharp criticism of Turner and his entire thesis.

Patricia Limerick, for example, in her essay, "The Adventures of the Frontier in the Twentieth Century," contends that the concept of the frontier, especially in the Turnerian sense, is indefensible. The "F-word," she argues, has been justly "pummeled for its ethnocentrism and vagueness," and she sets out five arguments challenging its validity. The first one she presents is the concept of the frontier, defined and defended reflexively by a largely white, English-speaking class of historians. The second argument purports to run geographically from east to west, ignoring the movements of people in a myriad of other directions, while the third contends that, despite Turner and the judgment of census officials in 1890, it is virtually impossible to define the beginning or end of a frontier (assuming the term is definable in the first place). The fourth argument sets forth the idea that the underlying conception of a frontier tends to ignore the elements of conquest. Finally, the fifth argument contends that the frontier thesis obstructs any critical understanding of the inevitable clash of cultures inherent in any definition adopted by a researcher.[4]

Turner's essay is subject to criticism on all five of these points: although reluctant to define the term at all, Turner nevertheless calls it "the meeting point between savagery and civilization,"[5] and adds, "The most significant thing about the American Frontier is that it lies at the hither edge of free land."[6] The crucial concepts of "savagery" and "civilization" and their relationships to the concept of "free land" are also left undefined. In light of these criticisms, the Turnerian thesis is probably most valuable to the researcher as a guide for what *not* to do in conducting border research. Therefore, this study of the Lake Huron "frontier" is, in part, a reaction to and rebuttal of Turner's ideas.

While Turner's "non"-definition of frontier is instructive in a negative sense, other researchers and essayists do provide more positive insights into the border and frontier phenomenon. In low-population-density definitions of the frontier, Alastair Lamb, for example, explains that a frontier evolves into a border when there are no more "turbulent tribes" to subdue just beyond the existing frontier line, and when a natural physical barrier halts their advance.[7] Kristof expands Lamb's definition by demonstrating that "frontiers" may give way to "boundaries" when states decide that it is important not only to keep the enemy out (as

Lamb would have it) but "because one's own citizens and re-sources have to be kept in."[8]

The land adjacent to a frontier/borderline, too, becomes zones of friction where "broad scenes of intense interactions" are often played out. These types of "borderlands" "have always been peripheral to the centers of economic, cultural, and military power and authority"[9] and often become areas where the effectiveness of central control is tested.[10] (That theory was put to a test January 1, 1994, when the indigenous people of Chiapas strongly challenged the Mexican central government's attempt to marginalize and threaten them through the imposition of the NAFTA regime). The United States, too, has never been immune to borderland conflicts; an analysis of the "frontier wars" points to classic "borderland" conflicts between indigenous people and the central colonial authority. Today, smuggling that takes place across both the northern and southern U.S. borders, as well as "illegal" immigration, widespread in the southwest, less so along the U.S.–Canada border, are instances of continuing borderland conflicts that challenge the effectiveness of central control.

In further tests of central control, borderland areas have often become places of refuge for indigenous people seeking to thwart governmental attempts to subjugate them. From colonial times until the present, the U.S.–Canada border has been rife with such examples: white "Indian" captives taken to Canada from New England,[11] the flight of the Nez Perce under Chief Joseph,[12] and the escape of Sitting Bull as well as Leonard Peltier to Canada, to mention just a few. One of the best examples of borderland use as a refuge, however, is that of the Apache under Geronimo, who fled to the U.S.–Mexico border to seek safety from pursuing American troops. It should also be pointed out that Mexican rebels used to seek refuge on the U.S. side of the border,[13] as did the Canadian Métis of Manitoba and Saskatchewan after their late nineteenth-century resistance to Canadian central authority.[14]

The above discussion should not be interpreted to imply that political conflict in the borderlands has always been instigated by and restricted to those who would challenge the central government's purposes. In his discussion of the British–Scottish borderlands, Anthony Goodman points out that the efforts to keep Northern England out of the hands of the "barbarians" to the north helped mold the emerging British nation-state through the common defense of the frontier and transformed British generals into politicians. This same process was obviously employed in the United States as well: generals Washington, Harrison, Jackson, Grant, and Eisenhower all rode victorious military parades to the White House. In the case of General George Custer, however, the failure to transform military exploit into political power constitutes, beyond a doubt, the most egregious counterexample.

"Borderland" Theory

While acknowledging its many possible definitions, John House offers an excellent and thorough interpretation of the term "borderland" as "a field of forces, changeable through time, within which there is economic, social, cultural, and political interaction between contrasting states, and even differing civilizations."[15] Strangely, this borderland interpretation has been applied to the U.S.–Mexico border region, but less so to the U.S.–Canada border, which encompasses the Lake Huron borderlands area.[16] McKinsey and Konrad argue that while the U.S.–Canada border may not constitute a single, coherent borderland region, it could be viewed as divided into several distinct "regional borderlands cultures" or six cultural landscape types relevant to a U.S.–Canada borderland paradigm.[17] Of these, two — the "empty areas" and the "divided cultural enclave" — merit some discussion, as they relate more pertinently to the present study.

McKinsey and Konrad describe the "empty areas" cultural landscape as "buffer zones with few inhabitants and little cultural interaction. An empty area has no focus or core on either side. The Yukon–Alaska border region, for example, [with its] low population density and historical interaction and cultural continuity in Native settlement, is the only borderland having this characteristic."[18] In the present study of the Lake Huron borderlands, these very qualities—obviously dismissed by others as insignificant—are of central importance.

The second borderlands cultural type is the "divided cultural enclave," a culturally homogeneous region split in two, separating Canada and the United States. McKinsey and Konrad suggest that examples of it "are rare because the boundary is seldom imposed in a well-established cultural region."[19] Yet the establishment of virtually the entire U.S.–Canada border, from the region of the Wabenaki Confederacy in the Northeast[20] to the Blackfoot regions of the Great Plains,[21] as well as the Native-occupied "empty areas" of the Alaska–Yukon border, cut through existing homogeneous Native cultural areas. Such "artificial" border constructions have given rise to any number of jurisdictional problems and controversies. Perhaps the most extreme example of this (using language that would be rejected by its sovereignty-minded residents) is the Mohawk reserve of Akwesasne, which is "split" by the U.S.–Canada border, occupying territory that is part of the state of New York and the provinces of Ontario and Quebec.

For reasons distinct from those cited above, other researchers also tend to ignore Native peoples in the borderlands because of the problems inherent in engaging in such a discussion. Principal among these is the use of biased language: a term such as "international region," for instance, presupposes a rejection of any claims to sovereignty that might be held by that region's Native people. As well as maintaining a sensitivity to the Native perspective of a region's political geography, researchers must also be sensitive to the imposition of other Eurocentric research paradigms, such as concentrating on the region's history since white contact, or restricting the Native to the role of reactor to white initiative. Harold McGee brings up another salient point for researchers to be mindful of: the complexity of Native communities. A "reserve community in North America," he claims, "has got to be one of the most complex social structures in the world. The [researcher] has to ferret out the influences of a number of competing Christian churches, various levels of foreign governments, the imposition of international states that portions of the community do not recognize, various Native associations . . . factionalism within each of these organizations . . . and on and on it goes."[22]

Despite these and other difficulties, many aspects of the Native experience along the U.S.–Canada border support a borderlands designation not unlike that utilized along the U.S.–Mexico border. Both the United States and Canada have similar federal Indian policies and Native histories that are quite distinct from the experiences — both historical and contemporary — of "Mexican" indigenous populations. Further, both the U.S. and Canadian Native people have treaties with their federal governments and discrete land bases that impart a degree of political sovereignty in their relationship to the U.S. and Canadian federal governments. These "quasi-national" qualities create within these Native groups a measure of homogeneity and "separateness" that can easily be viewed through a "borderlands" lens.

Defining the Lake Huron Borderlands Area
While this study recognizes the complexities delineated by McGee and the shortcomings of the McKinsey-Konrad borderlands culture area descriptions, it nevertheless explores the concept of the "divided cultural enclave," while specifically rejecting the imposition of the term "empty area" on Native-occupied borderlands of the "international" Lake Huron border region

of the upper Great Lakes. While it is true that Native density in any one region is invariably quite low, the homogeneity of the borderland region's population and its distinctiveness, relative to other adjoining areas, can justify designating an area as a "borderland."[23]

An analysis of current census data for both Michigan and Ontario shows that the concentration of Native people in areas bordering Lake Huron continue to reflect earlier patterns of occupancy. While the Native population of the entire state of Michigan is only .6 percent of the total population, the percentage of Native population in the thirteen counties bordering Lake Huron is 1.56 percent; the percentage of Natives in the fourteen counties *adjacent* to counties that border Lake Huron is essentially the same as the whole state (.58 percent or .0058). Therefore, the Michigan counties that border Lake Huron (from Chippewa County in the north to St. Clair County at the southern terminus of Lake Huron) contain an aggregate Native population that is nearly three times higher than both the adjacent counties and the state as a whole.

Breaking the data down geographically, the two northernmost counties, Chippewa and Mackinac, have Native populations of 11.0 percent and 15.8 percent, respectively, which represents a density of almost two to three times that of the neighboring counties (which themselves contain Native populations significantly higher than the rest of Michigan). Sanilac and St. Clair counties, at the southern end, show Native populations slightly below the state average yet claim a Native population 1.25 and 1.35 times that of their neighboring inland counties. Comparing the remaining eight counties in the central portion of the area to their adjacent inland counties reveals that Presque Isle and Alpena have a lower Native population, and Cheboygan and Iosco have Native population percentages virtually identical to their neighboring inland counties. The remaining four counties have Native proportions ranging from 1.2 times (Alcona County) to

1.5 times their neighbors (Arenac and Tuscola Counties). (Situated at the tip of the "thumb" of Michigan's lower peninsula, Huron County lies adjacent only to counties that also border Lake Huron and was thus excluded from this analysis.) There are eight federally recognized reservation areas within the thirteen counties that border Lake Huron; however, all but one are located in the Upper Peninsula. In Chippewa County, the Sault Ste. Marie Tribe of Chippewa Indians (Sault Tribe) maintains one reservation area within the city limits of Sault Ste. Marie and two smaller areas on nearby Sugar Island. Also in Chippewa County, the Bay Mills Indian Community has a reservation on Whitefish Bay just west of the Great Lakes area, and it, too, holds a small reservation on Sugar Island. The Sault Tribe also maintains two reservations in the eastern end of Mackinac County, one in St. Ignace Township and one in Clark Township. The only reservation area located in the lower peninsula counties adjacent to Lake Huron is in Arenac County's Standish Township and is maintained by the Saginaw Chippewa tribe, headquartered outside of the area in Isabella County.

Native population comparisons between American and Canadian portions of the Lake Huron borderlands area are difficult to make. Ontario counties, when compared to their Michigan counterparts, cover a much greater geographic area. (In northernmost Ontario, comparable political units are called "districts" and cover even greater areas than the counties of southern Ontario.) To further complicate data comparisons, the Canadian census does not ask questions that allow the respondent to claim Native heritage; in many cases that information must be inferred. Furthermore, in a sovereignty-building action, many Native communities in Canada refuse to participate in the federal census; consequently, in order to show the concentration of Native people in the Canadian portion of the Lake Huron borderlands, an approach different from the population analysis employed for Michigan counties is required.

Map 1. Contemporary Native Communities (United States and Canada)

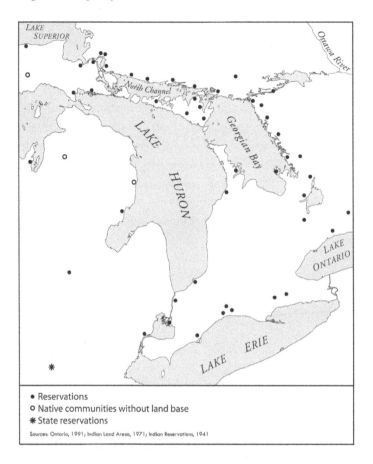

LAKE
SUPERIOR

Ottawa River

North Channel

LAKE
HURON

Georgian Bay

LAKE
ONTARIO

LAKE ERIE

*

• Reservations
○ Native communities without land base
✳ State reservations

Sources: Ontario, 1991; Indian Land Areas, 1971; Indian Reservations, 1941

    U.S. federal Indian policy in the early 1800s was concerned
with assembling the Native people from a region and concentrating them on a few reservations, typically west of the Mississippi River. During this same period, the Canadian government also sought to congregate Native people on reservations
(called "reserves" in Canada), but rather than moving them to
areas far from European settlements, as the Americans had, they
created several small reserves within the lands where the Native

people lived. As a consequence there are 116 reserves scattered throughout Ontario, the only Canadian province adjacent to Lake Huron.

Map 1, which situates the area's Native communities, shows that almost all of the reserves in Ontario counties bordering Lake Huron are islands or shoreline communities, demonstrating that the area's Native people are concentrated in the Lake Huron shoreline regions. Therefore, a borderlands approach to the study of this area's Native population appears justified in that they were — and are — a homogeneous, distinct, and concentrated population living in a region that straddles a border (one of the defining characteristics of a borderland).

Chapter 1 presents a more thorough discussion of these people and how they came to live in this area, but first it is important to establish an understanding of the Lake Huron borderland area's geological development and its very early inhabitants, because it helps clarify the reasons why Native people settled in the area in the first place, and why they were so reluctant to leave it.

The Geological Development of the Lake Huron Borderlands
The formation of the Great Lakes began during the Pleistocene era, about a million years ago. The repetitive action of receding and advancing glaciers, inaugurated by an ice age, carved out the lakes and established the waterways that now comprise the great inland seas of North America. However, the Great Lakes in their present configuration are of a more recent geologic formation (perhaps about two thousand years ago), which were caused by melting glaciers and water drainage patterns.

The northernmost point of Lake Huron, the rapids of the St. Mary's River, was formed when the earth was forced up at this point both by the weight of the receding glacier and by subsurface geologic forces that pushed igneous rock upward. The rise of the land was as much as four hundred feet in some places during the early postglacial era (3000 to 1500 BC) and one hundred

Map 2. The Lake Huron Borderlands Area

feet in other places during the period 1500 to 500 BC.[24] Behind the resulting quarter-mile-wide rock dam is the largest body of fresh water in North America: Lake Superior.

In their original state, the rapids at the Sault were undoubtedly magnificent, rivaling those of Niagara for their natural beauty. If we consider the width of the two falls in relation to their output, the falls at St. Mary's compared favorably with those at Niagara. The width of the rapids at the Sault is about 1,300 feet; the combined widths of the Horseshoe and American Falls at Niagara total about 3,600 feet. Over this escarpment Niagara sends a total of 205,000 cubic feet of water every second, which then falls

Map 3. The Northern Water Route to the St. Lawrence River

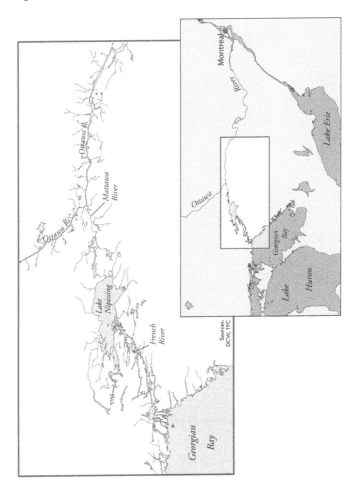

a distance of 180 feet to the level of Lake Ontario. Seventy-four thousand cubic feet of water per second flow over the rapids at Sault Ste. Marie, falling only 20 feet. Yet if we divide the widths of the two sites by their output (Niagara today and the Sault before diversion), we find that both sites would discharge about 55 or 56 cubic feet of water per second per foot of width. From this perspective, the two sites present virtually identical water flows.[25] Today, of course, the rapids at Sault Ste. Marie—creating what was once the greatest freshwater fishery in North America—have been greatly diminished, while the Niagara flow has only been minimally diverted.

At the other end of the Lake Huron borderland is Walpole Island, which presents an equally recent geologic history. The principal drainage pattern for Lake Huron during the formative stages of the Great Lakes was through a northerly route along the present French River–Ottawa River corridor (as seen in map 3). At that time the upper Great Lakes drained through the northern route, sending only a little bit of water south and draining into what is now Lake Erie. But when the glaciers at last receded and lake waters began to shrink, reaching nearly their present levels, the northern water route through the French and Ottawa rivers was cut off, so that the only outlet for the waters from lakes Superior, Michigan, and Huron was to the south through the St. Clair River, into Lake St. Clair, through the Detroit river, then on to lakes Erie and Ontario, and finally out to the Atlantic. The resulting water flow brought with it the soils that formed the rich and fertile estuaries and islands at the mouth of the St. Clair River—including Walpole Island, which is actually several islands—that constitute the southern terminus of Lake Huron. Interestingly, long after the cessation of glacial activity, early Native migrants and European explorers followed the geologically older northern water route to the Lake Huron area (fur-traders used the route as well).

The geologic action that formed the Great Lakes, and the resulting cutting action of this redirected flowing water, also worked to create another major geologic feature of the area: the island chain that stretches across the northern channel of Lake Huron from Manitoulin Island in the east, up the St. Mary's River, and to Sugar Island near Sault Ste. Marie. The major islands in this chain of hundreds of islands are (from east to west): Mani-

Map 4. Upper Lake Huron and St. Mary's River Islands

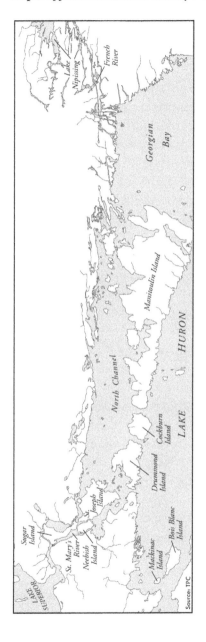

Source: TPC

toulin, Cockburn, Drummond, St. Joseph, Neebish, and Sugar (see map 4). Many of these islands, as well as Mackinac Island, which lies in the strait between lakes Michigan and Huron, will be discussed in detail as this study unfolds.

The First Native Inhabitants of the Lake Huron Borderlands Area

The first evidence of human occupation in the Lake Huron borderland area has been found at the Sheguindah site located in the northeast section of Manitoulin Island. The evidence there suggests that human occupation occurred sometime between 7000 and 6000 BC. Further evidence suggests that the north and south shores of what eventually became Whitefish Bay, just west of the Sault rapids, supported human activities during this same period.[26]

The very early occupants (from 7000 to 3000 BC), are placed in the Paleo or Early-Archaic-Indian category, while anthropologists have assigned later occupants (from 4000 to 1500 BC) to the "Old Copper" cultural mosaic.[27] Evidence shows that Old Copper occupants once resided on the northeast shore of Lake Superior in the Batchewana Bay area, about fifty miles north of Sault Ste. Marie, but abandoned the area about 1500 BC as they apparently followed the receding glaciers northward.[28] This abandonment of the area by the Old Copper people may explain why, at the time of European contact, the Native people of the area had no copper-working skills and possessed no copper tools. (Old Copper mining activity in the Keewenaw Peninsula in western Lake Superior continued until as late as one thousand years ago, but those mines were abandoned by the ancient miners who left the area as well, bequeathing no knowledge of copper-working to the area's subsequent inhabitants.)[29]

If the Old Copper people abandoned the Lake Huron borderland sometime during the period of about 1500 BC to 1000 AD, as the archeological evidence suggests, from where did the subsequent Native people of the region migrate, and how did they come to reside in the Lake Huron borderlands region? According to Anishnaabeg oral tradition, they had once lived on the Atlantic shore and then migrated westward to an area west of Lake Superior, where they came to reside more or less permanently. Modern accounts of the migration do not refute the oral tradition. Roland Dixon claims that in pre-Columbian times the Ojibway and the Micmac lived in close proximity near the eastern seaboard while several tribes moved north and east into the territory left vacant by the disappearance of the "Red Paint People." Elements of the Anishnaabeg were found to have settled along this route.[30]

George Quimby, in his article "The Archeology of the Upper Great Lakes Area," found that the archeological evidence does not refute an Anishnaabeg migration. He believed that "at the beginning of the historic period [i.e., the contact period] the Ottawa, Huron, and Chippewa were recent arrivals in the area. . . . The Potawatomi moved westward just prior to the historic period [and are] the best suspects as a Native population."[31] While his time estimates are perhaps too conservative, Quimby's speculation does support the westward migration of the Anishnaabeg—at the very least, nothing he says refutes Anishnaabeg oral tradition.

The pattern of settlement, as determined by archeologists, also supports Anishnaabeg migration. Comparison of the archeological sites for the period before 1400 AD with those carbon dated to the period after 1400 AD (until contact) shows areas of early habitation along the stated migration route to Sault Ste. Marie, which then spread into the Straits of Mackinac and northwest lower Michigan; the later sites are especially prevalent.[32]

Further evidence of migration exists in the form of several Anishnaabeg "migration scrolls," at least one of which has been carbon dated to the precontact era.[33] Figure 1 (p. xxxvi) depicts a record of Anishnaabeg migration as recorded by Sikassige, an

Ojibway elder. Sikassige explains that the migration began at the eastern saltwater lake, claimed as the original home of the Anishnaabeg. As depicted traditionally, the people are led westward by an animal (an otter, in Sikassige's account),[34] stopping when it stops, moving when it moves.[35] Selwyn Dewdney, who has uncovered several other Anishnaabeg migration scrolls, points out that the scrolls record not only the migration but also Midé beliefs and rituals.[36] His informants report that "God's messenger" gave the Midé religion to the Anishnaabeg on the Atlantic coast as a way of guiding them west, while saving the people from the ravages of disease rampant at that time.

While perhaps disagreeing on certain points and admitting that the various scrolls are not identical in their representations or interpretations, elders charged with interpreting the scrolls seem to agree on several points: that the origins of the Anishnaabeg are on a saltwater shore; that the Midé religion and the migration westward were divinely and simultaneously directed; that the religion and migration were both responses to some suffering experienced by the Anishnaabeg; and that the rapids at Sault Ste. Marie were an important point on the migration route in both the religious sense and the geographic sense. It should also be noted that these scrolls refer to a migration route that follows the drainage pattern of the ancient northern waterway from the upper Great Lakes through the French River and Lake Nipissing, then down the Ottawa River and out the St. Lawrence River to the Atlantic. As mentioned earlier, this is the same route, though in reverse, used by European explorers, fur-traders, and voyageurs as they moved into and through the area.

The fact that disease was the reason for the Anishnaabeg early prehistoric migration is supported by William Warren in his *History of the Ojibway Nation*. However, no direct evidence of disease ravaging the precontact Atlantic coast has been found. Nevertheless, Frederick Cartwright in *Disease and History* speculates that the great plague — known as the Black Death — that

Figure 1. An Anishnaabeg Migration Record

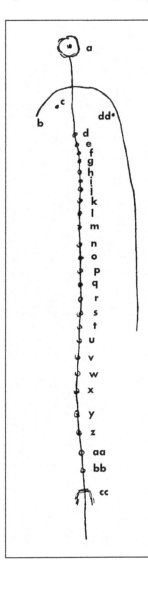

The circle at the top represents the original home of the Anishnaabeg; the curving horizontal line **b** divides the history between the pre-Midé and post-Midé periods. The dot at **c** represents the place where the Otter stopped to offer prayers and where the Otter began the journey west which the Anishnaabeg followed.

Other letters of Figure 1 represent places where the Otter appeared and the rites of the Midéwiwin were conducted; those indicative of places within the study area are **f**, Mackinaw, and **i**, Sault Ste Marie. **z** represents Sandy Lake, Minnesota, the last place where the Otter appeared. Designations **aa** through **dd** are not explained in the Mallery text (1972: 566-7).

ravaged Europe from 1346 to 1361 was carried to Greenland.[37] Inuit, having attacked the weakened Greenlanders, were probably also affected by the disease. What is not recorded is the transference of the disease from either Inuit or Norse populations to the Native peoples of the East Coast, an occurrence that seems more probable than speculative.[38]

The convergence of history, archeology, and oral tradition allow us, then, to conclude that both the Anishnaabeg migration and the Midé religion had their origins on the Atlantic coast, and that both were brought about by a complex set of circumstances involving the early establishment of "Vinland" on the North American continent, the transmission of the Black Plague in the fourteenth century from Europe to Greenland, and the recorded contacts of Greenlanders and Inuit during this period. Consequently it seems likely that the early Anishnaabeg did indeed migrate from the east before coming to settle in the Great Lakes region in precontact times.

Three Fires Unity

A Historical Accounting of the Anishnaabeg People

When Columbus landed in North America, one of his first acts was to rename and "take possession" of the islands he "discovered." In doing so, he also "took possession" of the people who lived on those islands, and in the process "bestowed" upon them the collective term of "Indians," a misnomer that persists to this day. Indeed, wherever the European people have settled during the past five hundred years, they have instigated this process of naming and "possessing" the lands and people of those areas. Despite this misnomer, indigenous societies all over the world have maintained their identities, the most evident being the name(s) that indigenous peoples use to describe themselves in their language. As mentioned earlier, the people from the Lake Huron borderlands call themselves the "Anishnaabeg."

To understand who the Anishnaabeg are, it is important to have some basic knowledge about their original beliefs, precontact history, and the various areas within the Lake Huron borderlands where they made their home. It is also important to take a close look at the individual tribes that make up the Anishnaabeg and the problems that occur when the historical record is inconsistent with reality.

We will begin by trying to trace the geographical history of the groups that composed the Anishnaabeg, a difficult task, as the first written records of contacts with these people came from European explorers and missionaries, who often made arbitrary and artificial distinctions. (Much later, actual Anishnaabeg migration scrolls were discovered that showed they were not at all adverse to frequent and far-reaching movements across wide territories. As a consequence, establishing their location at a particular place and time could, indeed, be quite problematic.)

In 1615 the Ottawa were first encountered by the French explorer Samuel de Champlain at a place surmised to be along the shore of the Georgian Bay of Lake Huron east of Manitoulin Island. Champlain called them the "Cheveux Relevez" — the Standing Hair People — in reference to their fashion of wearing their hair in a tall roach. Peter Schmalz, in *The Ojibwa of Southern Ontario*, consistently refers to them as "Ojibway," citing examples from the historic record to back his claim.[1] In 1634 the French explorer Jean Nicolet was sent by Champlain on a "peace mission" to the tribal people we now know as the Winnebago, in what is now Green Bay. The Huron, who had developed a close relationship with Nicolet, had apprised Champlain of the possible disruption of the fur trade by hostilities in the area. It was the Huron who led Nicolet to Green Bay, making him the first recorded European to have traveled the waterways into Lake Michigan. Out of the Nicolet mission came the first extensive European accounting of the tribes in the region.

Since there is no account of Nicolet's journey in his own hand, we must rely upon secondhand information provided by several people for a recounting of the tribes he visited. Not all of the accounts agree, and, indeed, some of the points in certain reports are disputed. Nevertheless, it is probable that Nicolet encountered sixteen different tribes. Of the sixteen, eleven are of historical significance to this particular study. (In the accounting that follows, the spelling of tribal names reflects modern convention, where such changes are appropriate.)[2] The first mentioned are the Outchougai, Mantoue, and Atchiligouan. These three groups appear to have been related to the Amikwa, who were also mentioned. At the time, the Amikwa were a large and powerful group closely allied with the Nipissing. They were, however, nearly destroyed by disease and war with the Iroquois early in the contact era and play virtually no role in the historic period. The remnants of the Amikwa seem to have merged with either the Nipissings or the Ojibways.[3]

The Noquets apparently lived on the far north shore of Lake Michigan in what is now the Bay de Noc area. Related to either the Menominees to the south and west, or to the Ojibways to the north and east, they eventually merged with one or both or these nations and ceased to exist as a separate tribe. The Winnebagos and the Menomineess are also mentioned in the Nicolet accounts. Both are fairly large tribes resident in extensive areas along the western shore of Lake Michigan both north and south of Green Bay and far inland. Wars and removal policy wreaked havoc on these people, who were pushed too far west of the area to be affected by the border issues under discussion.

Three other tribes referred to by Nicolet are the Baouichtigouians, the People of the Rapids at the Sault; the Ouasouarim, an Ojibway tribe of the Bullhead clan, who most likely were living in the Georgian Bay area at the time; and the Missisaugas, who also lived in the area along the north shore of the Georgian Bay, in the vicinity of the Missisauga River, and on Manitoulin Island. Keeping in mind the earlier discussion of the arbitrary nature of European naming, the Baouichtigouian, Outchougais, Atchiligouans, Noquets, Mantoues, and Ouasouarim can be considered "proto-Ojibway" people. The Missisaugas are also often classified as a division, or subtribe of the Ojibways, although they have, for the most part, retained a separate identity.[4]

The Ottawas are again mentioned in the accounts as having been visited on Nicolet's return to Quebec, as was a tribe identified as the Nassauaketon. Though referred to as a tribe separate from the Ottawas, the Nassauaketon—the People of the Fork—were a division of the Ottawas, who, in 1634, were most likely located on the south shore of Michigan's Upper Peninsula.[5] It is interesting to note that the name, Nassauaketon, went through some confusing changes. Butterfield, in his account of the Nicolet journey, wrote of a tribe called the "Mascouten," and located them at a six-day journey up the Fox River at Green Bay, in what is now Wisconsin. He added in a footnote that it was curious that Nicolet never mentioned them, although they were clearly one of the tribes living in the area at the time.[6] In fact, the "Mascouten" were actually the "Nassauaketon," an error made by the French, who mistakenly entered them into the European history under the former name.

Most historians have claimed that Nicolet visited all of the tribes mentioned in his accounts. This means that all sixteen tribes had to have lived along the water route from Lake Nipissing to the Sault, and from the Sault to Green Bay. There is some doubt that this is true.

The last four of the sixteen tribes in the "Nicolet accounts," the Potawatomis, Illinois, Assiniboines, and the Sioux are identified as tribes residing "in the neighborhood." James Clifton, in his book on the Potawatomis, doubts that any of these tribes were actually visited in their tribal location by Nicolet in 1634, since the Sioux, Assiniboine, and the Illinois lived too far away from the areas he visited, and the Potawatomis lived on the eastern shore of Lake Michigan at this time—out of the way of any direct route that Nicolet may have taken.[7] However, as Clifton notes, it could have been that Nicolet encountered members of these tribes in Green Bay, which was an important trading center at the time.[8]

In addition to the Nicolet accounts, one other vital contemporary group must be considered before attempting to create a map of tribal areas at the time of European contact. In 1671, the French administrator of Canada, Intendant Talon, well aware of the English presence to the north at Hudson's Bay, and the presence of the English and Spanish to the south and west of the Great Lakes, sent a party to Sault Ste. Marie to lay formal claim to the upper Great Lakes, as confirmation of French control of this vital fur trade area. Talon put Daumont de Saint Lusson in charge of the expedition and added the able explorer, Nicholas Perrot, to the party. Perrot's job was to travel to the far reaches of the area and invite the tribes to come to Sault Ste. Marie to attend the Native-French Council, now known as the "Pageant of St. Lusson." Sault Ste. Marie had been chosen as the place to hold this ceremony for two reasons: it was the central site of the fur trade area and it was also acknowledged as the historic meeting place of the Anishnaabeg.[9]

Perrot and other emissaries were successful in gathering together a number of tribes at the Sault. Most of the areas represented were the same as those encountered on the Nicolet journey (i.e., the Green Bay and the northern Lake Huron–Georgian Bay regions), but a number of tribes from the area north of Lake Superior were also in attendance. Some of these Native people have already been identified: the Potawatomis, Winnebagos, Menominees, Amikwas, Ottawas, and the Baouichtigouian, who were referred to by Perrot as the "Sauteurs," a French word with the same meaning as Baouichtigouian — People of the Rapids. Other groups claimed by Perrot to be residing at the Rapids at Sault Ste. Marie were the Achipoes (Ojibway), the Marameg (the Catfish Clan of the Ojibway), and the Noquets, which in Nicolet's time lived to the south and west of the Sault.[10]

Also at the 1671 Sault gathering were the Nipissing from an extensive area around the lake of the same name in northeastern Ontario, and the Hurons who lived south of the Nipissing in the area north of Lake Ontario. From the west, in addition to those already mentioned, were the Makomitek, an Algonquin group from the Green Bay area. Surprisingly, although they had to travel a great distance from their home in northern Ontario, the Assiniboines, Niscaks, Maskegons, Monsonis, and Crees were also in attendance. The Sauks from the lower peninsula of Michigan attended, but the Foxes, Kickapoos, and Miamis from the same area, did not. The Mascouten (as we now

Map 5. Tribe Locations at Time of Contact

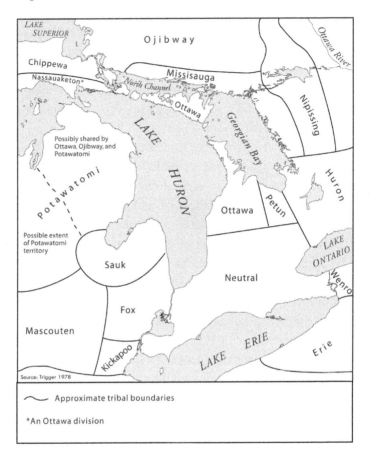

Source: Trigger 1978

‿ Approximate tribal boundaries

*An Ottawa division

know were the Nassauaketon) are missing from the historical accounts of this ceremony.[11]

In another account of the region's tribes at the time (1669), the French missionary, Father Dablon, claimed that members of twenty-two Indian nations came to the Sault to fish, but he named only nine of them. Four of the tribes, according to Father Dablon, were permanent inhabitants of the area: the Saulteurs, Noquets, Outchibous, and Marameg, and "the others [were] borrowers."[12] These "borrowers" were the Atchiligouan, Amik-was, Missisaugas (from islands in the northern Lake Huron region), the Cree, and the Winnebago (whom he called "wanderers," from the Lake Superior area).[13]

Many researchers of the Native peoples of this region have attempted to draw maps purporting to show tribal occupation at the time of contact. Please see map 5, which is a map developed by the Smithsonian Institution, on which there is a long disclaimer describing the difficulty in creating such a map.[14] Using the data on tribal locations gleaned from the accounts of Nicolet, Perrot, and Father Dablon, I have modified the map, which places the various tribes of Native peoples in the Lake Huron borderlands area in their most likely position at the time of European contact in the early 1600s.

This map raises some particular issues. To begin with, there are a few names on the map that have fallen into disuse. The Nipissings are now "officially" designated as Chippewas or Ojibways.[15] The Petun, located on the map just to the east of Lake Huron, have been historically referred to as the Tionontatis, or the Tobacco Nation.[16] Then there are the Mascoutens, which, as we already know, are a bit more problematic. Despite a popular myth that they comprised a "mysterious long-lost tribe which had disappeared from the pages of history without leaving a trace," Skinner claims that they were not at all "lost" but were, in truth, the "Prairie Potawatomis."[17] Clifton disputes Skinner's claim, arguing that "the Mascoutons were quite definitely a separate tribe which eventually merged with the Kickapoos."[18] To confuse matters even more, Hodge breaks the tribe into two groups and asserts that the southern group joined the Kickapoos while the northern group joined the Sauks and Foxes.[19] Fortunately, for the purpose of determining which groups were affected by borderland issues, it is sufficient to note that the Mascoutens appear to have merged with some other tribe and ceased to exist as a separate entity.

Other Native groups in map 5 are also unaffected by the Canadian–American borderland issues in the Lake Huron area. The Petuns, as we've already seen, are synonymous with the Tionontatis and eventually merged with the Hurons, who, along with the Neutrals and the Eries were so ravaged by the Iroquois during a series of bloody and devastating wars (apparently lasting from the precontact era until the mid-1600s) that they were either driven out of their home territory entirely, or, as their numbers were destroyed, merged into one tribe known as the Huron. This "Huron Confederacy,"[20] decimated by war, finally had to flee to "new" grounds, which eventually became the state of Michigan. The Huron Confederacy came to be called the Wyandot, which is claimed to have been the name of yet another of the "Canadian" tribes that fled before the Iroquois and joined the Huron group.[21] After being driven from Canada, the Wyandots lived in what is now the vicinity of Detroit and parts of northern Ohio. They were players in the Indian wars of the area but were eventually "removed" to Indian Territory in the early nineteenth century.[22]

Other nations on the map are the closely related Sauks and Foxes, the Kickapoos, and the Miamis. Most of the Foxes, having been driven from the area by the Ojibways, allied themselves with the Sauks. Eventually the allied Sauks and Foxes were forced west during the Removal period, as were the Kickapoos (many of whom moved eventually to Mexican territory) and the Miamis.[23] The five-nation Iroquois, the Illinois, the Menominees, and the Winnebagos (identified in map 5) all played important roles in the historic period but were not residents of the Lake Huron borderlands area. This leaves the Potawatomi living in the northern portion of Michigan's lower peninsula and along the eastern shore of Lake Michigan; the Chippewa-Ojibways making their home throughout northern Michigan and northern Ontario; and the Ottawas living on Manitoulin Island and the Bruce Peninsula, along the east shore of Lake Huron to the south. These three resident groups—Potawatomis, Chippewa-Ojibways, and Ottawas—became the resident tribes of the Lake Huron borderlands most affected by the eventual establishment of the U.S.–Canada border.

Orthography and Origins of the Three Resident Tribes of the Lake Huron Borderlands

The Ottawas or Odawas

The Ottawa people, despite having been called the "Cheveux Relevez" by Champlain, continued to refer to themselves as the "Ottawas," and Europeans began using this designation prior to the treaty-making period in question.[24] In Algonquin-based languages, the term "Ottawa"—and its variations—means "trader," and it was originally used to refer to all Native people who traveled the Ottawa River (running down from what is now northern Quebec into the St. Lawrence Seaway) to trade furs at the southern French posts.[25] Historically, the spelling of the word has varied considerably. Among some tribal members today, the preferred spelling is "Odawa," pronounced with a long "O" with the accent on the second syllable.[26] Consequently, "Odawa" is the term adapted for this particular study.

The Potawatomis

As James Clifton notes, the original meaning of the tribal designation "Potawatami" is also fairly straightforward. These people almost always refer to themselves as "Neshnabeks," meaning "People." During the early contact period, the French "blessed" the tribe with the name "Potawatamis" (which has up to 140 different spellings), a name with a less definitive meaning. Clifton suggests that the word is derived from an attempt by an Algonquin speaker to explain to a Frenchman (Nicolet?) that this particular group of people had something to do with blowing on a fire, "perhaps in irony or jest."[27] Whatever the truth, the designation itself is used consistently and unambiguously in the treaties and documents that affected their lives as Lake Huron borderland residents.

The Ojibways or Chippewas

The discussion on the third, and final, component of Anishnaabeg name origins and orthography is more problematic than the others, as early accounts of the various "proto-Ojibway" tribes indicate, as does the alternating use of the names "Ojibway" and "Chippewa." The tribal name "Outchibous," found in the Jesuit Relation of 1640, is more than likely the source for the modern designation of "Ojibways," or "Ojibwes," as it is now more commonly spelled. The designation "Chippewa" for the same tribe is presumably a corruption of "Ojibway." The fact that Bishop Frederic Baraga called his 1853 publication *A Dictionary of the Otchipwe Language* may be helpful in trying to understand how a single tribal designation came to have two distinct pronunciations over time.[28] However, the meaning of the word "Ojibway" and how it came to be applied to this nation, is more difficult to pinpoint.

Though the source of the tribal designation for this particular Native group has never been truly determined, many suppositions have been put forward. Literally defined, "Ojibway" means "roast until puckered up." One opinion posits the supposed practice of these people to "roast" their enemies over an open fire "until they are puckered up."[29] William Warren, in *History of the Ojibway Nation*, supports this interpretation, but his reference to the purported roasting of captured Fox warriors as its source relates to a time that would have occurred almost a century *after* the name "Outchibous" was first recorded. Warren, himself, admits that the "name does not date far back."[30] Further, in the view of E. S. Rogers, who authored an essay on the Ojibway for the Smithsonian Institution, such a translation is even "linguistically impossible."[31] It may also have been culturally impossible. Diamond Jenness, in *The Indians of Canada*, claims that the Ojibways never tortured their prisoners.[32] One may also assume that this included a proscription against their being "roasted."

The second meaning given to "roast until puckered up" was applied to the moccasins of the Chippewas, which, it was claimed, had seams that were puckered. According to this "translation," the Ojibways were people who wore moccasins with roasted, puckered seams. This definition is supposedly derived from their own language or, alternatively, from the "Algonquin language," although no evidence has ever been offered to indicate that these people ever created puckered seams by roasting their leather or their moccasins.[33] Modern tribal designations based on an article of clothing (or physical characteristic) are rare, but not unheard of, and are almost always names that have been bestowed upon a group by someone else—Native or non-Native—and not a name a tribe would apply to itself. It seems preposterous to believe that when asked, any group of people would refer to themselves as "The Roast Until Puckered Up People!"

Other suppositions included taking the word "pucker" and attempting to find meaning from it alone. In *History of the Ojibway and Their Connection with Fur Traders, Based upon Official and Other Records*, Edward Neill, rejecting the allusion to a moccasin style, presents two other possible meanings. First, quoting a missionary, Neill posits that the designation "Ojibway" might be related in some way to the word "shibew," which in turn is connected to the manner in which these people "draw out" syllables, producing a distinctive manner of speech. After implying that this meaning may be related to a "discernible *pucker* in their voice," Neill then dismisses this possibility.[34] In its place, he quotes Governor Ramsey of Minnesota as saying that a "more natural genesis of the word could probably be derived from a circumstance in their past history. Nearly two centuries ago (circa 1650) they were driven by the Iroquois, or Six Nations of New York, into the strait of Mackinaw, where lakes Huron, Michigan, and Superior, are "puckered" into a small channel or narrow compass."[35]

Other definitions, which make no reference to "roasting" or "puckering," have also been found. Henry Rowe Schoolcraft, the first U.S. Indian agent at the Sault, offers the rather dubious explanation that the term Ojibway "refers to the power of *virility*" (emphasis in original).[36] Harold Hickerson, on the other hand, suggests that Ojibway may be related to the Crane clan, which gained ascendancy at the Sault. He speculates that the word "Ojee-jok-bwa," "Voice of the Crane," may be one way to explain the origin of the Ojibway tribal appellation.[37] Edmund Danziger Jr., conjectured that the Ojibway name is corrupted from "o-jib-i-weg," which he claims means "those who make pictographs" and was a name bestowed on them by "neighbors."[38] Helen Tanner, in her *Atlas of Great Lakes Indian History*, seems to support Danziger by claiming that the word "Ojibwa" (the *Atlas* uses this spelling exclusively) refers "to the practice of recording information by drawing glyphs and signs on birch bark."[39]

In light of the above discussion, I would like to suggest yet another possibility for the origin of the tribal name "Ojibwa" (or "Outchibous"). Diamond Jenness, in his book on the Parry Island Ojibways, reports that the Ottawas of the island referred to themselves as the "Kitchibuans," or the "Great Medicine People."[40] A likely explanation might be then that, as a result of the passage of time (over three hundred years since the Europeans first made contact with the Anishnaabeg), a lack of spelling standards at the time, and the variations in the Ottawa and the Ojibway dialects (where it is not unusual for Native speakers to drop either the first or the last letter from a word), the transition from "Outchibous" to "Kitchibuan" is not too great.

Such a self-referential name would fit better with historical usage, and, as in the case of Sault Ste. Marie, we find, through oral tradition and the interpretations of migration scrolls, that the place "Bawating," or Sault Ste. Marie, has deep religious significance to the Anishnaabeg of the area. A tribal self-designation that refers to this sacred place and the people who live there makes far more sense than a reference to a moccasin seam, prisoner torture, or to sexual power. Although the controversy continues, Gerald Vizenor, in his book *Summer in the Spring*, has the last word on the subject. He concludes that the designation "Chippewa"/"Ojibway" is an "invented" name, the true meaning of which may never be known. He states, "Once recorded in treaties the name is a matter of law."[41]

The designations "Chippewa" and "Ojibway" should be considered synonymous throughout this study (although "Ojibwe" is the more common term in Canada, "Chippewa" the more common in the United States). For the sake of clarity and consistency, the term "Ojibway" is used in this study.

The Ojibways, the Odawas, and the Potawatomis all refer to themselves as the "Anishnaabeg" (or a variant of this spelling). Whenever a reference is being made to the three groups collectively, this study uses the term "Anishnaabeg"; "Ojibway," "Odawa," and "Potawatomi" are used to designate the individual groups whenever necessary.

Other Confusing Appellations

A caveat must be presented concerning other names that may be encountered when studying the Anishnaabeg. Another tribal group mentioned in the early accounts were the "Pahouiting-wach Irinis," which was a bad variant spelling of "Bawatingow-ininwuk," meaning "People of the Rapids," in modern Ojibway. Translating this into French gives us "Saulteaux" (pronounced, "So-toe").

The French word "saut" — at times spelled "sault" — has several translations, such as "to jump, leap, or vault"; as a noun, it stands for "falls," as in the "Saut du Ste. Mary," or, literally, the "Falls of St. Mary's." Lajeunesse misapplies the verb sense of the word "saut" and ludicrously claims that the term, "Saulteurs" was applied to the Native people from Sault Ste. Marie because they were "constantly on the move, hopping from one place to another."[42] The term "Saulteaux" is now generally applied only to the "Ojibways" who reside in the Lake Winnipeg region of Canada. Greenberg and Morrison argue quite convincingly that the application of this term to a group of people who now reside several hundreds of miles from where it originated does not necessarily signify a migration of these people from the Sault Ste. Marie area to Lake Winnipeg; instead it is more likely that the term itself migrated as Europeans misapplied "Saulteaux" to two separate groups of people speaking a common language and sharing the same culture.[43]

Another source of confusion is the similarity between the tribal names "Chippewa" and "Chipewyan." The Chipewyans are a rather large Athapaskan group that resides in north central Canada. The word is Cree in origin and may refer to the type of clothing these people wore, which included hoods that appeared to be "pointed skins" — although the Chipewyan people believe it is a term of reproach applied to them by their Cree neighbors and subsequently adopted into common usage. In contrast, the Chipewyans refer to themselves as the Denés.

A Brief Ethnography of the Anishnaabeg
While a complete ethnography of the Anishnaabeg is beyond the scope of this investigation, an understanding of some aspects their life is essential for comprehending their attitudes and actions in dealing with the Europeans.[44] Anishnaabeg political structure, for example, was quite different from the European models existing at the time of contact; consequently, misunderstandings on both sides led to many difficulties. One aspect of Anishnaabeg political life, in particular, was almost inconceivable to the European: the philosophy of individual liberty.

Among the Anishnaabeg, every person was (in European terms) "lord of the manor." Individual members of communities could not be compelled to do the bidding of any "chief." The term and concept of "chief" is a European invention, created to fit their preconceived notions of how societies "must" function. Furthermore, in contrast to the rigid, gender-based distribution of political (and social) power in European society, Anishnaabeg society was decidedly egalitarian.[45] Consequently, instead of exclusively designating male "chiefs," the Anishnaabeg relied upon the expertise of wise, experienced tribal members (who might be either men or women), who could be relied on to provide leadership when necessary. For example, a person well-versed in the healing arts would be the medicine "chief," the best hunter would lead the hunting party, one skilled in the ways of warfare would lead the war party, etc. Individual members were expected to follow these "chiefs" only as long as their performance inspired confidence in their leadership abilities.[46] As we shall see, this concept of individual liberty, especially as it relates to warfare, proved to be problematic when the Anishnaabeg were faced with British and American military threats.

The concept of individual liberty was somewhat mirrored within the community as a whole. The Anishnaabeg lived most of the year in small, semi-autonomous units, returning to central locations at various times of the year as social and subsistence demands warranted. These semi-autonomous communities were closely connected to others through marriage, and cooperation and unselfish hospitality were the ruling forces in community relations. These units could be reduced to autonomous family units, and these separate, or individual families (or larger "bands" of families) would, through traditional custom, return to the same areas for hunting, fishing, gathering, etc., year after year, although the concept of land "ownership" as the Europeans conceived of it was completely foreign to the Anishnaabeg. It isn't difficult to see that a political philosophy that embodies individual liberty and community autonomy faces certain disadvantages when faced with the monolithic concepts of "The British Empire" or the white Americans' self-proclaimed "Manifest Destiny." These disadvantages will be made evident as this study unfolds.

The French Period

The introduction of the European fur trade eventually brought a profound change to the Anishnaabeg way of life, although there is no doubt that trading was indigenous to tribal life long before the Europeans arrived in the upper Great Lakes in the early 1600s. However, the historical record shows that the French and other Europeans were concerned with more than just obtaining fur; minerals were also a large inducement to their continued and expanding presence in North America. In fact, a chunk of copper taken to Champlain in the early 1600s was partially responsible for the impetus to send Brulé on his northern expedition in 1618, and again in 1621. As time passed, the Europeans looked to other area resources for exploitation, including iron ore, timber, and eventually the land itself.

Since the French, however, proved to be more interested in the lucrative business of trading with the indigenous people of the North than in dispossessing them of their land, and because the French fur trade regimen gave them access to European trade goods, the Native people of the region regarded the French presence in North America as largely benign. It is, of course, much easier to view French policy in retrospect, as well as in light of what followed the end of French domination, but contemporary records of the period demonstrate that most northern indigenous groups with which the French came into contact were favorably disposed toward them. The increasingly less positive Native experience in New England with other European colonizers was well known to the Anishnaabeg, a fact that further added to their regard for the French regime. It could be said then that the Native people of the Great Lakes region were relatively content at this time, as they were not disturbed in their homes and were able to have access to European trade goods through the French fur trade regimen.

In the earliest period of the fur trade, of course, the English were not yet making territorial demands on the Great Lakes Native population, despite the keen competition between the French and English fur trading enterprises. Interestingly, it was well known among the Native people that the English were more liberal in their trading practices and that the English goods were of better quality than those the French supplied; in some cases the prices given for fur pelts (known as "peltries," for the way in which they were grouped together) that were brought to the British would be twice that given by the French. Yet the Anishnaabeg remained loyal to the French and ignored the lure of the more "liberal" British trading regime. Extensive inter-marriages between the French and Anishnaabeg also point to this compatibility.

The most notable exception to French favor were the Iroquois, who were first allied with the Dutch and then with the British. Shortly after the founding of Quebec in 1608, Champlain took the side of the Huron in their long-standing dispute with the Iroquois. With French aid, the Huron and their fellow Algonquin allies defeated the Iroquois, thus beginning a century of animosity between the Iroquois and the French (and adding fuel to the fire of long-standing Iroquois-Algonquin conflicts). Yet, the French were pressed by more than just the Iroquois strife.

One factor that weakened the French hold on the territory they did claim, apart from the Native land, was their policy of settling French colonists only near French trading posts. Although the vast Great Lakes region, from a European perspective, was "French," it lacked the kind of stability that agriculture provided for supporting English territorial claims. But the French also knew, perhaps as well as the Native population, that agriculture and industry would destroy the necessary environment for continued production of the fur-bearing animals who were the basis for this French enterprise.

The Iroquois Wars, ca. 1640 to 1667

As mentioned briefly in the passage above, the struggle between the Iroquois and the Anishnaabeg became greater during the period of the French alliance because the Iroquois were pushing harder into the Great Lakes region as a means of gaining territorial dominance. This Iroquois aggression arose from the fact that they had trapped out their homelands in the Hudson River valley and upstate New York by the 1640s and were faced with either expanding their territories or giving up the fur trade and the European goods it brought them. Not surprisingly, they chose to expand their territory. Their old enemies, the Huron, were the first to feel the heat of this expansion. The Huron controlled the territory (called "Huronia") between the Great Lakes and the French fur trade centers in Quebec and skirted that of the Iroquois to the south along the St. Lawrence. The advantageous trade route, which followed the ancient waterway from the French River near the eastern end of Manitoulin Island, through Lake Nipissing, and down the Ottawa River to Montreal, circumvented Iroquois land as much as possible. During this period, the Anishnaabeg were allies of the Huron; the Odawa, especially, were firmly ensconced within the Great Lakes–Quebec trading regime.

In 1641 the Iroquois began attacking Huron villages on a relatively small scale; in the summer of 1648, however, they launched a successful series of raids against the Huron, destroying their villages and killing, or widely dispersing, the residents. The Nipissing to the north of the Huron were also attacked and dispersed by the Iroquois during this, and subsequent, campaigns. It was at this point that the Iroquois raids also forced the Huron and their Petun-tobacco, Neutral, and Erie allies out of what is now

Canada. The Odawa and the Potawatomi, also living within Huronia at the time, were forced to flee as well. The Neutral, who had forcibly evicted the Anishnaabeg people from around Lake St. Clair earlier in this period of warfare, were, in turn, also expelled from that area. The Odawa and the Potawatomi, who had been living with their Huron allies in southern Ontario, fled to the western side of Lake Michigan, where they took up residence. Many Odawa, Huron, and Neutral reportedly took up residence at the Sault, while other remnants of southern Ontario tribes were dispersed throughout the Great Lakes region.

The Ojibway and their allies at the Sault were not spared the disruptions caused by these widespread and lengthy Iroquoian wars. Attacked by the Iroquois in 1650, many fled the area and joined the other Anishnaabeg in the western parts of Michigan's Upper Peninsula and Minnesota. Pushed back from moving farther west by their "little" enemies, the Sioux, and hemmed in by the Iroquois on the east, the Anishnaabeg spent several uncomfortable years confined to an area at the western end of Lake Superior.[1]

A 1653 engagement at Green Bay shows how far west the Iroquois had been able to push the Anishnaabeg and their Native allies in their attempt to conquer and control the upper Great Lakes. A large contingent of Algonquin peoples and other Native tribes, with French support, successfully defended the fur-trading fort from invading Iroquois, driving them back east. The Anishnaabeg were deeply involved in this engagement: about forty percent of the defending forces were Potawatomi, and another forty percent divided between the Ojibway and the Odawa. After the successful 1653 Green Bay defense, many Anishnaabeg were able to return to their homes in areas east of Green Bay. In a decisive battle fought in 1662, about twenty miles west of Sault Ste. Marie, on the southern shore of Whitefish Bay (now called Iroquois Point), upper Great Lakes Anishnaabeg drove the Iroquois from the area. Shortly after this, the Anishnaabeg returned to their ancient home at Bawating.

With the Iroquois vanquished and the area once again safe for Europeans, the French established a mission and trading post at the Sault in 1668.

Soon, Sault Ste. Marie became the trading center for the entire upper Great Lakes; furs from the Cree far to the west and north found their way to the Sault for assemblage and transport to Montreal. The French were firmly in control of this trade, engaging many Native people to accompany their flotilla of canoes across the north and into the Ottawa River to Montreal, hoping to stay far north of the Iroquois. By 1667 the Iroquois were finally forced into peace as a consequence of a series of military defeats both on the upper Great Lakes and south into New York.

The Post–Iroquois Wars Period

The Peace of 1667 gave the French the opportunity to solidify their hold over the upper Great Lakes territory. It was in 1671 that the "Pageant of Saint Lusson" had been staged in Sault Ste. Marie to insure the alliance of the Native people of the fur trade areas and to recognize the Sault both for its reestablished central role in the fur trade and its importance as an historic meeting place of the Anishnaabeg. With the defeat of the Iroquois and the resumption of the French fur trade, the Native people returned to their traditional homelands, and life in the upper Great Lakes returned to a more peaceful rhythm.

Unfortunately, the peace did not last long. Disruptions of Native life caused by European intrigues were becoming serious and widespread. One such disruption occurred when a contingent of Native troops trained in the upper Great Lakes in 1684 were sent on a military expedition to support a French commander, Monsieur de la Barre, in an attack on the Iroquois in their own territory. Warriors from the Odawa, Huron, Ojibway, Menominee,

Potawatomi, Illinois, Fox, Kickapoo, and Mascouten, who were forced to travel more than a thousand miles, complained that such a long absence would subject their families to possible starvation. They had little recourse, however, from abandoning the enterprise and were taunted about being cowards and were reminded that they had taken an oath of loyalty to the French. Unfortunately, the expedition ended in disaster for the French and their Native allies.

Despite the loyalty of their Native allies, pressure on the French to abandon their forts in the upper Great Lakes was beginning to grow. The British established the Hudson Bay Company in 1670 to further press the French from the north. By the late 1680s the Iroquois had resumed their forays into the upper Great Lakes, and the conflict with the British heated up. The British did manage to get eleven canoes full of trade goods to Michilimackinac in 1685, giving the Native people of the region an opportunity to see for themselves the difference between their own higher-quality goods and trade practices, and those of the French. While the French were able to drive the British from their forts on James Bay in the far north, during the 1680s and into the next decade, the pressure on the French was still intense enough to compel them in 1689 to abandon their post at the Sault in favor of the more southerly and defensible one at Mackinac.

However, the abandonment of the French forts in the upper Great Lakes was not so much the consequence of conflicts with the Iroquois and British as it was the result of growing economic and social constraints. The peace of 1667 had given new impetus to the fur trade activity, and by the latter part of the century the warehouses at Montreal were well stocked with furs. High supply meant low prices and reduced profits for Montreal merchants. Shutting down the northern posts, they calculated, would force Native traders to travel to Montreal with their peltry, thereby reducing the supply, eliminating the middlemen, and raising the prices.

The Jesuits, too, were demanding that the trading posts be abandoned. The fur trade, they complained to the French authorities in Quebec, was destroying Native life and failing to induce tribal members to exchange their idolatrous ways for Christianity. The real reason, however, was that the extremely volatile mixture of fur traders, Natives, rum, and women was leading the Jesuits to feel they had lost control over the northern missions. Their arguments, coupled with the desires of Montreal merchants, eventually led to the closing of the northern posts. Simultaneously, the licenses of all of the traders in upper Canada were also revoked in an effort to slow the supply of furs coming into Montreal.

The Establishment of Detroit and French-British Conflicts
French concern that the policy of abandoning its posts would mean, in effect, abandoning the region to the English was one of the arguments in favor of allowing Antoine Laumet de Lamothe Cadillac to set up, in 1701, a "model" fur trading post at what is now Detroit. Such a post at Detroit would lend authority to French territorial trade claims made earlier in the Sault. In the same year, a peace was concluded at Montreal between representatives of the Iroquois, Odawa, Potawatomi (also representing the Wisconsin tribes), Huron, Miami, Fox, and Ojibway, which boded well for the Detroit "experiment." Cadillac named his settlement Ponchartrain and set about convincing the Native people of the region to relocate to the area. Soon, Anishnaabeg and other people from the upper Great Lakes found themselves far south of their usual homelands.

The experiment at Detroit was an interesting and important departure from French policy during this era. Previously, the French had always set up posts in the Natives' own territory. In Michigan those posts were located at (using modern-day names) the Sault, Mackinac Island, St. Ignace, Port Huron, and Niles; elsewhere in the area were two forts north of Lake Superior, one at Lake Nipigon, and one further north on the Albany River. By contrast, the new Detroit post was an attempt by the French to gather the Native people from "French" territory into one place from where, it was assumed, they could better control the entire region. The French hoped, too, for better control of fur prices than was possible in the old system of licensing traders and operating far-flung trading posts. Moreover, Native people would presumably be more inclined to trade in Detroit with the French than to travel to English posts where they could get better prices but risk losses incurred by extensive travel.[2]

The policy of consolidating and controlling the region's Native people was at first successful: many tribes were induced to abandon their traditional homes and establish villages near each other at Detroit. Among them were the Ojibway and the Missisauga, who united in Detroit to form one village; the Odawa and the Huron from Michilimackinac, who left only a few of their number behind; and some Nipissing, Miami, and Amikwa. The Potawatomi, Fox, and Sauk also set up villages in the Detroit area.

But this success was short-lived. Long accustomed to relatively wide spaces between themselves and their neighbors, the tribes now found themselves in close proximity to each other—a situation that almost always led to trouble, either with the French, or among themselves. In 1706, for example, acting upon reports that the Miami were planning to attack them while they were weakened by an outbreak of hostilities between themselves and the Huron, some Odawa killed a missionary and a French soldier during an attack on some Miami, several of whom were also killed. The incident outraged the French, whose major goal (at least as far as Native people were concerned), was to keep peace between the tribes, while at the same time keeping the French themselves out of harm's way so that the fur trade could proceed unimpeded.

Miscouaky, an Odawa chief whose brother, Jean le Blanc,

was involved in the incident, traveled to Detroit to present the Odawa version of what happened to the Marquis de Vaudreuil. He placed most of the blame on the treachery of the Miami and the Huron, whom he claimed were in league against the Odawa at the time. However, it is not his defense of the Odawa that is important here, but rather Miscouaky's claim to speak for all of the tribes in the area, which, according to a list he had made, included the Odawa, Fox, Mascouten, Kickapoo, Winnebago, Menominee, Saulteurs (Ojibway), and Missisauga. (The list, of course, excludes the Miami and the Huron, since Miscouaky claimed to be speaking for all of the tribes that opposed the Miami and the Huron.)

This incident passed without further bloodshed, but it typifies some of the problems encountered by the various Native groups in the Detroit region and the undercurrent of hostilities that constantly kept them on the verge of war. Just five years earlier, for instance, the Odawa and the Huron had been very strong allies living near each other at Michilimackinac. As well, Father Marest, the Jesuit missionary at Michilimackinac at the time (1706) reported that an apparent split in the Odawa tribe had been mended. Yet in 1708 it appears that the Odawa were again divided, those tribes at Mackinac having refused to return to Detroit to join their relatives already there.

A 1711 French document recounts the recent conflicts between the various tribes: the Missisauga had raided the Miami; the Fox, too, were against the Miami and attacked the Wea and the Piankeshaw, while threatening the Huron; the Wea had attacked the Fox; and finally, the Fox and the Kickapoo were at war with the Illinois. The French explorer Nicolas Perrot also wrote of intertribal conflicts during this period. His account catalogs the struggles of a number of tribes: the Odawa were fighting the Fox (who once had helped the Odawa against the Miami); the Fox, who had once aided the Saulteurs, were now warring against them; the Miami, once allied with the Fox against the Sioux, were now opposing them; the Illinois, who had never made war on the Kickapoo or the Fox, were now battling them at Detroit. He wrote that the Potawatomi, who were also at war with the Sauk and Fox, were "half Sakis; the Sakis are in part Renards [Fox]; thy cousins and thy brothers-in-law are Renards and Sakis."[3]

Perrot concludes his account with a recitation of all of the area tribes responsible for the deaths of Frenchmen in this period: the Iroquois, Huron, Odawa, Ojibway (Saulteur), Missisauga, and Miami. It was the relatively high number of deaths of their countrymen that led the French to question the value of Detroit and that prompted some to press for abandoning it altogether in favor of a reinvigorated post at Michilimackinac. The French were still concerned, of course, that abandoning the experiment might induce the Native people at Detroit, now geographically closer to the English, to trade with them at the expense of the French. While it is true that the French, as might be expected, blamed much of the unrest on the English, they were not necessarily concerned with peace for its own sake; like the tribes, they, too, seemed inclined to make war in order to "keep the peace."

The most notable example of this came in 1712. During the winter, most Native people left Detroit to travel to their winter hunting grounds to trap furs; only a few Huron remained with the French, who numbered about thirty men. In late winter a group of Mascouten and Fox set up a village outside of the French fort at Detroit. Dubuisson, the fort commander, feared the worst and sent out messengers to reassemble the "Detroit" tribes to defend the fort from attack. The tribes summoned were the Huron, Odawa, Potawatomi, Sauk, Menominee, Illinois, Missouri, and Osage, as well as other more distant tribes. The report does not make clear exactly which tribes responded to the call but does imply that the bulk of the defenders were Odawa, Huron, Saulteurs, and Missisauga. Some tribes had split on the issue. There is some evidence, for example, that about twenty-five Iroquois were among those who had assembled to defend Detroit and that some Sauk were also in the attack contingent. It should also be noted that the Odawa and Huron, erstwhile enemies, were allies once again on the side of the French against the English and their supporters.

An important reason for the attack was that the Fox were fearful that their enemies, the Dakota Sioux to their west, would come under the French umbrella and gain access to firearms, thus further threatening their homeland. Dubuisson, however, was convinced that the attack was orchestrated by the English and the Iroquois. An incident that reveals the French distrust of—and perhaps disdain for—all Native peoples, occurred when the Native defenders of the fort at Detroit requested entry into it. Dubuisson, "seeing that they were too excited," allowed them to enter, although it had been his intention "to make them camp outside, near the wood, so that we should not be inconvenienced."[4]

The battle was finally engaged, with the attackers suffering more than the defenders; eventually the Mascouten-Fox village was placed under a siege. After nineteen days the Mascouten and Fox village was put on the run. They were able to secure a new position and withstand another siege of four days, but their stronghold was finally overrun. "All were destroyed," wrote Dubuisson, "except the women and children whose lives were granted them. . . . That, Sir, was the end of those two wicked tribes, with such evil designs, who disturbed the whole land."[5] Dubuisson's claim that the tribes were annihilated was optimistic, however. They, and their allies, were still a force to be reckoned with; indeed, the Fox continued to make war on the French and their Indian allies until the early 1740s.

The Fox War of 1712 was fought within a much larger series of European wars, which, at least for the British and the French, ended with the Treaty of Utrecht in 1713. This treaty required the French to return the James Bay trading posts to the British.

This, combined with the perceived threat of a British-Iroquois alliance that might renew forays into the heart of their territory, led the French to reestablish their post at Detroit. Its new commander, Sabrevois, proved, however, that he was no true friend of the Native people, going so far as to threaten to execute any Indian found trading with the British. Many Native people (foremost among them the Odawa and the Potawatomi) were so upset with Sabrevois that they set out in seventeen canoes to travel to the British post at Albany to trade their furs. But they were persuaded to go to Montreal instead and present their case to Vaudreuil, the governor general of New France, which they did on June 24, 1717. Fortunately, their complaints were well heard, and Sabrevois was removed from his post at Detroit.

Other posts were also established throughout the northern region as far west as Winnipeg in Manitoba, which essentially covered the territory of the Ojibway, Cree, Odawa, Sioux, and Menominee. The two new tribal names—the Sioux to the west and the Cree to the north—reflected yet another attempt by the French to expand their sphere of influence in the face of British competition. By 1712 Mackinac had once again become the center for these northern posts. The Native people of the north were encouraged to resettle there, especially the Odawa who had been living on Saginaw Bay, away from their Odawa relatives at Detroit. (Both groups had been convinced to abandon their homes on Michilimackinac in the early 1700s.)

Detroit became a lesser center for trade with and control of the more southern tribes under French influence: the Ojibway, Odawa, Potawatomi, Miami, and Shawnee. (Of the Anishnaabeg, the Ojibway and Odawa lived throughout the region, while the Potawatomi were only in the south.) Some of the Sauk, however, along with the Fox and Mascouten, were still outside the French sphere of influence, and a possible alliance of these tribes with the British and Iroquois continued to concern the French, who were determined to extend their dominance far to the south of the Great Lakes. In 1739 they mounted an expedition against the Chickasaw, the specific aim of which was to stop the Chickasaw from raiding French forts along the Mississippi and disrupting trade and communication in the southern portion France's empire in North America.

The Ojibway, Odawa, Potawatomi, Sioux, and Nipissing were called from the north to assist in this effort. Despite French concerns, some of the Sauk and Fox (both tribes were apparently split by this time) joined in the expedition against the Chickasaw.[6] Tribes further to the south of the Great Lakes region of New France—the Wea, Piankeshaw, Miami, and Illinois— became part of the offensive as well. The intent of the expedition was to attack the Chickasaw in their homeland in western Tennessee, but the results were inconclusive. The French were fighting too many enemies on too many fronts to be very effective; nevertheless, raids into Chickasaw territory continued into the 1750s.

The Period of French Decline
European-induced wars and the fur-trade competition continued to have a major disruptive effect on the lives and relationships of indigenous individuals and communities. In yet another instance of this, the Missisaugans had allied themselves with the Iroquois against the French, even though their relatives, the Ojibway, seemed to be firmly in the French camp at the time. As France's situation in North America grew more desperate and the need to retain their influence over "loyal" tribes increased, many tribal leaders were induced to travel to Montreal to be feted by the French authorities, who laded their visitors with presents and provisions for their people. Native peoples were induced as well to join a French expedition into the vast Ohio Valley in 1749 to claim the area for France.

The impetus for this action had actually occurred a decade earlier, when the Huron, who had made peace with the Chickasaw but were warring against their recently abandoned Anishnaabeg allies, broke with the French. In still another example of the complexities of Native life during this period of intense French-English rivalry, the Hurons, along with the Miamis, were able to lure some of the Odawas and Ojibways of Michilimackinac and Saginaw Bay into a conspiracy against the French at Detroit in 1647, a conspiracy that ultimately failed.

The Huron "defection" created a British stronghold on the shores of Lake Erie. This was eventually replaced by a Miami village that was also strongly pro-British. This British inroad into nominal French territory lasted until a "French" force of Odawas (from L'Arbre Croche in northern Michigan) and a few Potawatomis from the Detroit area managed to destroy the combined Miami-Shawnee fort in 1752.[7] In the same year, the French assembled a company of Potawatomis, Foxes, Sauks, Dakotas, Winnebagos, and Menominees to attack the Illinois, then considered to be wavering in their loyalty to the French. Interestingly, some Foxes and Sauks — resolute enemies of the French in the early 1700s — were now fighting *for* the French.

The British-French struggle for control of the area was manifest in the east as well, and Anishnaabeg from the Great Lakes found themselves far from home fighting for the French in places like Virginia, Maryland, New York, Pennsylvania, and Connecticut. With Montreal as the base from which the battles in these areas were fought, many Anishnaabeg never returned home for the annual hunting and trapping cycle: by this time they were full-time mercenary soldiers. (In keeping with tradition and policy, the French took care of the families of the warriors who accompanied them into battle, providing them with a large measure of "presents.")

In 1757 a pivotal event occurred in Native-French relations which led to a serious decline in the ability of the French to compete militarily with the British. A group of Native warriors who had attacked and scored a stunning victory against Fort William Henry, about fifty miles north of Albany, were unwittingly exposed to an outbreak of smallpox at the fort. The warriors took the disease home with them to the Great Lakes with devastating consequences for their population. Mistrust of the French followed in the wake of this catastrophe. Some Native people, once allied with the French, broke into open rebellion; one faction of the Menominee at Green Bay attacked the French in the winter of 1757–58. And it was becoming apparent that the many Natives who had allied themselves with the French had done so only to drive the British from their territory, and when that was accomplished they planned to drive out the French as well. The days of France's empire in North America were drawing to a close; Quebec City fell to the British in 1759, Montreal a year later. Although the military struggle was not yet over, the British were soon to be in control of the Great Lakes region where the Anishnaabeg would find themselves resisting these victors and their increasingly harsh policies more fiercely than they had ever done during the reign of the French.

The British and "Pontiac's Conspiracy"

Once the French were expelled, the British soon determined that they would not repeat the French mistake of becoming allies of the Native people of the Ohio Valley and the Great Lakes; instead, they decided to become masters over them. In place of the French policy of giving presents that insured the well-being and amity of their Native allies, the British decided that "presents" would be made only in payment for services rendered, or for items taken in trade, on an equity basis. The British also quietly instituted a policy of restricting the sale of gunpowder to the Indians.[8] When it became evident, despite some assurances to the contrary, that the British were beginning to man the abandoned French forts, the Native people understood that their worst fears were being realized: the British were planning to seize their lands. The British steadfastly maintained, however, that their policies were designed merely to foster good trading relations, which they claimed was their only goal where the Native people were concerned.

The new British policies soon proved to be costly ones. For one thing, the harmonious trade relationship never materialized; the posts were ill-stocked, and prices quickly rose far beyond the "official" rates and out of the reach of most Native people, who were quite destitute in the aftermath of the war and the disruption of trade caused by it. General Amherst, the British commander of the region, attempted to "control" the situation by further restricting the goods that could be traded: scalping knives, razors, gunpowder, flints, fowling pieces, and rum were all struck from the list of trade items. The Ojibways at Sault Ste. Marie killed some traders in 1762, some believe, as a direct response to this limitation on trade.⁹ Such restrictions, coupled with the British insistence that any and all British prisoners be returned, even those who wished to remain with their adoptive Native families, eroded whatever little influence the chiefs had over increasingly dissatisfied tribal members. In addition, intratribal hostility (and in many cases open warfare) and attempts by some tribes to forge alliances against the British, while other tribes wished to make peace with them, led to crises throughout the region. Thus, the lack of presents, the deterioration of the trading regimen, the restriction of goods, the occupation of the forts, and pestilence and disease blamed on the British, all combined to form a view in the minds of the Native tribes that the British were a malevolent force, and set up a nostalgia for the days when the French were the benevolent "fathers" to their Native "children."

Playing into all of this was the persistent rumor that the French would promptly return to the area if the British could somehow be removed from it. Of course, many Native peoples hoped that the British could be expelled without the return of the French. Either way, the exorcism of the British scourge became the overriding concern of the Native people throughout the region. Exacerbating the situation were rumors that France, far from coming to the aid of the Native population, was, instead, intending to cede Canada to the British. This particularly appalled the Native people of the Great Lakes, who had clearly never lost their territory, which included areas of Canada, to either the British or the French.

While a general sense of animosity and grievance toward the British became widespread, no systematic opposition, or centralized structure for resistance, existed. In what came to be known as "Pontiac's Conspiracy," beginning in the summer of 1763, the British were attacked by the Miamis, Delawares, Shawnees, Mingos, Senecas, Odawas, Ojibways, Wyandots, Weas, Potawatomis, and Missisaugas. But the participation of these various nations in the anti-British struggle was not always consistent or unanimous. The Ojibways from Michilimackinac took the British fort at the Straits, but the Odawas from L'Arbre Croche and St. Ignace redeemed the fort's prisoners and led them to safety in Montreal, demonstrating an obvious split between the Odawas of southern and central Michigan, who were following their chief, Pontiac, and the Odawas of northern Michigan, who were not. Nor did the tribes from the west — the Menominees, Winnebagos, Sauks, Foxes, and Iowas — join the fight against the British.

Even among those who did support Pontiac, there was little consensus. The Ojibways, who took the fort at Michilimackinac, later denounced Pontiac for inflicting cruelties that violated the Anishnaabeg moral code and offended the "Master of Life."[10] But perhaps the biggest blow to Pontiac's success came by way of the French refusal to come to the aid of the Native people besieging three important forts: Detroit, Fort Pitt, and Niagara. Without French assistance the "rebellion" was doomed to failure. The French, defeated when Montreal fell in 1760, had, in fact, been negotiating a peace with Britain, unbeknownst to the Native people. The 1763 Treaty of Paris was signed on February 10, months before Pontiac and his allies met in Detroit to plan the uprising that took place later that summer. The rumors that France would cede its territory in North America had been proven true after all. By the terms of the 1763 Treaty, the British acquired all the French territory east of the Mississippi, while the Spanish received the western portion of the French North American empire. The French and Indian Wars that had begun in 1754 were over, and the French had been defeated. Their Native allies, however, had not been signatories to that treaty signed in Paris by European diplomats.

While the French regime had lasted through several generations, and the introduction of European trade goods had profoundly affected Native life in the region, it was the brief, final throes of the French-British struggle for Native loyalty in the fur trade that was responsible for devastating the area's Native population. For the first time in their history, the Anishnaabeg—no strangers to war in defense of their homeland—faced the loss of their territory to a European power, a European power, moreover, that had never militarily defeated them. It has even been argued that throughout this entire period the Native people of the region were always firmly in control of the fur trade, although admittedly control often passed from one Native group to another.[11] Several reasons supporting the viability of this notion included the relatively low numbers of British and French in comparison to the larger Native populations, the strength of Native resistance, the shifting alliances, and the trade with *both* the British and the French during this period.

While Pontiac's action is called a "conspiracy" by western historians, Native peoples referred to it as the "Beaver War"—that is, a fur-trade war, albeit on a scale larger than any previous fur trade war, and with far more serious consequences. In truth, virtually all of this period's battles, sieges, expeditions, and raids were elements of this period's one long, protracted Beaver War. Pontiac's defense was just the last of a long series. Finally, by 1763, it can be seen that the area is already very much a "borderland" within the modern meaning of the term, i.e., the scene of intense interactions[12] which sorely test central (read "European") control,[13] punctuated by the clash of differing civilizations.[14]

The British Period

Pontiac's 1763 siege of Detroit was broken on November 5, but the reprovisioning of the fort at Detroit did nothing to bring the partisans of Pontiac into the British fold, and the area was far from solidly in British hands. The Native people were of the mind that since the French had ceded their territory in North America, they (the Native people) were sole proprietors of the land: the British had neither traded for nor purchased it from them. As a result, resistance from the Native people continued to keep the British at bay, despite the end of "Pontiac's Conspiracy." Yet the British came to terms with the various tribes, one by one. Even Pontiac, in late 1765, came to accept the British as his "father," but his recognition of British hegemony did little to bring peace to the region. Native people could see that, despite the Proclamation of 1763, which forbade English settlement west of the Allegheny Mountains, many whites were, indeed, moving into Native territories.

To allay Native fears and to solidify their fledgling alliances, the British renewed the French policy of giving presents and began replacing the French medals marking the status of chiefdom, with others marking British favor. The British policy of *choosing* chiefs, in the belief that this would allow them to control the Native population, did not always help them achieve the intended result. Pontiac himself came to believe that he was indeed the "chief" of the western tribes, but his arrogance soon provoked his fellow Odawa into abandoning him. He sought refuge with his relatives among the Illinois, but then greatly angered them by stabbing one of their chiefs. Finally, acting on a rumor that had him leading his (nonexistent) warriors against the Kaskaskias, Pontiac was killed by a Peoria warrior in the "French" village of Cahokia in 1769, thus putting an end to British presumptions of control.

Apparently, the British plan for their new territory was to create several separate Native alliances, arm all sides, and then sit back to watch the competing Native alliances destroy each other. But the plan did not work out as they had hoped. Instead, Native groups sought British mediation to smooth over the differences between the conflicting tribes. Soon, the British found themselves in the same position as the French had been in, distributing presents and mediating disputes. None of this, however, did anything to help the British become the "master" of the Native people in its new empire.

For the Anishnaabeg, the transition period from the French to the British Empire was filled with turmoil. For over a century, the Native people and the French had developed a system that was, for the most part, mutually beneficial and that left intact the basic village life of the Anishnaabeg. In the words of one Anishnaabe: "They never molested the places of our dead."[1] Moreover, although many warriors found themselves away from their village for extended periods during the French and Indian War, the understanding was always that their French "fathers" would look after their families in their absence; this was indeed the case, costly as it was to the French.

British attitudes toward the Native population were very different. While the French had been quite content to live with and marry into the Native tribes, the British were deathly afraid of their own subjects choosing to do this, believing that those who had "gone Native" would be impossible to control. Further, friction was created because white settlers, responsible for the rampant wholesale murder of Native people on the frontier, were rarely brought to justice under British law. Revenge murders committed by Native people, on the other hand, frequently were.

Anishnaabeg Land Tenure

Despite their displacement by the French and the ensuing war with Britain, Native people, by the end of these conflicts, were essentially still in control of the territory in which the Europeans had found them a hundred years earlier. In fact, from their perspective, the Anishnaabeg were in control of a much larger territory than that which they had occupied in the 1640s. This view is supported by a comparison of map 5, which shows tribal distribution in the Great Lakes region at the time of contact, and map 6, which shows tribal distribution in 1768.

The Sauks, Foxes, Mascoutens, and Kickapoos, residing in lower Michigan at the time of contact, had been pushed to the west by French policy and a century of conflict. In 1768 the Sauk and Fox could be found in an inland area west of Lake Michigan—territory that, a century earlier, had been occupied by the Sioux, Iowas, Winnebagos, and Menominees. In 1768 the remnants of the Huron Confederacy, now called the Wyandots, lived in a small enclave on the Canadian side of the Detroit River in extreme southwestern Ontario, as well as in a more sizable section of land along the south shore of Lake Erie.

The Menominees and the Winnebagos continued to occupy their homelands as they had for centuries, albeit on a smaller scale, since some of their land was now held by the Odawas and the Potawatomis. The Miamis, pushed out of the northern areas of their contact era holdings, now inhabited a larger area further to the south. The Illinois lost a sizeable portion of their territory to the Potawatomis, Kickapoos, and Mascoutens.

The Anishnaabeg's territorial gains included land of the Potawatomis, who had abandoned their northern Michigan territory and taken control of a wide belt of land that stretched all across southern Michigan, northern Ohio, Indiana, northeast-

Map 6. Native Settlement Patterns in the Mid-1700s

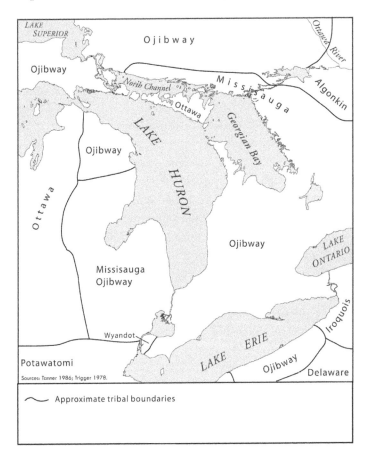

Sources: Tanner 1986; Trigger 1978.

ern Illinois, and along the west Lake Michigan coast — an area
that extended from Detroit nearly to Green Bay. At the time of
contact, this land had been occupied by the Kickapoos, Mascoutens, Miamis, Illinois, and Winnebagos.

The Ojibways and their close relatives, the Missisaugas, also
considerably expanded their territory, occupying the whole of the
Ontario peninsula, as well as northern Ontario, Michigan's Upper Peninsula, and the eastern portion of Michigan's lower pen-

insula. The Ojibways also enlarged their holdings to the west and southwest of Lake Superior, land once held by the Dakotas.

The third branch of the Anishnaabeg, the Odawas, regained their home on Manitoulin Island and moved into territory once occupied by their Potawatomi relatives in the western portion of Michigan's lower peninsula. They also held land all along the northern shore of Lake Michigan, including the Door Peninsula east of Green Bay; to the south, they could be found along the Maumee River in northwest Ohio.

All of the territory, then, that the Anishnaabeg held at the time of contact was still firmly in their control, as were large tracts of land abandoned, or forcibly vacated, by their former neighbors. In 1768 the Anishnaabeg occupied all of what is now Michigan; all of Ontario, except areas in the far east (Algonquins) and the far north (Crees); much of northern and eastern Wisconsin; northern Minnesota; some areas of northern Ohio and Indiana; and northeast Illinois. That is, they occupied almost all of the land that borders the five Great Lakes except the area to the south of Lake Ontario and a portion of southern Lake Erie, both held by the Iroquois, as well as small areas along the Detroit River and on the south shore of Lake Erie that were held by the Wyandots.

The Anishnaabeg viewpoint, that they were firmly in control of virtually the entire Great Lakes watershed, was not shared by the British who saw these areas from a completely different perspective and made attempts to control them. For the most part, these attempts were failures. The Native traders, who were supposed to obtain licenses from the British and then trade only with British merchants, were in open revolt. Many refused to cooperate with the British at all, obtaining their permits from other authorities and then trading freely in the "British" Great Lakes area. In addition, most traders sent their furs south through the Mississippi valley to New Orleans rather than sending them by the more costly route across land to British ports in the east.

The Anishnaabeg and the Struggle for Control of the Ohio Valley

The British trouble with trade was matched by the equally intransigent problem of settlers moving across the Appalachians. Despite the Proclamation of 1763, which had set up a monopoly system in both trade and land, the British found it impossible to control the influx of settlers, which continued despite attempts to evict them. This de facto negation of the Proclamation proved very costly to the British. The revenue from the fur trade had been intended to defray the cost of maintaining a North American empire by financing the expensive system of military posts and trading centers, helping pay the expenses generated by the French and Indian War, and paying for the presents given to chiefs for distribution in efforts to assure their loyalty to the Crown. Restricting the movements of settlers was, in effect, an attempt to maintain the Natives in their traditional hunting grounds in order to keep a steady supply of furs entering the British trading system. But for the colonists, the land—not peltry—was the valuable commodity, and the rich Ohio valley, off limits to them according to the Proclamation of 1763, was a prize too precious to ignore.

The first breach of "Indian Territory" since the Proclamation of 1763 was, in fact, a recognition that the tide of emigrants could no longer be held back. The Treaty of Fort Stanwix, signed in 1768 by the British and the Iroquois, granted the British rights to Kentucky, despite the claims and protests of the Delawares and Shawnees who, unlike the Iroquois, actually lived there. This treaty, and the British Act of 1774, again moved the border of Indian Territory, only this time west to the Ohio River, while simultaneously reaffirming that the area to the north and west of the river was an Indian state and declaring invalid all Indian land sales in this territory. This move was designed to placate the Native people who were growing weary of the colonists' encroachment. But to the colonists, who demanded that the whole of the territory be opened up to settlement, it was one more "intolerable act," which only fomented more discontent with British rule. When Britain went so far as to impose a tax on the colonies to defray the costs of defending the Indian Territory against settler depredations, the colonists rebelled, and, thus, the Revolutionary War began.

The Revolutionary War and the Anishnaabeg

Although the Native role in the Revolutionary War was small, and perhaps not decisive, when Native people did fight it was almost exclusively on the side of the British, and not one member of the Algonquin Nation (which included all of the Anishnaabeg) could be found that was friendly to the American cause. Among the Anishnaabeg, this included Potawatomi warriors from southwest Michigan who were reluctant partisans after 1780, and, to some extent, Odawa and Ojibway warriors from both Detroit and Michilimackinac, along with the Missisaugas.[2]

According to Indian agent Henry Rowe Schoolcraft, 5,000 Ojibways, 450 Odawas, 450 Potawatomis, and 250 Missisaugas — all Native warriors from the upper Great Lakes — fought in the Revolutionary War. (Schoolcraft also mentioned that all of these Native warriors were from "Canadian" territory.) Of course, all of British North America could be considered "Canadian" before the Revolutionary War; Schoolcraft makes no distinction as to whether these warriors were exclusively from territory that, subsequent to the war, was designated as Canadian as distinct from the territory of the emerging United States.[3]

The fact that the area's Native people fought on the British side should not be construed as their having any great love for the British; more likely it reflected a greater fear of the American settlers. Native people fought with the British against the Americans with the same fervor and for the same reasons they had fought with the French against the British — in defense of their homeland and with the hope of eventually ousting all non-

Native power. While this long-term hope was never realized, at least one change in British behavior during the war did benefit the region's Native people: the British policy, built on the concept of "master and subject," was gradually giving way to one built on "social capital." The British began to rely more and more on the old gift-giving patterns established by the French — gifts that solidified allegiance with the Native people. Chiefs were chosen for their loyalty to the British and lavished with extra gifts, councils were held, disputes were mediated, warriors and their families were fed and clothed at the forts, and gunpowder and shot were again freely distributed.[4]

By 1782 the British were suing for peace and had advised their Indian allies to return to their villages and engage in defensive measures only.[5] The Native people, who viewed the war mainly as a fight between two brothers, were justifiably apprehensive about the terms of peace. To the Anishnaabeg of the Great Lakes region, who had not been conquered by the Americans, why the British were suing for peace was a mystery, and they feared betrayal at their hands.[6] Unfortunately, the Native-European experience that followed the French and Indian War was about to repeat itself.

Protests followed. In a report of one floridly translated speech, most likely made in response to the recent peace overture of the British to the Americans, one unnamed Odawa chief told Captain Robertson at Michilimackinac, on July 6, 1783, that he "was afraid the Tree was fallen on the wrong side, and that [it] ought to have been laid before them, and [then] perhaps the Tree would still be standing straight. They are told the Five nations will keep the door shut . . . but I believe that all of you have been telling us *lies*, but this is our Ground."[7] A modern interpretation of the speech would likely be: "If you [the British] had been willing to allow us [the Odawa] to continue our war against the Americans, we and the Five Nations Iroquois could have held the Americans back, but you have given up the fight and now we are afraid you will betray our lands to the Americans."

Another unnamed Indian, a Wea, delivered the following speech in Detroit on June 28, 1783: "We are informed that instead of prosecuting the War, we are to give up our lands to the Enemy, which gives us great uneasiness—in endeavoring to assist you it seems we have wrought our own ruin." British major De Peyster's reply was to the effect that had they not gone to war, the Americans would have taken the lands anyway; besides, he did not yet know the terms of peace—the implication being that the Native people might yet be able to keep their lands.[8] Whether or not the British believed this to be true, their response to the concerns made by Native people was an admonition to keep the peace, "until told the contrary by their Fathers."[9]

The Second Treaty of Paris
The Second Treaty of Paris, signed by the United States and Great Britain in Paris on September 3, 1783, ended the Revolutionary War. The Native people were not treated too badly in the treaty—they were able to remain in control of their territory and the Americans were either to treat with them for their land, or purchase it. They were assured that they could not be forced off their land nor punished for their role in the war. Throughout the peace negotiations, the British had been assuring their Indian allies that they, the British, would not allow them to be molested by the Americans, and that the British still considered them to be the "King's children."[10] This assurance had some credibility with the Native people, since the peace treaty allowed the British to maintain their posts in the Great Lakes until some later and indefinite date. This was an important consideration as the post at Mackinac was handling as much as three-fifths of all of the trade in Canada's Upper Country.

Part of the reason for Britain's seemingly tough line against the Americans was that the Americans were still a very weak confederation without the ability to impose their will on the large numbers of hostile Natives of the vast western Indian Territory, for, despite the cessions of the Fort Stanwix Treaty, it was still considered to be "Indian Country." The Native people of the western region still refused to accept the concept of themselves as "conquered people" and were adamant that the land was theirs and not the Americans'.[11] The peace treaty that ended the Revolutionary War was, from the Native perspective, essentially a treaty of peace between the new United States and Great Britain; Native people felt less restrained by the treaty and continued to attack white settlements all across the frontier.

Great Britain, however, had not entirely given up its claims to the area. As late as 1786, it was still acting the "father" role when it attempted to broker a peace between the Ojibway and various other nations of the west through the issuance of presents and through the admonition that they were all still Children of the same Father and should not fight among themselves — mainly because it disrupted trade upon which they all relied.[12] Moreover, they continued to negotiate land claims with the tribes. For example, in 1781 the Ojibways and the Odawas did "surrender and yield up . . . forever, the Island of Michilimackinac" to the British, despite the fact that it quite clearly lay within the territory claimed by the new United States.[13] Obviously, the northern Anishnaabeg were still firmly within the British sphere of influence.

The Northwest Ordinance and Its Effect on Native People

During this same tumultuous period, the United States clearly understood that its hold over the Northwest Territories was tenuous at best. This understanding is subtly — even ironically — apparent in the one document most relevant to shaping the new nation's "frontier" and the future of the Native people living within the affected region. The Northwest Ordinance, passed by the fledgling government in 1787, set out the process by which the new territory would be divided into states and the manner by which these new states would be admitted to the Union.

The problem, of course, was that the United States had no control over these lands, which were quite firmly in the hands of their original inhabitants. The Native people were, in turn, strongly supported by Britain. Strapped with enormous debt from the Revolution, the United States could not purchase the lands from the Native people (assuming they would sell), yet saw the sale of the Northwest Territory lands as a source of revenue. The problem, then, became one of how to obtain the lands from the Native people at the lowest cost. The Northwest Ordinance purported to set out an orderly, non-military process by which the lands would become part of the expanding American empire. Article Three of the Ordinance (dealing with education and the treatment of the Indians) reads, in part: "The utmost good faith shall always be observed toward the Indians; their lands and property shall never be taken from them without their consent; and in their property, rights and liberty, they shall never be invaded or disturbed, unless in just and lawful wars authorized by Congress."[14] The government policy underlying the article was to encourage a gradual movement of the frontier westward, slowly opening the land to settlement, with the Native people gradually moving west behind this advancing frontier, until they would eventually move north into Canada or west of the Mississippi. At the time the Ordinance went into effect, the options of forced removal or conquest were unrealistic, both from a military as well as a financial perspective. Skeptics regard this article as "more a blueprint of political and social conquest"[15] than as basically humane policy of "good faith" and voluntary "consent."[16] In fact, Robert M. Taylor Jr. characterizes Article Three as "at best ironic and at worst hypocritical," since the Native people of the region were wholly opposed to further expansion of American settlements.[17] The Native people directly affected by this expansion were the Delaware, Shawnee, and Miami who now lived just north and west of the Ohio River, but who had already been pushed out of Pennsylvania and were adamant in their refusal to be pushed further. The Iroquois to the east and the Anishnaabeg to the northwest, indeed, all the "Western Indians," understood all too well that the dispossession of their homelands was the foundation of the Northwest Ordinance.

The Continuing Struggle for the Ohio Valley

In defense of their homelands, virtually all of the "western" Indian Nations entered into a single confederation, of which the Great Lake Anishnaabeg were a valuable part. In addition to the Six Nation Iroquois, the confederation sent warriors into the field from a number of tribes: the Cherokees, Ojibways, Delawares, Hurons, Kickapoos, Mascoutens, Miamis, Mingos, Munsees, Odawas, Piankeshaws, Potawatomis, Sauks, Shawnees, and Weas.[18] This much wider and more solid confederation than that assembled by Pontiac two decades earlier lit its Council Fire at Brownstown at the mouth of the Detroit River (on the "U.S." side).

The major impetus behind the confederation was the need to present a united front to the Americans. Its driving force was Joseph Brant, the celebrated Mohawk chief, and its model that of the Iroquois Confederacy. While the confederacy did represent virtually all of the tribes of the "Indian Territory," its major tenet was that the land west of the Ohio belonged to *all* of the Native people and could not be sold or treated for unless *all* of the tribes agreed. The power of the confederacy to hold sway over each individual tribe, "chief," and warrior was at best tenuous. Small village chiefs did, in fact, sign treaties with the new U.S. government, which then claimed the newly ceded territory, despite the wider confederacy view that such cessions were invalid. Eventually, a major breach in the confederacy was opened by members of the Huron-Wyandots who, due to an historic mutual animosity, resented the Iroquois' dominance of the confederation and made a bid for its leadership in 1788.

At the same time, while Brant was negotiating with the Americans to assemble a council to discuss peace and land cessions, the Huron unilaterally accepted an American offer and set up their own treaty process, which yielded the Treaty of Fort Harmar in 1788. This treaty essentially ratified the earlier land cession treaties entered into by village chiefs without the consent of the entire confederation. As it had done with the earlier village chief treaties, the wider confederacy repudiated this treaty. Though it had been signed by a large number of tribal representatives, including (in addition to the Huron) representatives from the Delawares, Odawas, Ojibways, Potawatomis, Munsees, and Sauks, none of the signatories were important tribal leaders and, for the most part, had little claim to the land being ceded. The situation was so untenable that even the leading Huron chief refused to sign the treaty.[19]

As a stratagem to achieve ascendancy at the expense of the Iroquois, the Treaty of Fort Harmar was a failure for the Huron and discredited both tribes in the eyes of those western tribes that had—and wanted—no part in the negotiations. Although the confederation itself was not destroyed by the Huron action in 1788, the leadership did change, evolving to the Shawnees, Miamis, and Delawares who were most affected by the land cessions agreed to by the Fort Harmar Treaty. Not coincidentally, these Native people would gradually emerge as the most militant within the confederation, since it was they who were most reluctant to accept the "peace" of 1783 and were the tribes most endangered by unauthorized western settlement.

While the Native people were entering into their confederacy, and the British were attempting to foster better relationships with the upper Great Lakes Native people, the Americans were preparing to send troops into the region in attempts to subdue the Native people who were raiding the settlements in southern Ohio and Kentucky. In 1790 a U.S. expedition led by General Harmar was ambushed by warriors, and the American expedition was destroyed. A year later, General St. Clair led another American force into the same area with even more disastrous results: over six hundred were killed and nearly three hundred were wounded. The defeat of St. Clair was a stunning blow to the Americans and a glorious victory for the Native warriors. In spite of these victories, the Harmar and St. Clair battles revealed the weakness of the Indian Confederacy — they could not keep the warriors in the field for any sustained engagements. These were Native warriors, not army regulars, and when the battle was over they went home. Moreover, the Native concept of individual liberty meant that Native warriors were free to follow their war chief or abandon him as they evaluated the conflict — they could not be compelled to fight. Keeping these troops supplied on the battlefield was another serious problem, and it gave the British, who had recognized this weakness and become the supplier for the Native troops, increasing influence over the confederacy and further drawing it into British-American disputes.[20]

After the defeats of Harmar and St. Clair, both sides — that is, the Americans and the Natives — sought peace. The Americans, for their part, accepted the fact that the Indian nations had not been defeated and thus that Native territory could not be taken without their agreement. The Native people were prepared to make peace only if the Americans could insure that no colonizing settlements would be allowed within their territory. The only sticking point to the negotiations was the question of where the boundary between the two nations would be drawn: the confederacy demanded that it be the existing Ohio River boundary; the Americans pressed for a Muskingum boundary that would have given them eastern Ohio (essentially the position agreed to by the Huron-brokered Treaty of Fort Harmar in 1788). It seems that the only thing both parties could agree on was that the "permanent" Indian boundary set out in the Proclamation of 1783 was no longer the Appalachian Mountains. Disagreements among the Native people themselves about where to locate the boundary weakened their solidarity and widened their dependency on the British.

The situation came to a head in 1794 when, despite being routed by American troops under Gen. Anthony Wayne, the British failed to come to the aid of the badly divided confederacy, leaving the Ohio Indians to fight Wayne's troops alone.[21] Following the "Battle of the Fallen Timbers," many Native groups reconciled themselves to making peace with the Americans, and many Anishnaabeg from the upper Great Lakes became part of the Indian force that met General Wayne late in 1794 to negotiate the Treaty of Greenville, signed in 1795.[22] These negotiations contained assurances that the United States agreed that the lands west of the Ohio were sovereign Indian territory, and that the Americans held no claim to them, other than that which would be freely granted by the Native people to the United States through treaty and purchase — essentially the same provisions agreed on earlier by the British and the Americans. In return, the United States demanded that the Indians recognize the United States as their "protector," and if they wished to cede any lands, they would "treat" only with the U.S. government when doing so. A compromise had been struck: Indian territory was exclusively Native, but the United States was now the Indians' new and only "father." The transfer of power from the British to the Americans appeared to be firm and irrefutable.

Certainly the Greenville Treaty gave little advantage to any side, whether British, American, or Native. It was essentially a document that recognized the fact of stalemate. It had drawn a line separating the Indian from the settler, leaving the Native people of the Great Lakes in control of their territory and permitting the British, while chastised, to buy some time to salvage what they could of their fur trade monopoly. The stalemate was, however, highly unstable, and what followed led to its inevitable devolution to American control.

The United States and the Division of the Anishnaabeg Homeland

Presents and British Posts

The British did agree to abandon their posts with "convenient speed" in the 1783 Treaty of Paris that ended the Revolutionary War, but "convenient speed" turned out to be more a figure of speech, because the British took a decidedly long time to leave. They were still in possession of their posts in the upper Great Lakes in 1795 when the Americans were pressing their case at the Battle of Fallen Timbers.

This limited "victory" led the Americans to again demand that the posts be abandoned at once. Their objections to the British posts were manifold. First, the American government wished to open the Ohio valley to settlement and use the proceeds from the resultant land sales to help retire the new nation's debt. Secondly, the United States' hold on the territory was tenuous without control of the British posts. The Native people of the region, maintaining that the recent war between the Americans and the British had been a struggle between brothers, regarded the resultant peace treaty as a resolution to that conflict only, not as a land cession treaty involving Native people. Despite the Treaty of Greenville, the Native people continued to insist that the Fort Stanwix Treaty line was the valid eastern boundary of "Indian Territory." They looked to the British to help them maintain their hold on the territory and keep the Americans out. Consequently, though the British were not anxious for another war with the Americans, the presence of British forts did give tacit support for the Native claim to the region.

Third, in recognition of their weak hold on the territory, the

Americans justly complained that the British forts were being used to supply the Native people with guns and ammunition, which posed a persistent threat to their interests. The British, however, were not quite ready to relinquish their own (commercial) interests in the area; aware that the Native people of the region still held the balance of power, they wished to maintain Native loyalty and alliance as a way of maintaining hegemony in the region. As the British had learned, the distribution of gifts helped preserve this loyalty, and in 1794 the British distributed them at Swan Creek, south of Detroit—ostensibly U.S. territory—to the Nanticokes, Duquanias, Cayugas, Tuscaroras, Mingos, Oneidas, Mohawks, Delawares, Connoys, Munseys, Cherokees, Mahicans, Delawares, Shawnees, Miamis, Pickaways, Kickapoos, Maquitches, Waliatamakis, Chillicothes, and Odawas.[1]

The "Indian Buffer State"

While the British desired the loyalty of the Native people, they were not always willing to reciprocate. The 1768 Treaty of Fort Stanwix had declared, for instance, that the region in question was called "Indian Territory." This declaration had not been reasserted by the 1783 Treaty of Paris, which referred to the area as the "Old Northwest." This omission gave the region's Native people a reason to suspect British motives and loyalties. In hopes of averting an Indian uprising, John Graves Simcoe, the British governor who had been appointed in 1791, sought to placate the Indians by retaining the British posts in the area.[2] They also proposed to the Americans that the area be set aside as an "Indian Buffer State," the maintenance of which would continue to serve British commercial interests. The British merchants and their Canadian counterparts understood that the new American government wished to open the Great Lakes area to settlement, an action which would inevitably destroy the Native hunting grounds and seriously impair the fur trade. An Indian Buffer State, which would require a redrawing of the U.S.–British North

Map 7. Proposed Indian Buffer State

Proposed Indian
Buffer State

International boundaries
desired by Great Britain at
the Treaty of Ghent, 1814

American boundary established after the Revolution, would interpose another "state" between the two countries (thereby decreasing the size of the U.S. territory).

According to early British designs, the Indian Buffer State would include all of the "Old Northwest," give Britain access to a navigable portion of the Mississippi River, and include much of the Great Plains up to the Rocky Mountains.[3] A map that shows the boundaries of the United States, Canada, and a scaled-down Indian Buffer State, as actually proposed by British officials, is shown in map 7. Of course the British proposed as well that the Indian Buffer State be under their protection, hence the necessity of maintaining their posts in the region.

Jay's Treaty

A further complication came in the form of "Jay's Treaty," named after its chief negotiator, John Jay, the first chief justice of the U.S. Supreme Court. The treaty's official title is The Treaty of Amity, Commerce, and Navigation. Negotiated in 1794 in the midst of the battle of Fallen Timbers, Jay's Treaty was designed to settle the differences not resolved by the Treaty of Paris ending the American Revolution. Article III of Jay's Treaty relates to traders and the Native people of the region and is significant in the context of the continuation of the British posts. The relevant text of Article III is quoted below:

> It is agreed that it shall at all times be free for His Majesty's subjects, and to citizens of the United States, and also to the Indians dwelling on either side of the said boundary line freely to pass and repass by land or inland navigation, into the respective territories and countries of the two parties, on the continent of America, (the country within the limits of the Hudson's Bay Company also excepted,) and to navigate all the lakes, rivers and waters thereof, and freely to carry on trade and commerce with each other. . . . No duty of entry shall ever be levied by either party on peltries brought by land or inland navigation into said territories, nor shall the Indians passing or repassing with their own proper goods and effects of whatever nature, pay for the same any impost or duty whatever. But goods in bales, or other large packages, unusual among Indians, shall not be considered as goods belonging bona fide to Indians.

This early North American "free trade" agreement clearly conflicted with the Treaty of Greenville. To help the United States gain control over the lucrative fur trade, the Fort Greenville treaty had stipulated that the traders in the upper Great Lakes needed a license from the U.S. government, whereas the provision of the Jay Treaty quoted above allowed citizens of both countries and the Native people to pass freely and trade throughout the territory. The British used the uncertainty created by this discrepancy to once again refuse to abandon their posts in the upper Great Lakes, thus insuring that the area's lucrative fur trade was firmly in their hands and that its Native inhabitants remained, despite the Greenville Treaty, firmly within the British sphere.

In short, for the United States, the situation was completely unacceptable: the British were still in possession of their forts throughout territory which, in theory, belonged to the United States; the fur trade continued to be controlled by the British; and, due to continuing Native land claims and Native opposition to the new U.S. government, the area could not be opened for settlement. The War of 1812 was the nearly inevitable result.

The Anishnaabeg and the War of 1812

Just as Pontiac has come to be associated with the principal action of the French and Indian Wars, Tecumseh is regarded as the key Native leader in the War of 1812. Tecumseh was a Shawnee who, with his brother Tenskwatawa (The Shawnee Prophet), reassembled the members of the earlier pan-Indian confederacy in the Old Northwest. The involvement of the Anishnaabeg in this confederation was significant. A document published in 1812 prior to the outbreak of hostilities recounted that "considerable numbers" of Potawatomi, Odawa, and Ojibway were with Tenskwatawa at the confederacy's village of Prophetstown in Indiana.[4] Tecumseh and many other Native leaders had never accepted the terms of the Treaty of Greenville. Their position, supported by a great number of Native groups and based on the provisions of the earlier confederacy, was that the validity of any land cession was dependent upon agreement by all the region's tribes.

The 1812 report further claimed that gifts "more abundant than usual" were being accumulated at Fort Malden, which was just south of what is now Windsor, Ontario, and that Indians from the north and south of Detroit were repairing there. The fact that many Indians, including the Sauk, were also visiting the

British at St. Joseph Island at the far end of Lake Huron was cited in the report as well.[5] Apparently, the U.S. government used this reported increase in present-giving activity as justification for its preemptive raid on Prophetstown in 1811. The report was, of course, not made public until after the raid.

Many Anishnaabeg fought with Tecumseh and the British in the course of the war, despite having considered the British their enemy only a generation earlier; the post–Pontiac British gift policy, redesigned to follow the earlier French example, was serving the Native people well. By contrast, the American policy had been altered to mirror the previous British one of granting gifts only as payments for debts. The British policy of "disguised exploitation" was, moreover, less harsh than the American policy of displacing Native people with white settlers. The Americans were now the enemy.

Hence the attack on Fort Michilimackinac, one of the few Great Lakes posts that the British had abandoned earlier to the Americans.[6] Together with other Native people, over 300 Odawas, under their chief, Amable Chevalier, of Lower Canada, participated in the attack, which was deployed from St. Joseph Island. Notable among the raiders were two white fur traders from Sault Ste. Marie, John Johnston and Charles Ermatinger, both of whom had married into influential Native families. Johnston had wed a daughter of Waubojeeg, a distinguished Sault chief (and one of Johnston's daughters, Obaabaam-waawaagezhegoqua—The Sound Which Stars Make Rushing Through The Sky—would later marry Indian agent Henry Rowe Schoolcraft).[7] Ermatinger was married to Charlotte Katawabide, "the daughter of an Ojibway chief."[8] According to one source, Johnston, Ermatinger, and the Native people assembled on St. Joseph Island for the Michilimackinac raid were present at the behest of the traders of the Southwest Fur Company and the Northwest Company, evidence supporting the notion that the War of 1812 was a fur trade war fought mainly for commercial reasons.[9]

While Johnston, Ermatinger, and others were engaged in the raid on Mackinac, the U.S. Army seized Ermatinger's property and "plundered and destroyed" John Johnston's in retaliation. (As a result of the war, Charles Ermatinger moved to the north shore of the St. Mary's River where he set up a new trading post in violation of American Fur Trading Company policy, i.e., he held no license from the company, while John Johnston rebuilt his post on the south side of the river.)

Records show that Shingwauk, the Ojibway chief from the Sault, had fought with Tecumseh and that other Ojibways from the Sault lost their lives at the Thames River battle where Tecumseh fell.[10] With Tecumseh's death the War of 1812 was essentially over, and any Native hopes for driving the Americans out of their territory were dashed. The British, while lamenting the death of Tecumseh, were pleased that they and their Native allies had kept the United States out of Canada and, thus, regarded the war as a "victory."

The Postwar Period

There is ample evidence that the British had used Native fear of the Americans' desire for more land—Native and British land, to be more exact—to exhort the warriors to fight for the "British" cause since it was, indeed, their cause as well. In this vein, British Lieutenant Colonel McDonald delivered a rousing speech in 1814 to the Native chiefs assembled at Mackinac:

> You have now proved that you merit the benevolence and friendship with which your Great Father [the British King] has always treated you; be assured that the interests of his Red Children will never be forgotten by him, that he will keep his word and the promises which he has made to you, my children. . . . The Great Spirit smiles on our just cause, but frowns on that of the deceitful Americans because they have cruelly oppressed you [and if they win] you will be gradually driven beyond the Setting Sun.[11]

Despite these reassuring words, the Native people of the region had once again sided with the losing faction, though they had not, themselves, been conquered. Indeed, after the war of 1812, the Anishnaabeg were still in control of all of the upper Great Lakes territory. Again, Lieutenant Colonel McDonald urged the Indians to have confidence in the security of their position:

> Should the King, your Great Father, deign to listen to the proposal which the enemy have made for peace, it will be on the express condition that your interests shall be first considered, your just claims admitted, and no infringement of your rights permitted in [the] future. My Children, doubt not that this will be the case. . . . He will never abandon his Red Children.[12]

Despite the rhetoric, the Native people doubted that the British would represent their interests in negotiations with the Americans, and they were correct in their suspicions: the area was, in fact, ceded to the new U.S. government and the British abandoned the posts purportedly on "U.S." soil. In return for their loyalty, the Native people were instructed by the British to "be on good terms with our neighbors, the Big Knives" and to treat the American traders with respect.[13] In a response to McDonald's speech delivered to a contingent of "western Indians," including Winnebago, Sauk, and Fox warriors, the Sauk chief Black Hawk, apparently referring to the Americans, declared that since the British had made peace with the United States "a black cloud is overrunning our country."[14]

For one thing, the American determination to put an end to Britain's control of posts on "U.S." territory would significantly impact the all-important distribution of presents. Mackinac Island, ceded to the British in 1781 by the Ojibways and the Odawas, was one of these posts. The British had maintained their presence there (prodded by Jay's Treaty) until 1796 when they moved their operations to St. Joseph Island, at the western end of Lake Huron's North Channel. In 1797 the annual distribution of presents took place there. St Joseph Island had been ceded by the Ojibways to the British in 1798 and, for a period of time, was the main British post for the distribution of presents, as well as serving as the supply point for combined British and Native forces in the War of 1812. After that war, the British again returned to Mackinac Island. The Treaty of Ghent (1814), however, which formally ended that war, stipulated that the British must again abandon their Mackinac fort. Michigan's territorial governor, Lewis Cass, felt strongly that the fort posed an imminent threat; accordingly, he petitioned the secretary of war to mount a naval blockade of the island to starve out the British and harm their Indian allies. According to Cass, another good reason to blockade Michilimackinac was to disrupt the distribution of presents there. In his view, "[a] great proportion of the Ottawas with nearly the whole of the numerous Nation of the Chipeways are hostile . . . restless, turbulent, and insubordinate. . . . [The blockade] would at all events prevent the accustomed supply of Indian goods and would destroy the influence, which distribution of presents is ever calculated to produce over venal savages."[15] Though the blockade was never mounted, the British abandoned Mackinac on July 18, 1815, leaving Mackinac Island irrevocably under U.S. control.

To protect their political and economic interests in the region, the British continued to require a regional post that would allow them to maintain their alliance with the area's Native people, who were still considered to hold the balance of power in the region. This necessitated a convenient post at which the annual distribution of presents could be made. Moreover, thousands of Native people, some from as far away as the Mississippi River Basin and the Red River area of Manitoba, were accustomed to reporting to the upper Great Lakes area for their annuities and presents. With the understanding that the terms of peace between Britain and the U.S. prevented them from distributing presents on "American" soil, the British began their search for a new site for a fort.

Due to considerations of convenience, the Sault was eliminated as a possibility. Problems with the previous site on St. Joseph Island doomed it as well. The British commander at Mackinac, Lieutenant Colonel McDonald, settled on Drummond Island, noting that: "The situation combines several important advantages, viz., an admirable harbor, proximity to the Indians, and will enable us also to command the passage of the detour . . ."[16] (see map 4). According to Samuel Cook, in *Drummond Island: The Story of British Occupation: 1815–1828*, the island, "for military purposes was well nigh useless, but as a rendezvous from which to retain influence over the Indians [it] was admirably chosen."[17] Here, too, the Treaty of Ghent was unclear as to the ownership of Pontaganipy—the Native name for Drummond Island—but for the sake of propriety, McDonall had Nebawg-naine, an Ojibway chief from Saginaw still loyal to the British, ceded the island to them where, in 1816, the British resumed their annual distribution.

In 1818, this time at a Native council on Drummond Island attended by 350 representatives of the Odawas, the Ojibways, and the Winnebagos, the Odawa chief Ocaita complained that "bad spirits" — that is, the Americans — were taking over Odawa land without treating with them for it, and that furthermore the British were not halting these American seizures despite their earlier promises to protect the rights and lands of the Native people. Ocaita further complained that the Americans "treat us worse than dogs," and that the British have abandoned us and "delivered us up to their mercy" (that is, to the Americans).[18]

In an earlier council, the British had heard the complaints of other Native leaders. A Winnebago chief insisted that because the Native people had not made peace with the Americans, the British had no right to give their land to the Americans. The cession of Mackinac Island, in particular, was greatly protested. Makataypenesee, the Odawa chief from L'Arbre Croche, called the Island "the most important place this side of Quebec," and pleaded with the British to retain the island, offering in its place land on the mainland for the American fort and suggesting, as well, that the border between the two interests be drawn through the Straits of Mackinac.[19] (The recorded date of this council, which took place on Michilimackinac, appears to be in error; the place and the context would place it prior to the abandonment of the island by the British).

While it is true that the British had largely abandoned their War of 1812 allies with respect to U.S. territorial claims, they did not desert them entirely. Still attempting to solidify their alliance, the British continued to deliver gifts to the Native people without regard to their residence on either side of the border; virtually all Native people from the newly ceded Old Northwest were eligible. As early as 1808 an accounting of the presents distributed at the Grand River in Ontario (home of the Six Nations), shows the breakdown of Native people from U.S. territory, comparing it with those residing in Canada: 1,924 were from Canada, 2,292 from the United States.[20] Such statistics reveal the obvious importance of the "American" Native people to British interests.

Other accounts of gift distributions show a more detailed delineation of recipients. In addition to the members of the Six Nations, a June, 1814, accounting of presents distributed at the Grand River shows that the following First Nations were represented: Shawnee, Kickapoo, Munsey, Moravian, Sauk and Fox, Delaware, Seneca, Cayuga, Odawa, Ojibway, and Potawatomi. Of these, the Odawa, Ojibway, and Potawatomi were included under one count and, when considered as a unit (as the British thought of them), they constituted the largest group outside of the Six Nations themselves. Of the 830 men who, with their families, traveled the long distance from their homelands in the western Great Lakes region to the Grand River for gifts, 428 were Odawas, Ojibways, and Potawatomis.[21]

At another distribution later in the year, the same pattern held: of the Nations traveling to the Grand River for presents, the Anishnaabeg again constituted the largest group.[22] It is important to point out that it was fairly common practice for Native people to collect presents from both the Americans and the British, and to do so at several locations if possible, claiming perhaps to be Ojibway at one post, Odawa at another, and Potawatomi at still a third. It is significant as well that the distribution of presents was not totally one-sided: the visiting Native people supplied the garrisons with foodstuffs and, more importantly, traded their furs—furs still being the primary reason for the continued British presence in the region. Nor was the securing of loyalties the aim only of the British or the Americans. The issue was sometimes openly broached by the Native people themselves as they attempted to gain greater concessions from one side or another.[23]

The 1820 Treaty of Sault Ste. Marie and American Control over the Sault Area

In the face of this continuing British-Native relationship, the U.S. government attempted to establish control over the Lake Huron borderlands, manning the abandoned British posts at Detroit and Michilimackinac. Sault Ste. Marie, at the northern terminus of the area, had never been the home of a British fort and was proving to be a difficult area for the Americans to secure. In 1815, according to George Johnston, son of the fur trader John Johnston and a government interpreter:

> [T]he Indians [of the northern Great Lakes] were lords of the soil, free and independent, and fierce as the northern autumnal blast. At this time the Indians were numerous and yet still hostile to the Americans, from the fact of their having lost many of their friends

and relatives during the war with England which broke out in 1812. Their wounds were not yet healed, nor was their aversion to the American name lessened, and . . . the least pretext would have called forth the tomahawk and scalping knife to avenge the deaths of their relatives killed in the war.[24]

Into this situation at the Sault stepped a contingent of U.S. Army soldiers, intent upon showing the flag and surveying the new "U.S." holdings. Upon their arrival, they received word that the Indians were planning to raid their camp that night. Sentinels were posted, and though they were not molested in any way, when day broke, "it was considered most prudent" that the general and his soldiers leave the area immediately and give up on their plans to visit Lake Superior.[25]

In July of the following year (1816), a group of Native people attacked another army contingent under General McComb as it made its way to Lake Superior after an uneventful stay of several days in the Sault. This party also "thought it advisable to put about and return. . . . So end[ing] the expedition."[26] Thus, once in 1815 and again in 1816, U.S. Army patrols had been prevented from passing beyond the rapids at the Sault by hostile, Native forces. In 1818 the United States was again fired upon, this time when they were above the rapids.[27] (This was occurring at the same time that Ocaita, in the council cited above, was complaining to the British about American activities in the area.)

It wasn't until 1820 that the Army made yet another attempt to secure the area. They were accompanied by Governor Cass, who in 1819 had expressed fear that the Great Lakes Native people were still under the influence of Tecumseh's brother, Tenskwatawa (The Shawnee Prophet), and had been plotting at the Malden gift distribution in southern Ontario to reform the confederacy to resume their attacks on the United States (Tenskwatawa lived in this area for years after his brother's death). Cass included the Sioux, Sacs, Winnebagos, Shawnees, Kickapoos, Menominees, Potawatomis, Odawas, and Ojibways as members of this new "conspiracy," which was purportedly planning an offensive for the spring or fall of 1820.[28] In the very midst of the rumored planning for this attack, Cass traveled to the Sault to secure a land cession from the Ojibways in order to erect a fort. A council was called for the purpose of discussing the particulars, although subsequent events proved that the important Native leaders were not in attendance.

Among those who were there was the Ojibway "young chief" Sessaba, who had apparently lost a brother at the Battle of the Thames and was still loyal to the British cause. At the very start of the council, Sessaba upbraided the assembled subchiefs when they went to pick up and smoke the tobacco thrown on the ground to them by an army interpreter—an obvious insult. Sessaba immediately left the council room and returned to the village, where he raised the British flag. Word of his action touched off a potentially serious confrontation between his followers and the army, and the "treaty" council was dispersed. The elder chiefs, who were not present at this council, were urged to confront Sessaba to put a stop to his protest and threats of violence. The chief chosen to confront Sessaba was Shingwaukonce (Little Pine), the "British Chief" from Garden River, just east of the Canadian Sault. Shingwaukonce was an important ally of the British who had fought with them throughout the War of 1812, including the siege of Detroit.

Although he suffered a blow from Sessaba's war club, Shingwaukonce managed to secure a peaceful end to the crisis. The British flag was struck and the flag of the United States hauled up in its place. Once the council resumed its proceedings, Cass was able to extract from the Ojibway a cession of sixteen square miles (though his instructions had been to obtain a maximum of ten).[29] The Ojibway did reserve the right to fish in the rapids and to maintain an encampment along the shore for this purpose. They wished, as well, to retain a small burial ground within the sixteen-square-mile area, which (in the words of Cass), "they regard with peculiar veneration. . . . [as it] contains the bones of their ancestors, objects of great solicitude, mingled with religious feelings."[30]

Cass's letter to John C. Calhoun, the secretary of war, details these and other particulars of the negotiations, but it is instructive in other respects as well. He wrote, "I did not require the Indians to cede to us a larger tract . . . because it is important to our character and influence among them, that our *first* demand should be distinctly marked with moderation" (emphasis added).[31] This makes clear that the land acquired in the 1820 treaty was not the only cession that Cass wished to extract from the Ojibway of the upper Great Lakes. Interestingly, there is no mention in the letter of the resistance Cass encountered; certainly nothing in the treaty itself revealed Cass's close encounter with disaster on the shores of the St. Mary's River at the hands of Ojibway people who were obviously still hostile to the U.S. presence in the region.

Cass's letter also neglects to mention any discussion of the residency status of the treaty's Native signatories, conveniently avoiding, it would seem, the question of whether or not those signatories had the authority to cede the land. For example, Shingwaukonce had lived in various places throughout the Upper Peninsula of what is now the state of Michigan, as well as at Saginaw in the lower peninsula; most often he resided on the northern shore of the St. Mary's River at Sault Ste. Marie in Canada.[32] He and his son, Ogista, had also been living in Canada when they became signatories to the 1819 Treaty of Saginaw—also negotiated by Cass—whereby the Ojibways ceded the remaining southeast portion of Michigan's lower peninsula not already ceded in 1807, which comprised all of the lands surrounding Saginaw Bay and extending into central south Michigan. Shingwaukonce and Ogista are listed in the treaty registry respectively as "Shingwalk" and "Shingwalk, jun."[33] (From about this point on, Shingwaukonce apparently preferred to be known as "Shingwauk" [The Pine] dropping the last part of his name, "-once" which signified "little").

It is interesting to note that Shingwauk signed the 1820 treaty as "Augustin Bart," his French name, and, after the treaty-signing, resumed his residence on the "British" side of the St. Mary's River.[34] Other accounts have him signing as "Lavoine Bart," apparently another of his assumed names. Shingwauk's son, "Ogista / Shingwalk, jun.," also signed Canadian treaties as "Augustin."[35] The significance of the use of these various names at treaty-signings will be clarified in the chapters that follow.

In 1822 the Native people who were traveling to British forts from American territory for their presents were reportedly being threatened by U.S. authorities with imprisonment and beatings as they passed by Michilimackinac. Since the presents were distributed at Drummond Island, British authorities there had been quick to offer their protection to the Native people, who were justifiably concerned that the Americans would act on their threat.[36] Responsibility for this threatened hostility on the part of the U.S. authorities may be attributed to Governor Cass himself, who, in his 1820 letter to Secretary of War, Calhoun, wrote: "The farther I penetrate into the Country [the upper Great Lakes], the more apparent are the effects produced upon the feelings of the Indians by the prodigal issue of presents to them at the British Posts of Malden and Drummonds [sic] Island. . . . There will neither be permanent peace nor reasonable security upon this frontier, until this intercourse is wholly prevented."[37]

In spite of Cass's securing of a land cession at the Sault for a military fort and his reports of Native hostilities toward the surveyors years after the war with Britain had been concluded, the federal government had still not appropriated monies for a military defense of the area.[38] In the winter of 1824 in yet another attack on a surveyor crew, Cass reported to Calhoun that "the Indians during the whole winter have appeared unfriendly, that they have taken up his [the surveyor's] posts and obliterated his marks and numbers upon the trees, that they forbade his proceeding, and that finally they attacked and fired upon his men." The surveyor, Cass noted, "left his work the day after this attack."[39]

Based partly upon these recurrent attacks on government surveyors, Cass considered the Old Northwest frontier to be "the weakest and most exposed in the Union" and admonished the war secretary for his plan to withdraw the military garrison from Michilimackinac. The British distribution of gifts continued to disturb Cass, too. "Large bodies of Indians are always found here during the summer season, he complained, "stopping here on their way to and from Drummonds [sic] Island."[40] In the same letter, Cass also bemoaned Fort Malden, the British "Indian Headquarters" directly opposite Detroit, which was, in his words, "where . . . the influence and operations of the department [are] concentrated and directed," and the post to which "almost all of the Indians on [the U.S.] side of the Mississippi resort annually." The effect of all these "British counsels and presents—freely distributed," argued Cass, "may be traced in all our disputes with the Indians from the treaty of 1783 to this day."

In this dispatch to Calhoun, Cass made special mention, as well, of the "Potawatamies, Ottawa, and Chippewas, amounting. . . . to about twenty thousand" and claims that "garrisons four or five hundred miles from them can neither control nor restrain them. . . . [A]nd if there be no force stationed upon the boundaries of their Country, nor in its interior, there is nothing to produce an effect upon them."[41] Disregarding the existence of twenty thousand Anishnaabeg living "upon this peninsula," Cass called for the protection of "the whole population [of European-Americans, which] does not exceed eleven thousand," informing the secretary that he had ordered the garrison at Mackinac to remain in place because of his conviction that "some unfortunate occurrence will demonstrate the impropriety of the evacuation."[42] In lower Michigan, Cass was pressing for a fort to be built on the Saginaw River to counter the threat of the Ojibway there, "who have proved themselves more troublesome than any other Indians . . . always unquiet and insolent." The Ojibway, Cass claimed, had always been loyal to the British and "present formidable obstacles to the progress of settlement."[43]

After the securing of the cession at the Sault, the U.S. government installed Henry Rowe Schoolcraft as Indian agent in 1822. More sensitive than Cass, perhaps, to balance-of-power issues in the region, the federal government instructed Schoolcraft to foster good relations with all of the area's important Native leaders without regard to their residence, that is, without regard to whether they lived on the American or the Canadian side of the border.[44] At this time, however, the border through the upper St. Mary's River was still in dispute. Essentially, British and U.S. officials could not agree on ownership of Sugar Island (also known as St. George's Island). Officially, the border was supposed to follow the usual shipping lanes in order to avoid forcing one party to intrude on the territory of the other while navigating the Great Lakes system; at Sugar Island, this precept was put to the test. According to John Bassett Moore's 1898 book, *History and Digest of the International Arbitrations to Which the United States Has Been a Party*, the deliberations concerning Sugar Island and the Treaty of Ghent required that the boundary line pass "to the north and east of Isle à la Crosse, and of the small islands numbered 16, 17, 18, 19, and 20, and to the south and west of those numbered 21, 22, and 23, until it strikes a line... passing across the river at the head of St. Joseph Island, and at the foot of the Neebish rapids, which line denotes the termination of the boundary directed to be run by the sixth article of the treaty of Ghent"[45] (see map 8).

The "line passing *across* the river denot[ing] the *termination* of the boundary" is simply the obfuscating language of diplomacy (emphases added). A more faithful rendering would state the obvious: "Because we can't agree on where the boundary

Map 8. Disputed Boundary in St. Mary's River

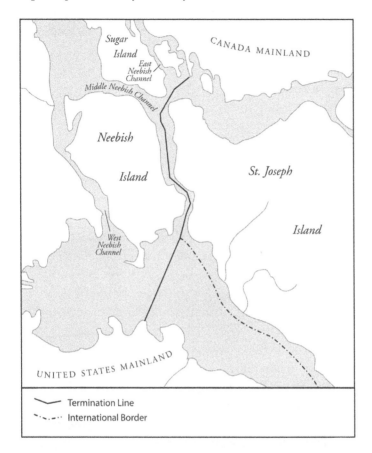

Sugar Island

CANADA MAINLAND

East Neebish Channel

Middle Neebish Channel

Neebish Island

St. Joseph

West Neebish Channel

Island

UNITED STATES MAINLAND

⌒ Termination Line
–·–·– International Border

goes after this point, the boundary ends here; we'll pick it up at the other end of Sugar Island" (this section of the border was not drawn until 1842; more will be said of this odd situation in the Epilogue). The instructions to Schoolcraft, in part, may have reflected this border ambiguity. Since it was not clear whether the residents of the large Native settlements on the island were "American" or "Canadian," it seemed preferable to treat all of the Native people equally. Doubtlessly helping to shape this conclusion was the fact that the area was far from being firmly under U.S. control: not only were the British still honoring their earlier commitments to Native people and maintaining their alliance through the distribution of presents, but the attacks on the surveyors had not yet stopped.

Presents Redux

The British commitment to the presents' policy depended, of course, upon reciprocation in the form of Native loyalties; American land grabs of Native territory continued to shore up such loyalties. The Indian Council held in June of 1816, when the annual distribution of presents was resumed on Drummond Island for the first time since the War of 1812, is instructive on this point. Shouapaw, a Winnebago proclaimed that "[t]he Saux [Sak], Renards [Fox], Agovois [Odawa], Kickapoos, Fallavoines [Menominee], Chippewas, and the Winnebagos have entered into a league not to suffer any encroachments to be made on our lands, at the same time, we will wait a little time for an answer from our great Father, before we have recourse to violent measures."[46]

Several other chiefs spoke in the same manner, and although the British military men gave the chiefs no encouragement in their threatened hostilities against the Americans, yet another anti-American, pro-British, pan-Native confederacy was being formed to defend the Native homeland. (Although the Potawatomi are not listed in Shouapaw's speech, they, like all Anishnaabeg have always played a significant role in these confederacies.) Despite such organized resistance, a series of "peace" treaties had been negotiated by the U.S. government in 1815 whereby various "western" tribes agreed "to be under the protection of the United States, and of no other nation, power, or sovereign whatsoever."[47] Four of these treaties were signed by various bands of Sioux. Subsequently, at the 1816 Drummond Island distribution, the Sioux delegations received only a scant portion of presents from their British Fathers." Their chief, Little Crow, understood the meaning behind this slight (as, in fact, did all the assembled tribes) and the Sioux soon left the council and the island, ending the relationship between the British and the Sioux Nations.[48] Though the War of 1812 against the Americans was over, the consequences of alienating the British were evident to all the indigenous Nations in attendance.

Indigenous loyalties were not sought by the British alone. The Americans, too, solicited the loyalty of the Anishnaabeg of the upper Great Lakes, and Schoolcraft, as Indian agent, began his own gift distribution. The important Native leaders at Schoolcraft's first presents allotment were the chiefs Shingabawassin (Image Stone), Shewbeketone (Man of Jingling Medals), Kaugaosh (Bird in Eternal Flight), and Wayishkee (First Born Son), in addition to "others of minor note."[49] These were important chiefs, indeed. Along with Shingwauk, they were signatories to the 1820 land cession treaty extracted by Governor Cass. Shingabawassin, referred to as "first chief of the Chippewa nation," had also signed the 1825 treaty, which established peace between the Sioux and several tribes of the Great Lakes region. Three of these same four chiefs (Kaugaosh was the exception) also signed the Butte des Morts Treaty in 1827. "Maidysage" represented Kaugaosh (who was possibly absent from the proceedings), on the 1836 Michigan land cession treaty.[50]

The absence of Shingwauk at this first distribution is notable, considering his role in the 1820 Cass land cession treaty mentioned above. In Schoolcraft's words, Shingwauk was "a person of some consequence among the Indians. . . . His residence is . . . for the most part, on the British side of the river, but he traces his lineage from the old Crane Band here."[51] The allusion to Shingwauk's Crane clan affiliation affirms his importance as a Native leader. According to the oral tradition of the Anishnaabeg, Kitchi Manitou (the Great Spirit) made the Crane and sent it down from the sky to make its abode on earth. The bird was endowed with a loud and far-sounding cry, which was heard by all. Seeing the rapids (Bawating) and its multitude of fish, the Crane decided to make its home here. Upon hearing a loud cry sent out by the Crane, the Bear clan, Catfish clan, Loon clan, and Marten clan all gathered at Bawating. The Rapids then became the gathering place for the five major clans[52] of the Ojibway Nation, and the Crane clan (the Echo Makers) was chosen to preside over all councils.[53]

The wording of Schoolcraft's remarks about Shingwauk is significant in two other respects as well. First, his phrase, "for the most part," implies that Shingwauk does, on occasion, reside on the American side of the St. Mary's River. Secondly, the reference to Shingwauk's Crane clan membership places him, in all likelihood, on the Sault Ste. Marie, Michigan side. The implication is that *lineage* is as important—perhaps more important—than *residence* in the determination of leadership and identity associated with a *place*. In addition to living on both sides of the St. Mary's River, Shingwauk was known to have resided at Portage Lake in the Keewenaw peninsula, on Grand Island off of Munising, at Bay de Noc on Lake Michigan's north shore—all in Michigan's Upper Peninsula—and on Saginaw Bay in Michigan's lower peninsula.

As a consequence of these diverse residences, Shingwauk's children were born in areas that came to be separated by the U.S.-Canada border. Also, through marriage, he had formed alliances that stretched from Little Current on the east end of Manitoulin Island, through Sugar Island and Sault Ste. Marie, and on to L'Anse in the central portion of Michigan's Upper Peninsula. Various treaty signatures show that not only Shingwauk but other Sault area chiefs had, at one time or another, resided at Saginaw, Prairie du Chien, the Butte des Morts, and Fond du Lac, as well as at the Sault. Moreover, evidence exists that chiefs from the Sault area traveled to Detroit and Washington DC to negotiate U.S. treaties.

"Residence," then, must be viewed as a flexible circumstance. With few exceptions, Shingwauk's broad geographical migrations are probably little different from those of most of the area's Native population. Practical aspects of Native life in the area dictated seasonal moves; notably, the people's hunting grounds ran from the St. Mary's River north to the Hudson's Bay, while their summer camps were generally maintained in the southern areas.[54] Any attempt, then, to designate an individual upper Great Lakes Native person as "American" or "Canadian" before the 1820s—especially since the border had not yet been established—was, at best, merely an academic exercise.

Drummond Island

Although the 1816 resumption of annuity distributions took place on Drummond Island, the British never really developed Fort Drummond because of unresolved border issues and the question of ownership. The island was finally awarded to the United States in 1822, although the circumstances surrounding this decision are in dispute. The popular story of the Americans getting the British party drunk and then tricking them into accepting the notion that the main shipping channel was to the east of Drummond Island (thus situating Drummond in the United States), cannot be substantiated.[55] C. Colton, in his *Tour of the American Lakes, and Among the Indians of the Northwest Territory, in 1830*, posits that St. Joseph Island was an American possession and that it was traded to the British in exchange for Drummond Island.[56] However, this explanation also fails to fit the facts.[57] Whatever the nature of the Drummond Island grant to the United States, the British did not abandon the fort until 1828. For over ten years, then, it remained as the prime British post in the upper Great Lakes region and the focus of the Anishnaabeg in their relations with the British.

Presents and the Incentive to Immigrate to Canada

As early as 1795, in the aftermath of the Fallen Timbers battle, the British, anticipating both American objections and internal administrative obstacles (such as expense), began to associate the annual distribution of presents with migration to and permanent settlement in Canada. The continuing strength of the British-Native alliance after the Revolutionary War had been made possible by the maintenance of several British posts, the policy of distributing gifts, and the lack of anything more than a token U.S. military presence in the area. However, the completion of the American border posts in 1826, the settlement of some of the outstanding border questions, and the strong American criticism of its gift allotment policy led the British, after 1828, to finally abandon their posts on American soil. They did not, however, abandon the Native people, who began traveling to Canada to receive gifts.

Schoolcraft, of course, admonished these travelers to Canada, just as he had earlier criticized them for traveling to Britain's "American" posts. (Among the area's notables taken to task were the chiefs Oshawano, Wayishkee, Neegaubeyun, Kabamappa, and Keewikonce.)[58] From the viewpoint of the Americans, this attempt at dissuasion met with little success; for the most part, the area's Native people simply went on receiving presents on both sides of the border. Their persistence may be partly accounted for by the favorable British rates of distribution. On Drummond Island, the British annual allotment served an average of forty-five hundred Native people per year;[59] in contrast, Schoolcraft's annual gift dispersal apparently accommodated about three thousand Ojibways per year.[60]

Accustomed to visiting the British either at Mackinac or Drummond, the Native people, however, were often finding it difficult, or even dangerous, to reach Britain's most northern Great Lakes post, situated at Penetanguishene in the extreme southeast corner of Georgian Bay. For those in the northern Lakes, travel to Penetanguishene considerably increased the distance they had to travel, and for others who found the waters unfamiliar or who had to cross the width of Lake Huron in fragile canoes, travel was dangerous. These serious drawbacks acted as an inducement for northern Anishnaabeg to settle in areas of Canada where access to Penetanguishene was easier and safer. Additional impetus to migrate came from a suggestion by President Monroe in 1825 that some of the area's Native people be removed to an area north of Illinois and west of Lake Michigan, and others to an area west of the Mississippi, in order to "shield them from impending doom [and] promote their welfare and happiness."[61] Native people from the American areas of the Old Northwest, whose animosity toward the United States was increasing, now saw themselves being forced to decide between emigration to Canada or removal by the United States to strange lands west of the Mississippi.

However, whether or not to "voluntarily" "repair" to Canada was a decision that both the Anishnaabeg and other Native people had had to make long before the introduction of Monroe's policy. Even before the Revolution, some Native groups had been forced to move to Ontario and Quebec for refuge after white settlers forced them from their lands. Immediately following the Revolution, Ojibway, Odawa, Delaware, and Wyandot peoples also emigrated to Canada.[62] In 1784 Joseph Brant, the Six Nations leader, also led a sizeable portion of his people to Canada, where they established a reserve on the Grand River. In 1793 the Lenni Lenapes (the Delawares) moved from Ohio to Canada, with others following in 1800.[63] In the same year, a group of Munsees moved to an area on the Thames River in Ontario,[64] and a Potawatomi band, whose leader had fought with the British in the War of 1812, moved to Canada after the war and settled in the Lake Simcoe area in southern Ontario.[65] Also living in southern Ontario (for the most part on or near Walpole Island) were many Anishnaabeg who had found themselves in Canada after the War of 1812 and had chosen to stay.[66] And, in 1818, the Odawas sought assurances from the British authorities that they would be permitted to return to Manitoulin Island in Canadian territory, if they chose to do so.[67]

In order to distinguish between those Native people who lived in Canada and were therefore automatically eligible for presents, and those who resided primarily in the United States, the British set up two categories of Native people: "Resident" and "Visiting." Besides the Anishnaabeg, "visiting" Natives included the Hurons, Senecas, Delawares, Shawnees, Sauks, Foxes, Miamis, Kickapoos, Sioux, Winnebagos, Menominees, Nanticokes, Peorias, Creeks, Cherokees, Chickasaws, Missouris, Osages, Otoes, and "smaller numbers of visitors from the northeastern states and from New York and Pennsylvania."[68]

In addition to the "resident" and "visiting" division, the Native people at the annual distributions were further divided into two classes, one designating "deserving chiefs and warriors," the other "common warriors." Those regarded as "deserving" were, of course, being recognized for their military achievements in wars against the Americans; their presents—greater in quantity and often in quality than those allotted to people in the "common" category—were, essentially, a form of pension for war service. The "deserving" category also included the families of those wounded or killed in action against the Americans. The "common" category was essentially for the families of those who fought with the British.

With the passage of time, and the decline of the ranks of "deserving" Indians, virtually all of the "common" warriors of the War of 1812 era came to be included in the "deserving" class. "Common" then became the designation for all other Native people, many of whom had been too young to have served the British militarily but who constituted an ever-growing constituency.[69] Table 1 cites the totals for each category of Native people at the British post at Amherstburg (near Windsor, Ontario) in 1824 and presents a typical accounting.

The figures given in table 1 show that the Anishnaabeg accounted for 80 percent of all people receiving presents in 1824 at Amherstburg, the post most active in this annual distribution. The

Table 1. Native People Receiving Presents at Amhertsburg, 1824

Nations	Category One	Category Two
Chippewa	47	2223
Potawatomi	28	1492
Ottawa	32	1081
Munsee & Moravian	32	282
Huron (Wyandot)	11	261
Six Nations	8	237
Shawnee	8	225
Sauk and Fox	5	69
Miami	1	34
Kickapoo	0	34
Delaware	0	14
Total	172	6,131

Note: Category One = Deserving Chiefs, Warriors, Wives, and Widows; Category Two = Common Warriors, Women, and Children.
Source: Adapted from Clifton, "Visiting Indians in Canada."

second most active post was at Penetanguishene, and, because it was closer to the Anishnaabeg homelands, it may be safely assumed that the Anishnaabeg would easily have constituted this post's majority as well. These numbers, together with the fact that the posts at York (Toronto) and Kingston (at the far northeastern end of Lake Ontario) played a lesser role in the annual gift allotment than did the Amherstburg and Penetanguishene posts, reveal the importance of the Anishnaabeg in both the historic and postwar British-Native alliance.

A later accounting for Manitoulin Island in 1838 (as represented in table 2) reflects the additional breakdown of those Natives considered American and those considered British.

In the material used to compile table 2, the "British Nations" included the Ojibway/Odawas, Potawatomis, and Ojibways. (The double listing of the Ojibways, first in combination with the Odawas and then separately, reflects the residency aspects of British accounting procedures: the Ojibways and the Odawas lived together at some reserves in Canada but at Saugeen and at

Table 2. Native People Receiving Presents at Manitowaning,
August 20, 1838

	The British Nations				
	Deserving		Common		
Chiefs	Warriors	Wives	Chiefs	Warriors	Women
13	6	10	17	492	501
	+ boys and girls — for a total of 1,749 Native people				
	The American Nations				
	Deserving		Common		
Chiefs	Warriors	Wives	Chiefs	Warriors	Women
2	4	0	5	219	285
	+ boys and girls —for a total of 848 Native people				

Source: Adapted from Clifton, "Visiting Indians in Canada."

Owen Sound there are no Odawas residing with the Ojibways.)
The "American Nations" included Ojibways from Sault Ste. Marie, Bay de Noc, Drummond Island, St. Ignace, and Grand Tra-
verse, Odawas from "Wau-qui-huc-see" (L'Arbre Croche), and
Menominees from Green Bay.[70]

The circumstances surrounding this 1838 accounting of presents distributed on Manitoulin Island are significant: during the
1836 presents distribution there, the lieutenant governor of Canada, Sir Francis Bond Head, declared that within three years
visiting "Indians" must become residents of Canada in order to
continue receiving their presents.[71] The 1838 distribution represented the third year. Head explained that this change in policy was necessary for two reasons: first, visiting Indians were
subjects of another state (the United States) and thus Canada
should not have to support them; secondly (reflecting U.S. objections), part of the annuity included guns and ammunition,
and international agreements precluded Britain from continuing to arm American subjects who might then turn those arms
against the United States. Head's reasoning was no doubt met
with amazement by many Anishnaabeg, who considered themselves to be loyal Anishnaabeg, not "American" or "British" sub-

jects. (The annual distribution of gunpowder was, in fact, continued until 1844.)[72]

Head neglected to tell the assembled Native people some of the other reasons for the new presents policy. Foremost among these was the simple fact that the annual distribution was a costly affair and represented a financial burden that the government wished to reduce. Moreover, by the late 1820s Britain no longer harbored illusions of fighting a border war with the United States and, by the early 1830s, it was evident to both the Americans and the British that the Native people of the Old Northwest were no longer the military threat they had once been.

The period running from about 1820 until the 1836 pronouncement on Canadian residency requirements was an unusually turbulent one for the Anishnaabeg. If the British and the Americans easily recognized the decline of Native power in the area, the Native people themselves certainly must have felt an increasing inability to control their own destiny. The experience of Shingwauk, one of the most respected chiefs in the region, is a case in point, demonstrating how extensive the "geopolitical" shifting between borders was during this period, even for a single individual. (His "allegiances," relative to various Canadian and U.S. treaties, will be treated in the next chapter.) Prior to the incident at the Sault in 1820, which had nearly derailed Governor Cass's attempt to acquire Ojibway land, Shingwauk had lived on the American side of the St. Mary's River; after 1820, he moved to the Canadian side. In 1826 he moved back to the U.S. side, reminding Schoolcraft that he had helped Cass in a very delicate situation and assuring him that he was to "live permanently on the American side of the river and put himself under [Schoolcraft's] protection."[73] In 1827 Shingwauk returned to the Canadian side at the request of the British.

In 1836, while living on the American side, he was recognized by the British as chief of all the Ojibways from Thessalon to Goulais Bay (an area along the North Shore of the Georgian Bay, in Ontario). In 1838, while still living on American soil, he was again recognized by the British as the leader of all the Western Indians at the annual distribution on Manitoulin Island. In 1841 he moved to Manitoulin where he lived for a year. He moved again in 1842 to Garden River, Ontario, near the Sault. His shifting loyalties and residences finally came to an end in 1845, when he formally reasserted his loyalty to the British. Shingwauk's repeated relocations in the decades following open hostilities between the British and the Americans have a contemporary significance that goes far beyond his personal narrative given that the Anishnaabeg in the Sault Ste. Marie area — on both sides of the border — will always refer to Shingwauk and his leadership to bolster their claims of sovereignty and treaty rights made to both the U.S. and Canadian governments. Yet, nothing they had faced was more difficult than the impending land cession and removal period. The next chapter presents a more thorough examination of the events of this climactic period.

5

Anishnaabeg Treaty-Making and the Removal Period

Land Cession Treaties

The Fort Stanwix Treaty of 1768 and the Treaty of Greenville in 1795 were the first meaningful threats to the integrity of the Native homelands in the Great Lakes area generally, but over time, virtually all of the Native lands in the area were ceded. This chapter examines the land cessions through which the Anishnaabeg lost control over most of the Lake Huron borderlands. This necessitates a recounting of the land cession treaties; the synopsis that follows is constructed chronologically without regard to whether the non-Native signatory was the United States, Britain, or Canada.

The first treaty directly affecting the Anishnaabeg homeland was the Ojibway cession to the British of the "Island of Michilimakinak" in 1781. This treaty, labeled "No. 1" in the Canadian government's treaty books because it was the first treaty between the British-Canadian government and Native people following the American Revolution, is interesting because the territory it cedes is clearly claimed by the United States. Obviously feeling free to ignore any American objections, the British opted instead to recognize that it was the Ojibway "who have or can lay claim to 'La Grosse Isle,'" as it was called by the Canadians. Four years later, however, in 1785, the U.S. government signed a treaty with the Wyandots, Delawares, Ojibways, and Odawas wherein they "reserved to the sole use of the United States . . . the post of Michillimachenac [*sic*] with its dependencies, and twelve miles square about the same."[1] Although it appears that this does not refer to Michilimackinac *Island*, but only to the *fort* on the tip of Michigan's lower peninsula (a short distance away) that shares the same name, the situation makes clear the conflicting territorial claims to the area.

Helen Tanner, in her *Atlas of Great Lakes Indian History*, states that, "[in] 1785 the British acquired control of the Severn River route from Lake Simcoe to Matchedash Bay, a southeastern arm of Georgian Bay."[2] Chronologically, this would be the next cession affecting the Anishnaabeg; the Canadian government's three-volume set, *Indian Treaties and Surrenders*,[3] however, makes no mention of it.

The next treaty, in 1790, is another Canadian one — only this time it was between British authorities and "the principal Village and War Chiefs of the Ottawa, Chippawa, Pottowatomy, and Huron Indians Nations of Detroit," who ceded to them the extreme southwest portion of the Ontario peninsula.[4] That this treaty is between the British government, the village, and war chiefs of Detroit once again demonstrates the extent to which the Anishnaabeg and the British authorities could essentially ignore U.S. political claims to the area in the early years of the republic.

The fourth treaty affecting the area was signed by the Ojibways in 1796 and ceded to Canada the land lying east of, and adjacent to, the lower half of the St. Clair River. The treaty after that is also Canadian, signed in 1798 with the Ojibways, who relinquished the "Island known by the name of the Island of St. Joseph and also by the name of Cariboux Island and in the Ojibway language by the name of Payentanassin, situate, lying and being in that strait which joins the Lakes Superior and Huron."[5] Small portions, adjacent to southeastern Georgian Bay in Canada, were also ceded by the Ojibway in 1798 and 1815.

The 1795 Treaty of Greenville, the 1807 Treaty of Detroit, and the 1815 Treaty of Spring Wells were all instrumental in ceding that portion of lower Michigan that contains Detroit and the surrounding area. The 1815 treaty was merely a reaffirmation

of the Greenville treaty, with added provisions deemed necessary to restore "the relations of peace and amity" between these
tribes and the U.S. government that existed before the war. That
the major players "associated with Great Britain in the late war"
were the Anishnaabeg is indicated by the 1815 treaty's distinction between "the Chippewa, Ottawa, and Potawatomi *tribes*"
and "'*certain bands*' of the Wyandot, Delaware, Seneca, Shawnee, and Miami tribes" (emphases added).[6]

In 1819 the Ojibway signed a major land cession treaty whereby
they transferred the central portion of lower Michigan, as well as
the area bordering the lower half of Lake Huron, to the United
States. In 1820 the United States asserted sovereignty over its
claimed portion of the Sault Ste. Marie area when the territorial governor, Lewis Cass, traveled to it to establish a fort and
raise the U.S. flag. The ensuing threat of hostilities persuaded
the Native people to sign a treaty ceding land for the American
fort. Also in 1820 the Odawas and the Ojibways ceded the Saint
Martin Islands (small islands in the Straits of Mackinac area) to
the United States.

In three treaties signed in 1822, 1827, and 1836, the Ojibways
ceded to the Canadian government the remaining portion of the
Ontario Peninsula, with the exception of the Bruce Peninsula
and the territory to the south of it which borders Lake Huron.
The 1836 treaty, through which the Ojibways surrendered the
"Saugeen Tract" of 1.5 million acres (607,057 hectares) was, and
is, surrounded by controversy. It appears that no Native people
with authority signed the treaty and that the Anishnaabeg had
circulated war belts, preparing to fight for their lands.[7] The threat
of a Native uprising over the Saugeen lands dissipated at the on-
set of the Rebellion of 1837, a civil conflict in which some Ojibways even volunteered to fight for the government.[8] However,
following the rebellion (about which more will be said later), the
Saugeen Ojibways continued the fight for their lands, this time
through legal channels. In 1846 they received some compensa-

tion for the ceded lands, along with an annuity, a few small reserves, and a deed to 450,000 acres on the Bruce Peninsula, just north of their homelands.[9]

In another 1836 treaty, the Odawas and Ojibways ceded to the United States the remaining portion of Michigan's lower peninsula, as well as the eastern portion of the state's Upper Peninsula. In another interesting example of the ongoing U.S.-Canada dispute over the border in this area, the treaty used the "boundary line in Lake Huron between the United States and the British province of Upper Canada . . . as established by the . . . treaty of Ghent" as the boundary for the land cession, despite the fact that the boundary line had not yet been finalized.[10] In fact, Sugar Island, located in these disputed boundary waters, was reserved for the use of the Ojibway in the 1836 U.S. treaty, even though the island had not yet been declared either U.S. or Canadian territory (see map 8).

Schoolcraft related a highly instructive incident involving this 1836 treaty that underscores the seeming absence of the border in the Sault area, as well as uncertainty about any claims to authority over the area. Schoolcraft's brother, James, who was in charge at the Sault during the period when several Native chiefs, including Whaiskee, were in Washington for negotiations, reported that "since Whaiskee's departure the whole Sault has been troubled."[11] A council was held in response, led by the "British chief" Gitshee Kawgaosh. Kawgaosh complained that it was not right that Whaiskee had been sent to Washington to represent "the ancient band of red men whose *totem* is the lofty crane" (emphasis in original), since he was not even from the area ancestrally, but from La Pointe (in Wisconsin).[12] It is clear from the council and the events surrounding it that the Sault Ste. Marie–area Anishnaabeg recognized the authority of the traditional clan structure and were quite prepared to ignore, or dispute, the federal government's claims to its control.

Again in 1836, the Odawas and the Ojibways agreed with Canada that Manitoulin and adjacent islands be set aside as a common reserve for all of the "many Indians who wish to be civilized."[13] This was, in effect, an effort by government authorities to establish a kind of Canadian "Oklahoma" in Upper Canada. The lieutenant governor, Bond Head, felt that the "greatest kindness [the government] can perform toward these Intelligent, simpleminded people is to remove and fortify them as much as possible from all Communication with the Whites."[14] The treaty also contained a provision whereby the British would withdraw any claim that they may have had to these islands. (While this is not, properly speaking, a "land cession" treaty, it is included here because it sets the stage for more permanent Native land losses on the island in a subsequent treaty.)

The next major land cession treaties in the area were the Robinson Treaties of 1850 between the Canadian government and the Ojibway people of northern Ontario. The negotiations took place between the government and two separate Ojibway leaderships, one under Peau de Chat representing the Ojibways of Lake Superior, and the other under Shingwauk and Nebenaigoching on behalf of the Ojibways of Lake Huron.

Various circumstances surrounding the activities of these two Lake Huron chiefs is worth reporting in some detail, because they resulted in what was, very likely, the final military action of the Lake Huron borderlands' Anishnaabeg. In November of 1847 Denis-Benjamin Papineau, the commissioner of Crown Lands, sent to the Sault area to gather information prior to the treaty negotiations, claimed that the tribal bands in the Sault area did not inhabit the north shore of the St. Mary's River before the Conquest of 1763 (i.e., before the defeat of the French in the region) and therefore could not be considered the "original inhabitants" of the region. The commissioner also determined that the bands were too loosely organized to be considered a "nation." Together, these two assertions led Papineau to declare that the bands, represented by Shingwauk and Nebenaigoching, had no right to the land they inhabited.[15] Furthermore, it was claimed that the two chiefs, both former residents of the United States, had only recently immigrated to Canada.[16]

The chiefs' reply to these arguments was that because their forefathers had hunted the land in question since time immemorial, they were indeed entitled to them. In a poignant letter to the governor in Montreal, Shingwauk tried to drive his point home:

> When your white children first came into this country, they did not come shouting the war cry and seeking to wrest this land from us. They told us they came as friends to smoke the pipe of peace . . . at the time we were strong and powerful, while they were few and weak. But did we oppress them or wrong them? No! . . . Time wore on and you have become a great people, whilst we have melted away like snow beneath an April sun [and] you have hunted us from every place as with a wand, you have swept away all our pleasant land, and like some giant foe you tell us "willing or unwilling, you must go from amid these rocks and wastes, I want them now! I want them to make rich my white children, whilst you may shrink away to holes and caves like starving dogs to die." Yes, Father, your white children have opened our graves to tell the dead even they shall have no resting place. . . . Drive us not to the madness of despair.[17]

Shingwauk most certainly must have felt despair, but he also appeared determined to demonstrate Native control of the area as a prelude to treaty negotiations. This motivated Shingwauk (who had earlier threatened a land surveyor) and Nebenaigoching to lead a band of between 30 and 100 men to a mining settlement on Mica Bay (some two hundred miles north of the Sault on Lake Superior), where they attacked and drove off the miners in November of 1849. The chiefs, along with two white and two Métis raiders, were subsequently arrested for the raid and jailed in Toronto. Conveniently, all were later released and pardoned in time to participate in the Robinson treaty negotiations that took place in the fall of 1850.[18] The 1849 raid was probably the final military action of the Lake Huron borderlands Anishnaabeg. (Canada's last gasp of military bravado directed against the Americans most likely preceded this: in 1846 the British Indian superintendent George Ironsides (whose mother was Native) openly broached a plan to arm Britain's Indian allies throughout the upper Great Lakes and launched a war against the United States, with the first goal being to "recapture" the Michilimackinac fort.[19] Nothing came of the proposal.)

In spite of the obvious difficulties, the Robinson treaties were signed on September 7 and 9, 1850 (both in Sault, Ontario). By way of these treaties, the Ojibway ceded to the Canadian government all of the lands adjacent to the northern and eastern shore of Lake Superior and those adjacent to the northern shore of Lake Huron "inland to the height of land which separates the territory covered by the charter of the Honorable Hudson's Bay Company from Canada."[20] In the first of the two Robinson treaties, the land relinquished by the Lake Superior Ojibways under Peau de Chat extended as far west as the Pigeon River, which forms the U.S.-Canada border at the northwest end of Lake Superior.

The extent of the land ceded under the second Robinson Treaty—to which the first two signatories are Shingwauk and Nebenaigoching—is still in dispute. The Teme-augama Anishnabais have laid formal claim to about 10,000 square kilometers (about 3,900 square miles), proposing joint control with the Ontario government over 3,100 square kilometers, and exclusive control of another 7,300 square kilometers. The 1850 Robinson Treaty land cession, the Teme-augama assert, extended east only as far as the French River–Lake Nipissing–Ottawa River waterway. The Canadian government, on the other hand, claims that the Teme-augama chief, Nebenegwune, met Robinson on Manitoulin Island a few days after the treaties were concluded at Sault Ste. Marie and that at the meeting Nebenegwune was offered twenty-five dollars, the acceptance of which constituted, the government alleges, an agreement to cede the land. But as early as 1877 the Teme-augama were asserting that they did not come under the provisions of the 1850 Robinson treaties.[21]

To further complicate the Temagamis' claim (the spelling of Teme-augama used in geographical contexts), a map titled *Indian Treaties*, published by the Canadian government in 1970 (revised in 1977), shows the disputed land to have been ceded under a 1923 treaty.[22] More recently, an Ontario government publication shows the land to have been ceded by "Pre-Confederation Treaties." (The same publication shows Manitoulin Island as part of the Robinson Treaty cession, which, as shall be shown, is not the case.)[23] Other maps indicate the area as ceded under the Robinson treaties, although Helen Tanner's *Atlas* shows the area as not having been ceded.[24]

Robinson treaty language does state that the cession includes "[t]he eastern and northern shores of Lake Huron from Penetanguishene to Sault Ste. Marie," including all land north and east to that claimed by the Hudson's Bay Company.[25] However, in the schedule of reserves set aside for those bands represented at the signing, virtually all are Lake Huron shoreline communities (the exceptions are in the Lake Nipissing area): clearly, there was no representation of the inland Teme-augama at the Robinson Treaty negotiations. While admitting that the Teme-augamas were not signatories to this or any other treaty, the Canadian Supreme Court nevertheless ruled in 1991 against their land claim. The Court claimed that, by accepting annuities and a reserve, they had relinquished any claim they may have had.[26] Since that time, the Teme-augama Anishnabais and the Temagami First Nation have reached a tentative settlement with the Ontario government that will create a large reserve of approximately 127 square miles (330 square kilometers) in the Lake Temagami area.[27]

The Bruce Peninsula, which forms the western boundary of

the Georgian Bay, was not part of the 1850 Lake Huron Robinson Treaty, but was ceded by the Ojibways during the period from 1854 to 1857. The last major cession in the area came in 1862 when most of Manitoulin Island and the other islands of the North Channel were ceded to the government by "Chiefs and Principal Men of the Ottawa, Ojibway, and other Indians occupying the said islands."[28] This is the same "Canadian Oklahoma" that in 1836 had been set aside for all Indians who wished to settle there and "be totally separated from the whites," and that had been part of Lieutenant Governor Head's plan for Native resettlement in fulfillment of the new residency requirement for receiving presents.[29] The language of the 1836 Manitoulin Treaty guarantees protection of the Native population of the island:

> [V]arious circumstances have occurred to separate from your Great Father many of his red children, and as an unavoidable increase of white population, as well as the progress of cultivation, have had the natural effect of impoverishing your hunting grounds it has become necessary that new arrangements should be entered into for the purpose of protecting you from the encroachments of the whites. In all parts of the world farmers seek for uncultivated land as eagerly as you, my red children, hunt in your forest for game. . . . but uncultivated land is like wild animals, and your Great Father, who has hitherto protected you, has now great difficulty in securing it for you from the whites, who are hunting to cultivate it.[30]

By 1862 it was clear to the Canadian government that white encroachments on Manitoulin were only going to increase, and that they would have to force the Native people to give up their lands in return for small reserves. The sharp contrast in the language of the two treaties points to the quite casual disregard of the governments for the treaties they negotiated with Native peoples: "[I]t has been deemed expedient . . . to assign to the Indians now upon the island certain specified portions . . . and to sell the other portions thereof fit for cultivation to settlers."[31]

Not surprisingly, many Native people living on the island were quite adamant in their rejection of the government's proposal to cede the entire island, and after much intense negotiation and threats of hostilities, they succeeded in retaining the eastern end of the island for unrestricted Native use and occupancy. This area is now the Wikwemikong Unceded First Nation, designated by the Canadian government as Indian Reserve Number 26.

Although the Anishnaabeg on both sides of the border saw their land bases diminished even further in subsequent years, the 1862 treaty was essentially the last major expanse of land to be ceded to one of the two governments. As extensive as these territorial losses were to Native people, it is nevertheless important to note that in all of the U.S. and Canadian land cession treaties, not only were some areas "reserved" for Native use, but Native people also frequently retained—in the words of the 1836 U.S. treaty—"the right of hunting on the lands ceded, with the other usual privileges of occupancy, until the land is required for settlement."[32] In the words of the 1850 Robinson Treaty: "Her Majesty and the Government of this Province, hereby promises and agrees to allow the said chiefs and their tribes the full and free privilege to hunt over the territory now ceded by them, and to fish in the waters thereof, as they have heretofore been in the habit of doing, saving and excepting such portions of the said territory as may from time to time be sold or leased to individuals or companies of individuals and occupied by them with the consent of the Provincial Government."[33] Map 9 shows the lands ceded by the treaties cited above. Land cessions outside of the Lake Huron borderlands are not shown.

The U.S. Removal Period and Its Effects on the Anishnaabeg

Occurring simultaneously with these land cessions was the implementation of the United States' policy of Removal. This idea was first brought forward by President Thomas Jefferson in 1803, who later suggested that the land from the Louisiana Purchase

Map 9. Lake Huron Borderlands Land Cessions

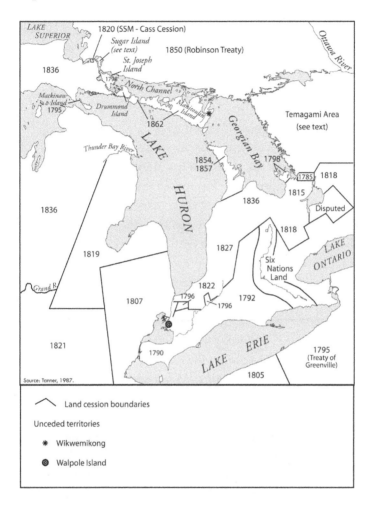

Source: Tanner, 1987.

Land cession boundaries

Unceded territories

* Wikwemikong

◉ Walpole Island

be set aside for the Indians removed from the east. The idea
was still very much alive two decades later in 1825, when President Monroe justified his plan for Native people by suggesting that they be "removed" in order to "shield them from impending doom [and to] promote their welfare and happiness."[34]
Monroe suggested the area west of Lake Michigan and north

of Illinois as a Removal location for some of the Native people. While the tragic effects of the Removal period on the Five Civilized Tribes of the southeast is well documented and need not be recounted here, what is less well known are the effects of Removal on Great Lakes Native people, both in the United States and Canada.

The Canadian "Removal" Period

In Canada a formal Removal policy was not implemented, but the government did attempt a less stark version of it with its "Manitoulin Experiment," formulated as a policy of isolating Native people from white society. The policy became official under Lieutenant Governor Head. Head's apartheid-like approach to the Native "problem" was never fully implemented, however, since he was removed from power after only two years in office for his mishandling of the 1837 Rebellion in Upper Canada (Ontario). Slightly earlier, a rebellion in Montreal in Lower Canada (Quebec) had broken out over the rising power of the English-speaking commercial and banking elite at the expense of the French-dominated elected assembly. Head sent the provincial militia of Upper Canada to Montreal to support the British government. During their absence a populist uprising in Upper Canada was launched by William Lyon Mackenzie, the Reform party leader and a supporter of an American-style republic, who led an ill-prepared attempt to take Toronto by force.[35]

Native people in Upper Canada were of two minds about the uprising: while some sought to remain adamantly neutral, others were willing to support the British-Canadian government. Apparently aware only of the latter opinion, Indian agent J. B. Clench wrote: "I rejoice to be able to bear testimony to [the] devoted loyalty [of] the Munsees, Moravians, and Chippewas [who are] to a man . . . ready and willing to take the field.[36] Clench's exaggerated claim was countered by the St. Clair Chippewa, who recommended that it would be best to spread our matts [sic] to sit-down & smoke our pipes and . . . remain quiet. . . . we can gain nothing by fighting. [Furthermore, we] cannot be compelled to go & fight for any party, [we] are free men and under the control of no one.[37]

Clench, in response, wrote that the "sentiments [of the St. Clair Chippewa] [are] so selfish, unfeeling, and disloyal that the parties deserve . . . the severest censure."[38] Despite all the recriminations and counsel both for and against involvement in the Rebellion, Native people were neither called to active duty in 1837 nor found to have actually supported the rebels in any way.[39]

The initial uprising in Upper Canada was quickly quelled, but many rebels fled to the United States, where they found willing allies who wished to see British rule overthrown in Canada. From bases there, these so-called "patriots" led a series of raids into Canadian territory in the summer of 1838, making incursions into Ontario and all along the border between Canada and the United States, from Windsor in the west to Prescott in the east.[40] Native people (with the exception of those who again remained neutral) supported the British, who in 1838 asked the Mohawks for military assistance in the east, as well as the Delawares, Chippewas, and Potawatomis in the west.[41]

The usefulness of Native people during the Upper Canada Rebellion in 1838 was not, unfortunately, limited to the military defense of Canada; the patriots whose cause they fought against found that the Native defenders could serve their purposes, too, though in a less overt way. Many Canadians who otherwise may have felt only mild sympathy for the rebel cause fell prey to rumors of an impending "Indian uprising" or, barring that, "revenge killings" against those whose loyalties the government suspected.[42] These colonists organized local militia to defend themselves from Native people who were rumored to be "[b]reaking into people's houses stealing guns and committing other outrages," while falsely proclaiming support for the rebels. The rebels found that they were able to use these fears of an "Indian uprising" as a recruiting tool for the patriot cause.[43]

The various accounts of the 1837–38 crisis report very little Native activity overall. In the 1837 phase, Native people (including Chippewas and Potawatomis) were called out but not deployed.[44] Mary Fryer, in *Volunteers, Redcoats, Rebels, and Raiders: A Military History of the Rebellion in Upper Canada*, found that Native warriors were among the defenders in the Windsor border area in 1838,[45] and Colin Read reports one incident where Indians in the Western and London districts, under the command of Colonel Maitland, shot and killed one Nathan Allen, a "notorious horse thief" and suspected rebel.[46] Aside from these few details, research into the contemporary accounts of the conflict seem to indicate an overwhelming silence on the subject of Native participation. This silence seems not to have gone unnoticed at the time by British-Canadian officials, who assumed that the Native role in this crisis was of scant importance and played no significant part in the military defense of Canada. This provided them with seemingly irrefutable evidence to support their growing belief that the Native people of the Great Lakes were no longer a military threat. Hence, Head's suggestion that annual gift distributions be ended became a reality.

While this aspect of Head's Indian policy was affirmed, his dream of an Oklahoma-style Manitoulin was more or less abandoned after his resignation in 1838. Instead, Canada returned to its policy of establishing "model villages" based on the supposed "civilizing" effects of a Christian farming life, paying for it out of funds acquired through the sale of ceded Native lands. This policy of assimilation did give Native people in Canada a way to resist Head's Removal scheme while retaining title to small reserves throughout Canada. Map 1 shows the results of this policy in the Lake Huron borderlands: it produced a rather large number of reserves, many in areas coveted by the advancing European agriculturalists. However, while the Canadian Anishnaabeg were able to resist Removal, they could not avoid dispossession. A complete transformation of their traditional hunting-fishing-gathering life was the eventual price they paid for retaining their reserves as vast tracts of land, and the life-sustaining natural resources embodied within them, were ceded. The Temagami region of Ontario is now the only place where the history of this dispossession is still being challenged.

Lower Great Lakes Removal-Era Migrations: The Potawatomis

The experience of Native people in the Great Lakes area during the U.S. Removal period begins in the southern reaches of the Lake Huron borderlands area. While some Potawatomis from lower Michigan had been moved earlier to Kansas and Oklahoma, most were reluctant to leave the region, preferring either to remain quietly on their traditional homelands in the United States or to move to Canada. Some Michigan and Wisconsin Potawatomi found ways to escape both Removal and migration, often by merging with their Anishnaabeg relatives on lands reserved for the Odawas and Ojibways.[47] Of the approximately 9,000 Potawatomis in the United States in the 1830s, Clifton claims that about 3,000 did settle permanently in Canada in the decades that followed.[48] Regrettably, all Potawatomi migrations to Canada were the migrations of refugees, as they could no longer lay claim to any homelands east or north of the Great Lakes. However, like many of those who remained in the Unites States, Potawatomi immigrants to Canada were frequently able to merge with their Anishnaabeg kin there and settle in virtually every reserve along Lake Huron, from the village of Spanish in the North Channel of Lake Huron to Walpole Island in the south.

In 1794 British superintendent-general Alexander McKee had established Walpole Island as a reserve for loyal Native people shortly after the American Revolution, mainly to accommodate those from the United States who felt threatened by the American forces in the lower Great Lakes. At the time, it was estimated that as many as 3,000 Odawas and Ojibways may have been preparing to move from the United States to the Walpole Island area.[49] These post-Revolution refugees joined the Hurons, Potawatomis, Saulteurs (Ojibway from the Sault area), and Missisaugas who had lived on Walpole since the early 1700s, having been induced to move there by Cadillac in his attempt to assemble the Great Lakes Native people in the Detroit area. The Potawatomis of the Removal period greatly preferred Walpole Island to Manitoulin Island, which, under the Canadian plan, would have confined them to an unacceptable way of life. Complaining that they were not accustomed to canoes and fishing but to horses and hunting, they found Walpole Island a much more hospitable environment. While the Potawatomis hoped that Walpole would be a sanctuary for Potawatomi cultural survival, other factors, including the old Potawatomi-British alliance, their antipathy toward the U.S. government, and the need for goods in the form of gifts also influenced their decision to move there.

Major Richardson claimed that before 1837, when the Canadian government announced its presents policy as an inducement for Native people to move to Canada, about 300 people, mostly Ojibways, attended the distribution of presents on Walpole Island. In 1842 over 1,140 were in attendance (table 3 presents the breakdown of native groups receiving gifts).

While Richardson's account does not specify the origins of the Ojibway immigrants, the record clearly indicates that the Odawas and the Potawatomis were from Michigan, having been displaced by the U.S. Removal policy. The period of 1837 to 1843 saw the greatest numbers of Potawatomis migrate to Walpole Island. It has been claimed that following migration, the Potawatomis sometimes returned to the U.S. side to hunt but did so at their own risk, as the American authorities did not allow such cross-border hunting.[50]

Parry Island and Christian Island were other reserves, which

Table 3. Native People Receiving Presents at Walpole Island, 1842

Native tribe	Total from tribe
Chippewas, old residents	319
Chippewas, arrived within the year	197
Potawatomis and Ottawas from Michigan	507
Others "on their way to settling"	117
Total	1,140

Source: Adapted from Richardson, *Tecumseh and Richardson*, 107.

saw a number of Potawatomi immigrants during the U.S. Removal period. Historic accounts claim that although some Potawatomis originally settled on Christian Island in about 1865, these former Michigan residents finally moved to Parry Island. In 1935 Parry Island had a Native population of about 250, of which about 100 were Potawatomis descended from the Michigan Anishnaabeg.[51] Other Potawatomis migrated to the Owen Sound and Saugeen reserves during this period,[52] and the Ojibways of Rama welcomed their fellow Anishnaabeg and a band of Potawatomis from Drummond Island to settle there.[53] In July of 1837 approximately 300 Potawatomis from the Chicago area moved to Manitoulin.[54] It has been claimed that Potawatomis from Wisconsin also petitioned the Canadian government for permission to move to Canada during this period, although no direct evidence of them having done so has been found.[55]

Lower Great Lake Removal-Era Migrations: The Odawas
Northern Ohio was squarely in the midst of the wars and turmoil that followed the 1795 Greenville treaty signing. This motivated many Odawas from the area to follow other Odawas who had migrated to Canada after the Revolutionary War. Following the War of 1812 and the implementation of the Removal policy that had been enacted into law in 1830, still more Odawa moved to Walpole (as evidenced by table 3). Other Odawa from both Michigan and Ohio did remove to Kansas in the 1830s, but

by the late 1830s and early 1840s most had left Kansas and migrated back to the area, to Walpole Island in particular.[56] As late as 1864, those Odawas still in Kansas petitioned the Anishnaabeg of Walpole to set aside land for their resettlement, which the Walpole Natives allowed in 1869.[57] It is claimed that by 1949 the Odawa descendants made up the majority of the Native people on Walpole Island.[58]

The Odawas also joined their Anishnaabeg relatives on Christian Island. These Odawa migrants, moving to Canada in the mid-1850s, were from the northern Lake Michigan area and were under the impression that the U.S. government was about to cease paying them their annuities and remove them to the west. Many chose instead to migrate back to their ancient homelands—the islands of the Georgian Bay.[59] McClurken, in his discussion of the Odawas during this period, claims that these northern Michigan Odawas were mainly Catholics who had split from their Anishnaabeg kin in southern Michigan who were either Traditionalists or Protestants. The southern Odawas resisted Removal for the most part, and many managed to remain in Michigan on lands bought with their own funds.[60]

Lower Great Lakes Removal-Era Migrations: The Ojibways
The 1807 treaty ceding the vast area surrounding Detroit contained provisions for certain Ojibways to remain on reserves set aside for their use in the area north of Detroit. In 1836 another treaty was signed by these "Swan Creek" and "Black River" Ojibways that ceded other reserved portions of land within the 1807 cession area. Negotiated by Indian agent Henry Rowe Schoolcraft, this was *not* a Removal treaty; however, in 1839 he recommended several changes in the treaty—without consulting the affected tribes—that were designed to force the removal of these Ojibways. Among the harsh provisions Schoolcraft endorsed was one that halted U.S. annuity payments for ceded lands for Native people who traveled to Canada for presents. Schoolcraft further

decided that any future annuity payments would only be made in Kansas—not at Port Huron, Michigan, as was the custom—and that the cost to the government for their Removal west would, moreover, be deducted from any payments due.[61]

Although some Swan Creek Ojibways did remove to Kansas, it seems that many of them chose Canada instead, since, on the other side of the international boundary, the Ojibways of the St. Clair reserve in Ontario saw a doubling of their pre-Removal population in the period immediately following the treaty's revision.[62] In 1839 Schoolcraft reported as well that a group of Saginaw Chippewas—who generally resisted Removal west—were on their way to Manitoulin Island with twenty-two orphans.[63] Finally, as table 3 indicates, 197 Ojibways came to Walpole Island in the early 1840s.

Upper Great Lakes Removal-Era Migrations

The experience of Removal for the Anishnaabeg of the northern reaches of the upper Great Lakes begins with the typical U.S. government attempt to force Native people west but ends with Canada's somewhat atypical "Manitoulin Experiment." The 1836 land cession treaty of northern Michigan contained no "Removal" language as it was originally negotiated: it was unlikely that the Anishnaabeg of this region would ever have agreed to move west. But the treaty, as it was being considered by the U.S. Senate for ratification, was "amended" by that body to conform with the U.S. federal government's plan to move all Native people to western land considered unsuitable for white settlement. The amended 1836 treaty stipulated that the reserves granted to the Anishnaabeg were "to be held in common . . . for the term of five years from the date of the ratification of this treaty, and no longer; unless the United States shall grant them permission to remain on said lands for a longer period."[64]

The treaty also made arrangements for Removal: "[A]s soon as the said Indians desire it, a deputation shall be sent to the southwest of the Missouri River, there to select a suitable place for the final settlement of said Indians. . . . When the Indians wish it, the United States shall remove them."[65] In the mid-1830s, some Anishnaabeg did send delegations to view western lands that the government deemed suitable, but this can be regarded as a diversionary tactic, and the surveys favorably impressed very few.[66] Of the approximately 8,000 Great Lakes Anishnaabeg who were "encouraged" to "remove," only 651 actually left their homelands.[67] Most of those removed were the southern Michigan Potawatomis, whose earlier experience with a violent military Removal had served as a lesson to all Anishnaabeg from the Great Lakes area.[68] The Anishnaabeg of the Sault did not "desire" or "wish" Removal under any circumstances and vowed to resist it, refusing even to send delegations to the west.[69]

While the Anishnaabeg and the American government were struggling with the question of Removal in the northern Great Lakes, as well as with the increasing encroachment of settlers on land still designated as "Indian Territory" on the other side of the border, the Canadian government was contending with two simultaneous problems in forming its Indian policy. To resolve them they chose to develop their own version of Removal in the form of the Manitoulin Experiment. The first problem was that the U.S. government was insisting that Canada cease its aid to "American" Indians in the form of presents, which included guns and ammunition. The other came from increased misgivings about their own distribution of presents.

As the Canadian government saw it, Native people no longer represented the balance of military power in the region, and Canada itself no longer had any geopolitical interest in the United States. They would lose little, they reasoned, by refusing to give presents to "their" Indians. Moreover, it was claimed that the presents, once distributed, were immediately traded for other goods near the trading grounds and that rum was one of the hottest trade items. These factors strengthened their resolve to rid themselves of the ever-increasing financial burden of presents allotment. At the time, the average number of "visiting" Indians was put at 3,270, with "residents" numbering 6,500; annual costs were estimated at $8,500. Eliminating presents to visiting Indians would mean, Head estimated, an annual savings "of say $4,000."[70]

Within the Canadian government, two factions had been fighting over whether or not to continue presents as usual or eliminate them altogether. In 1836 a compromise was reached declaring that after three years annual presents would no longer be issued to any Native person who was not a resident of Canada. The policy was formulated in such a way as to induce all of the region's Native people — both "American" and "Canadian" — to come to reside on Manitoulin Island, since that was the only place that would be designated for present distribution.[71] The cost, Head suggested, could be offset by selling the lands of those Native people who could be induced to move to Manitoulin Island.[72] In other words, the Canadian government was proposing that the Indians pay for their own presents out of the proceeds from the sale of their ceded lands. This Canadian "Oklahoma" was to "benefit" the non-Native population in other ways as well. Although it had been presented to the Native people as a means of isolating them from the predations of whites who were "hunting" for farmland, Head clearly saw it as a way to "remove" "Indians who are now impeding the progress of civilization in Upper Canada."[73] Moreover, he explained, while the island chain was well suited to the habits of Native people "as it affords fishing, hunting, bird-shooting, and fruit," no white settlers would want it anyway.

At first glance, it appears that Head's encouragement of "visiting Indians" to migrate to Manitoulin would increase the costs to the government over time, but he shared the view of most non-Natives that the Indians were a vanishing race: "I feel certain that though a few would at first immigrate to Canada, they would not long remain there. . . . We have only to bear patiently with them for a short time and . . . their unhappy race, beyond our power of redemption, will be extinct."[74]

Originally opposed to Head's plan as contrary to American interests in the area, Schoolcraft assumed it would ultimately fail, though not necessarily because Native people would become extinct.[75] The Native people were too enamored of the presents given to them by the U.S. government, he believed, to risk losing them by moving to Manitoulin Island. While Schoolcraft perhaps understood the appeal of Manitoulin's natural bounty to Native people, he argued that Head's plan was doomed as well by the island's poor agricultural prospects. His advice to the Anishnaabeg was that if they wanted fertile land, they should accept the U.S. government's offer of land west of the Mississippi.[76]

Indeed, despite the rhetoric of Manitoulin's suitability to the traditional lifestyles of the area's Native population, the Manitoulin Experiment had been, in part, predicated upon the supposed "civilizing" effects of an agricultural way of life, which, in combination with an adherence to Christianity, was regarded as "the key to the civilization, if not the very survival, of the [Manitoulin] tribes."[77] The pursuit of agriculture, it was reasoned, would keep the Native people from their seasonal migrations, and therefore, conveniently insure that they were never far from the missionaries. The reflections of one such missionary on Walpole Island, the Rev. James Coleman, epitomized this attitude. Hunting and fishing, he acknowledged, are "fascinating to the human mind," while agriculture and mechanical trades are, in comparison, "disagreeable labor." Coleman went on to pose the "obvious" question:

How then is it to be expected that the Indian . . . will, in favorable situations for success [in agriculture], relinquish his former enjoyments of hunting and fishing, for those which are less profitable to him, and attended with, to him, much greater fatigue? . . . I observed, that until game became so scarce in the neighborhood . . . they did not apply with any energy to agriculture. [Therefore] it is necessary that the Indian youth should be prevented from becoming hunters or fishers, and this can be alone done, by locating the village where there are no facilities for either. . . . Christianity and civilization have made much more rapid and effectual progress [where] there is no game.[78]

Coleman's analysis fits the Manitoulin plan to establish an agricultural community on the island, where game was becoming more scarce as more Native people moved there. Government and church authorities, however, had only limited success in convincing the Anishnaabeg to become Christian farmers; the Native people simply extended the time spent elsewhere on hunting and gathering activities, which, in turn, kept them from the island for longer periods of time. This was, of course, exactly the opposite of the original intent.

Nevertheless, due to its historical antecedents and the annual distribution of presents, Manitoulin Island was indeed an important Anishnaabeg center in the early 1800s. Head's plan to assemble all Great Lakes Native people there permanently added to that importance. But all Anishnaabeg were not in agreement with the proposal. At the 1836 council on Manitoulin, Shingwauk made an impassioned speech calling for the council fire to be moved to the Sault and declared that he would not move to Manitoulin.[79] Returning to Garden River near the Sault, Shingwauk launched a plan for a pan-Ojibway settlement there. Part of his strategy was to work with all of the upper Great Lakes Anishnaabeg chiefs to build and maintain loyalty to the British crown, which he partially accomplished by establishing alliances through marriage with the Anishnaabeg from Little Current in the east to L'Anse in the west. At the 1838 distribution of presents, Shingwauk was recognized by the British as the leader of all the "Western" bands (comprising all of the upper Great Lakes Native people).[80]

But unifying the Anishnaabeg was difficult due to overt attempts by both governments to keep the "American" Indians out of Canada; Manitoulin generally notwithstanding, concentrating the Native people in any one place — whether in the United States or in Canada — was considered potentially dangerous by both governments. In addition to this attempt to divide the area's Native people by forcing them to accept European-style national identities, both U.S. and Canadian authorities tried to divide the people along the lines of religious affiliation, a tactic that had served in part to divide the Odawas of Michigan.[81]

Due to the early French presence, Roman Catholic influence could be found throughout the area. But after the suppression of the Jesuits in France in 1761 and the assumption of British rule in Canada in 1763, the Catholic missions in Canada were fiercely opposed by missionaries from the Church of England who enjoyed some small success on Manitoulin Island and other places. The Methodists, too, were active, working among the Ojibways of the Saugeen and at Sarnia, Owen Sound, and St. Clair, as well as on Walpole, Rama, and Snake Islands.[82] In the United States, the Ojibways were at times also split by Protestant-Catholic rivalries. According to other reports, the Potawatomis were the least susceptible to Christian conversion, rarely associating themselves with any of the various denominations; in fact, they were at times referred to as "heathen" Potawatomis.[83]

George Copway, an Ojibway and Methodist missionary, acknowledged the inroads made by Roman Catholics throughout the Native communities of both the United States and Canada; his data reveal that the success of other denominations, however, was less bi-national. In the mid-1840s, Methodist missions in Canada outnumbered those in the United States by nearly a three-to-one ratio, while the Presbyterians and the Baptists in the United States had no Canadian counterparts. On the other hand, Episcopalians enjoyed a six-to-one advantage in Canadian versus U.S. missions.[84] Despite all of this missionary activity, however, it should not be assumed that all of the Anishnaabeg became Christians. An 1858 report on the religious affiliation of Walpole Island residents shows that over 40 percent were not associated with any Christian denomination.[85]

While large numbers of Anishnaabeg never converted to Christianity, the religious differences among those who did were real and persistent and had serious effects on people's lives. McClurken claims that the Anishnaabeg were often willing to claim an adherence to a particular mission since a rejection of Christian tenets could easily translate into open opposition from the resident "Indian" agent, resulting in a failure to secure rations, annuities, blacksmith services, and other necessities.[86] Andrew Blackbird reports that while the Odawas at L'Arbre Croche were mostly Roman Catholic, a dissident group of Protestants he led had been ostracized by the Catholic Native community, many of whom moved to Manitoulin Island.[87] Bleasdale claims that religious denominationalism so disrupted the once harmonious lives of the Native population that it became necessary to establish separate communities on the island that, essentially, kept the Roman Catholics and the Protestants apart.[88] In addition, the island's Potawatomi had most likely set themselves apart from the Ojibways partly because of religious differences, "[t]he resident missionary having been unable to induce them [the Potawatomis] to listen to his instructions."[89]

In spite of this religious factionalism, the Native leadership—both religious and secular—continued to make efforts during this turbulent period to maintain Anishnaabeg unity. Copway, the Ojibway missionary, had obviously been engaged in "cross-border" work, since at one point he claimed that the Canadian government refused to grant him any annuities "for several years . . . because I had been *too much with the Americans*" (emphasis in original).[90] At Garden River, Shingwauk complained to the Reverend O'Meara that he and his band were being "annoyed" by the efforts of Baptists and Methodists in an effort to draw them from their adherence to the Church of England.[91] Despite the seemingly sectarian nature of this charge, Shingwauk was not a religious partisan; in fact, he steadfastly worked to preserve solidarity among the Anishnaabeg in the face of active government and church attempts to use religion to divide and thereby weaken Native people.[92]

Movements to Manitoulin Island

As noted, after the War of 1812, the Odawa were openly discussing with Canadian authorities their possible return to Manitoulin Island.[93] In 1835, Captain Thomas G. Anderson, Canadian superintendent of the Western Tribes, visited the Odawas and other Anishnaabeg in Michigan and along the North Shore of Lake Huron and found that many expressed a willingness to move to Manitoulin Island. Furthermore, he found the Odawas of northern Lake Michigan preparing for Removal there.[94] It is very probable that these were the same Odawas who had requested permission to reemigrate to Manitoulin in 1818 and who were under the leadership of J. B. Assikinock, an influential Odawa chief from L'Arbre Croche.[95] Schoolcraft reported in 1839 that Chingossamo, an Ojibway chief from the Cheboygan area, left for Manitoulin with thirteen families comprising about eighty people (leaving behind in that area about forty-five Anishnaabeg);[96] in 1845 another group of about eight families from the north shore of Lake Michigan went to Manitoulin.[97]

In early 1850 a group of about 100 Roman Catholic Indians requested permission to settle on the west end of Manitoulin Island, claiming to have always been attached to the British government.[98] There is no indication in the correspondence of the U.S. location of the petitioners. The reply from George Ironsides, Indian superintendent at Manitowaning, was that the island was reserved for Native people from the north shore of Lake Huron and that "American" Indians who went to Manitoulin would therefore be interfering with the rights of "British" Indians.[99] This is in obvious contradiction to the original intent of the Manitoulin Experiment, which was to concentrate *all* Native people there, but does support the claim (specifically made in this case) that the government considered it easier to control the Ojibway if they remained divided by national (British or American) affiliation.[100] While there is no indication in the record of whether or not this group of "American" Catholic petitioners ever migrated to Manitoulin, the fact that by 1850 the Native population on the island was reportedly declining and that the Manitoulin Experiment itself was in serious trouble seems to indicate that they did not.[101]

The End of the Manitoulin Experiment

The final breakup of the Manitoulin Experiment was an ugly affair. At a treaty council in October of 1861, the island's Native people rejected the government's cession terms agreement, which was the official basis for initiating the Manitoulin "solution." In the words of one Native council member:

> The whites should not come and take our land from us: they ought to have stayed on the other side of the salt water to work the land there. . . . This land of which I speak, I consider my body; I don't want one of my legs or arms to be taken from me. I am surprised to hear you say the island belongs to white men.[102]

The divisions on the island were geographic and religious, represented by the two main settlements. One was Manitowaning, the main government outpost and site of the annual gift giving exclusively affiliated with the Church of England. The other was Wikwemikong, the predominantly Roman Catholic settlement at the eastern end of the island. Despite the treaty of 1836 setting aside the entire island chain for the use of all interested Native people, the 1862 treaty ceded most of the island to the Canadian government. It was this 1862 treaty that caused the turmoil on the island and further divided the loyalties of the island's Anishnaabeg.

The chiefs at Wikwemikong argued that the signatories to the 1862 treaty reported to be representing them had been either appointed illegally or were without the authority to represent them. Consequently, they never recognized the validity of the 1862 treaty, which led them, in July of 1863, to eject a white family and some Native people from the community, and to force chief Tehkummeh, a signatory to the 1862 treaty, to seek refuge at Manitowaning.[103] They also harassed the government surveyors.[104] The end result of these troubles was that the east end of Manitoulin Island became "unceded Indian territory" (a status that it enjoys to this day). Despite this defiance, most of the remaining land on the island was eventually surveyed, and in 1866 sold; Head's "Manitoulin Experiment" had come to an inglorious end.[105]

Although many Native people did move to the island, including a few Potawatomi from the St. Clair Reserve in southern Ontario,[106] the majority of them had already arrived by the time of Anderson's survey of the population in 1835. But within a few years many drifted back to their homelands either in the United States or in Canada, although some "American" Indians settled elsewhere in Canada. James Clifton, in *Visiting Indians in Canada*, claims that the total number of "visiting Indians" who had left the island but remained in Canada during this period was between 5,000 and 9,000.[107] Many of the Potawatomis returned to the St. Clair River area, while some Ojibways left for Lake Michigan in the early 1840s. Later, others left to join the Newash band on the Bruce Peninsula, with still others joining Shingwauk at Garden River.[108] In the final analysis, as a "Canadian Oklahoma," the Manitoulin policy was a failure as many

Anishnaabeg who did move there did so only temporarily; many simply returned to their home communities after only a short stay (staying there for one hunting season, for example). That may not have been much of a disappointment to the Canadian Government. In 1838 Head wrote, "I do not think the Indians of the United States could or would complain of the above arrangements, and I feel certain, that though a few would at first probably immigrate to Canada, (i.e., to Manitoulin Island) they would not long remain there."[109] He was right.

Canada–to–United States Migrations

With the exception of those who left the United States for Canada and eventually returned to the United States, almost all of these Anishnaabeg migrations were from the United States to Canada. However, an understanding of the fluidity of Native migrations in the area would not be complete without citing the few known cases of migrations from Canada to the United States. The *Journals of the Legislative Council of the Province of Canada* for 1858 reported that the population of the Sarnia Reserve had declined due to emigration from Canada to the United States, although no numbers are given.[110] Bleasdale, in describing the exodus of Native people from Manitoulin Island in 1841, reports that "some Canadian Ojibway . . . left for Lake Michigan."[111] Another report shows that "several members" of the Wyandots living in Anderon Township in southern Ontario "removed to Missouri where they received money and grants of land from the United States Government."[112] The same source claims that Moravian Indians, who had originally come from Pennsylvania, "surrendered much of their land in 1836 to make way for incoming settlers, and in 1837, 230 Indians from Fairfield [Ontario] went to Missouri."[113] Other Moravians had earlier left Canada to return to the United States.[114] In 1840 some Wyandot who had earlier moved from the United States to southwest Ontario left Canada for Missouri. Another source asserts that some Native people from Sarnia had moved to the United States "some years past."[115]

Shingwauk, Garden River, and a Pan-Ojibway Settlement

In the midst of the debacle that Manitoulin was becoming, Shingwauk was still actively pursuing his own version of a pan-Ojibway settlement at Ketegaun Sebee (Garden River). Part of his plan was to convince those "American" Natives dissatisfied with their treatment in the United States and considering the move to Canada that they should settle at Garden River. For the purposes of this study, what is important about the several groups in this category is not whether or not they finally reached Garden River, but that their lack of commitment to either the United States or Canada meant that they could readily change residences when the need arose, and that they could be expected to relocate in areas in accordance with their always overriding commitment to other Anishnaabeg people.

In 1845 Blackbird and Neokema, Ojibway chiefs from La Pointe, Wisconsin, representing about 500 Anishnaabeg, requested permission to immigrate to Canada, citing mistreatment by U.S. officials who referred to them as "English Indians" and tried to deprive them of their English medals and flags.[116] Canada's evolving policy since 1840 had permitted a new category of Native people, the "wandering Indians," to receive presents.[117] This category included those Native people who had moved to Canada from the United States but had not as yet permanently settled at a particular reserve or mission whose influence was expected to "civilize" them.

In 1847 Shingwauk and three other chiefs signed a petition to the Canadian government asking that Anishnaabeg from the United States be allowed to move to Canada. (All were Crane Clan chiefs and therefore entitled to represent the Anishnaabeg of the Sault area.) The reason given for the proposed move was that the Native's land was being sold by those "who were satisfied to renounce the fostering care of England for the cold hearted policy of the United States."[118] Later, a petition signed by Lake Superior Ojibway chiefs from Leech Lake, Red Lake, Chippewa River, Lac du Flambeau, Trout Lake, Grand Portage, Lac Chelec, Ontonagon, Bad River, Pigeon River, and Fond du Lac requested permission to settle on Native lands in the Canadian Sault area.[119] Up to 2,000 Native people were represented by the petitioners.[120] There is no indication of whether or not this request was granted, but as the rejection of the "American" Catholic Native peoples in 1850 showed, the Canadian government was not always inclined to welcome Native people from the United States.

In early 1855, sixteen chiefs petitioned Washington to remain on ancestral lands in upper Michigan: "We love the spot where our forefathers bones are laid, and we desire that our bones may rest beside theirs also." The Anishnaabeg had been struggling since the 1830s against Removal; in the 1854 Treaty of La Pointe and the 1855 Treaty of Detroit, both negotiated with the Ojibways, the government finally acceded to Anishnaabeg demands and lifted the threat of Removal from their lives.[121] Consequently, the motivation to move to Garden River or to Manitoulin was diminished as well.

By the late 1850s, when the Manitoulin Experiment was no longer considered viable, the Canadian government negotiated a treaty with Ojibways in the Sault (Ontario) area which amounted to tacit approval of Shingwauk's plan for a pan-Ojibway settlement at Garden River: in 1859 the Batchewana and Goulais Bay Bands agreed to cede the land reserved for them under the 1850 Robinson treaty (except for small islands used as fishing stations) in return for land on the Garden River reserve.[122] Just over half of the Anishnaabeg displaced by this 1859 treaty did settle at Garden River; the rest were scattered throughout the area.[123]

In 1856, in the midst of all these movements and machinations, the Canadian government ended the distribution of presents to *all* Native people. In the government's view, the annuities from the ceded lands would provide them with sufficient support. While the government was discussing this policy, the Odawa chief, Assikinock (Blackbird) reminded them of their perpetual obligation and threatened to shift his loyalties back to the Americans if present allotment was ended. The chief's strong stance on the subject was an indication of just how willing most Anishnaabeg were to shift residences and loyalties in order to maintain the tribal structures and relationships they regarded as essential to their survival as a people.

The extent to which Native people were willing to shift loyalties can be partially measured by a summary of gift distribution. Overall, the number of Native people receiving presents throughout Upper Canada was at its lowest in 1837, that is, in the year following Head's announcement that "visitors" would no longer receive presents. The 1837 number was 7,706. The highest number was in 1842, when 14,670 Native people received presents from the British regime. This near doubling of present recipients, it seems safe to assume, is partly, if not largely due to the increased numbers of "American" Indians in Upper Canada that year. There is little doubt that the "American" Indians of the Lake Huron borderlands saw this period as one of enormous upheaval, largely due to the unusual number of migrations—for which threats of Removal were, to a considerable extent, responsible. Certainly, the implementation of the U.S. policy of Removal had worked in sinister synchrony with the 1836 Canadian notice of the elimination of presents for "visitors" to profoundly disrupt the Anishnaabeg way of life.

Because of its wide-ranging ramifications, the establishment of the Canadian-American border has been among the most disruptive influences on Anishnaabeg life since contact. That these Native tribes neither felt nor recognized the border (a feeling and a perspective that persists even today) became vividly apparent in the council proceedings conducted in Detroit between

the Odawas and Ojibways and the U.S. government (to negotiate the 1855 Treaty of Detroit, the same treaty responsible for
eliminating the threat of Removal for the upper Great Lakes Anishnaabeg). At various points in the proceedings, the Native negotiators raised issues of concern to "Canadian" Natives, convinced that certain rights under the treaty should be available
to them no matter where they lived. At one point, Ossagon, of
Cheboygan, asked about the annuities to "our Indians [who]
went over to Canada."[124] At another, the Sault Ste. Marie chief
Waubogeeg brought up an issue of concern to the "Garden River
Chief," namely, the fact that in a recent annuity payment the
Garden River people received only half of what other (presumably American) people received. The response was that Agent
Sprague had been given instructions not to pay them, but that
in view of their (the Canadian Indians) "urgent . . . request," he
paid them four dollars per head, when "they ought not to have
received anything." Agent Gilbert's reply also reflected the le-
galistic status quo: "It is just such a case as occurred at Mackinac last fall, when I was applied to and did pay Canada Indians
small sums of money."[125]

The official council proceedings do not contain any discus-
sions that refer to the question of whether or not "Canadian"
Indians can be accommodated within the language of this U.S.
treaty; nevertheless, such accommodations were made in the case
of Garden River Anishnaabeg, whose concerns are addressed in
Article 1, Section 8: "The benefits of this article will be extended
only to those Indians who are at this time actual residents of the
State of Michigan . . . but this provision shall not be construed
to exclude any Indian now belonging to the Garden River band
of Sault Ste. Marie."[126]

Like the 1836 land cession Treaty of Washington, the 1855
Treaty of Detroit shows that the ties that bound the Anishnaabeg to each other were strong, while those binding the Anishnaabeg to the governments of either Canada or the United States

appear to have been very weak indeed. These examples, and several others that follow, make it clear that the loyalties of the Anishnaabeg are *Anishnaabeg* loyalties, akin to the modern concept of nationalist loyalties. An analysis of the signatories to U.S. and Canadian treaties gives a clearer understanding of what "Anishnaabeg nationalism" brought to bear upon the increasingly more difficult situation in which the Native peoples of the Lake Huron borderlands found themselves.

United States–Canada–Anishnaabeg Treaty Connections
As was observed earlier, several of the treaties signed by the Anishnaabeg with both the United States and with British authorities show a decided lack of concern for geopolitical boundaries. An analysis of these treaties and other relevant documents—both U.S. and Canadian—reveals many more examples of the porosity and nebulous character of the "international" border during this period of land cessions and treaty-making. This lends support to the idea of a continually existing "Anishnaabeg Nation State" in the Lake Huron borderlands. Through a process of comparison of those Anishnaabeg individuals who were treaty-signers or who were mentioned in both U.S. and Canadian Lake Huron borderland treaties, it can be shown that certain individuals were involved in the treaty-making processes on both sides of the border. Such cross-border identifications seem to imply that the designations of "Canadian" or "American" were in many cases irrelevant when applied to those individuals whose chose the Anishnaabeg leaders, as well as to those so chosen to represent them at treaty negotiations with agents of either the U.S. or Canadian governments.

Before analyzing the results of this investigation—presented in table 4—the process by which the information in the table was assembled needs explanation. The names of all signers and those otherwise mentioned in Lake Huron borderlands treaties and in other relevant documents (both U.S. and Canadian) were entered into a database along with a code for the treaty in which the name was found. The resulting list of over 1,500 names was then sorted alphabetically and examined for names that appeared in both U.S. and Canadian sources.

Many duplicate sets of names produced by this analysis are not included in table 4 due to perceived geographic distances or chronological gaps that rendered their inclusion suspect. For example, the names of those who were likely to have been at too great a distance from the treaty proceedings, or unlikely to have even been alive at the time in question, are not included. Rather than incorporate sets of names with dubious integrity, only those names able to withstand close scrutiny were included. The wide variations typical for the period in the spelling of names as they appear in treaty documents also frequently complicates the process of comparison; as a result, many other seemingly duplicate sets of names were also omitted from table 4.

As an example of the decided lack of spelling conventions, the Potawatomi chief Topinabee—to use the current post office spelling of the extant Michigan village—was signatory to several treaties, variously listed as Thupenebu (1795), Tuthinpee (1803), Topanepee (1805), Toopinnepe (1814), Topeeneebee (1815), Tuthinepee (1818), Topennebee (1821), Topnibe (1822), Topenibe (1826), Topenebee (1828), and Topenebe (1846).[127] On many occasions, the spelling of a name varied even within the same document. For example, an 1833 treaty contains the spellings Topenebe and Topenebee, together with the probable misspelling "Jo-pen-e-bee."[128] In sum, among the fifteen references to Topinabee (including the modern village name), there are thirteen orthographic variations—and this for a name whose spelling does not appear to present any great difficulties in comparison to others in the analysis.

Throughout this study, the most common spelling of a name has been the one most often used. But in table 4, as well as in table 5, which follows, the spellings are given as they appear in the cited source. In these tables, the name of the individual is followed by a number, which designates the year of the treaty or other source, and is labeled either "A" for the United States or "C" for Canada, depending on which country the treaty was being made with. The "S" designation refers to the source of the information: 1839-s refers to the Ottawa and Chippewa payroll of 1839 from the Schoolcraft Papers; the more recent sources for this data, 1985-s and 1991-s, are referenced in table 4. The 1850-v designation refers to the Robinson Treaty Voucher #2 from Sault Ste. Marie, Canada, and represents individuals who were paid by the Canadian government for cessions in the Huron–Robinson Treaty of 1850. "MI-EUP" refers to the Eastern Upper Peninsula of Michigan. An explanation of these references, treaty descriptions, and other sources are in table 6 in the appendix.

Three important leaders known to be associated with the Sault Ste. Marie area can be found in table 4: Shingwauk, Oshawano, and Waubojeeg. Their roles as signatories, as well as their names and the variant spellings of their names, reviewed below, are well-known and not in dispute.

In addition to his participation in the 1820 cession at Sault Ste. Marie, Shingwauk was a signatory to the 1817 and 1819 lower Michigan cession treaties, the 1850 Robinson land cession treaty, and other treaties associated with the Garden River reserve near Sault Ste. Marie. His son, Augustin, who was listed in the 1819 Michigan treaty as "Shingwalk, jun.," also signed several Garden River treaties.[129] The table shows that Tagoush, another son of Shingwauk, also signed treaties for both the United States and Canada.

Oshawano was another important chief from the northern reaches of the Lake Huron borderlands area. His grandfather, Kichiokamichide, was the first chief at Bawating (the Sault), and his father was Auchaswanon.[130] Oshawano's first name was Kasakoodangue (or Cassaquadung); he also used the name Weenikiz and was known to add "Kewazee" to the name of Oshawano,

Table 4. Anishnaabeg–Canadian–U.S. Treaty Signers

Signer Name	Treaty	Treaty Signing Location and/or Comments
Sheganack	1817-A	Northern Ohio
Sigonak	1819-A	Saginaw
Assekinack	1836-C	Manitoulin Island
Assikinock	1850-C	Sault Ste Marie
Assiginack	1862-C	Manitoulin Island
Chemokcomon	1817-A	Northern Ohio
Kitchmookman	1819-A	Saginaw
Chemogueman	1820-A1	L'Arbre Croche & Mackinac
Kitchemokman	1836-C	Manitoulin Island
Gitchy Mocoman	1836-A	Washington DC (No. MI-EUP cession)
Keezhigo Benais	1836-A	Washington DC (No. MI-EUP cession)
Keghikgodoness	1862-C	Manitoulin Island
Keywaytenan	1790-C	Detroit
Kewaytinam	1819-A	Saginaw
Kimewen	1836-C	Manitoulin Island
Kimmewun	1836-A	Washington DC (No. MI-EUP cession)
Kemewan	1839-S	Ottawa/Chippewa list
Macounce	1796-C	Thames River
Macquettequet	1807-A	Detroit
Eshtonoquot	1836-A1	Washington DC (St. Clair region)
"Little Bear"	1985-S	[1]
Ishtonaquette	1991-S	[2]
Meatoosawkee	1798-C	St. Joseph Island
Maidosagee	1836-A	Washington DC (No. MI-EUP cession)
Magisanikway	1836-A	Washington DC (No. MI-EUP cession)
Mahgezahnekwa	1859-C	Garden River
Megissanequa		Moved to Garden River by 1840[3]
Mosaniko	1836-A	Washington DC (No. MI-EUP cession)
Mosuneko	1836-C	Manitoulin Island

continued

Table 4. Anishnaabeg–Canadian–U.S. Treaty Signers (*cont.*)

Signer Name	Treaty	Treaty Signing Location and/or Comments
Nanguey	1795-A	Greenville
Nangee	1796-C	Thames River
Nangy	1800-C	Windsor
Nawogezhick	1855-A	Detroit
Nawwegezhick	1855-A1	Sault Ste Marie
Nawwegezhick	1855-A2	Detroit (Sault cession)
Nahwegezhig	1859-C	Garden River
Naway Kesick	1867-C	Garden River
Negig	1796-C	Thames River
Nekiek	1805-A	Fort Industry (No. Ohio)
Negig	1807-A	Detroit
Negig	1827-C	Amherstburg
Nemekass	1795-A	Greenville
Annamakance	1796-C	Thames River
Nemekass	1807-A	Detroit
Animikince	1827-C	Amherstburg
Nimekance	1991-S	"Chief of Sarnia Band"[4]
Paanassee	1815-A	Spring Wells
Panaissy	1850-C	Sault Ste Marie
Paimausegai	1836-C	Manitoulin Island
Pamossegay	1836-A	Washington DC (No. MI-EUP cession)
Shawanoe	1820-A1	L'Arbre Croche/Mackinac
Kewayzi Shawano	1836-A	Washington DC (No. MI-EUP cession)
Oshawano	1850-C	Sault Ste Marie
Shawano	1855-A	Detroit
Oshawano	1855-A	Detroit
Oshawawno	1855-A2	Detroit (Sault cession)
Ouitanissa	1790-C	Detroit
Wetanasa	1789-A	Fort Harmar
Penash	1790-C	Detroit
Penosh	1814-AA	Greenville

Signer Name	Treaty	Treaty Signing Location and/or Comments
Penashee	1832-A	Tippecanoe
Penashi	1842-A	LaPointe
Penashe	1859-C	Garden River
Peyshiky	1796-C	Thames River
Peeshickee	1826-A	Fond du Lac
Sagunosh	1819-A	Saginaw
Shaganash	1820-A1	L'Arbre Croche/Mackinac
Saganash	1827-C	Amherstburg
Chigenaus	1836-C	Manitoulin Island
Saganosh	1836-A	Washington DC (No. MI-EUP cession)
Saugassauway	1819-A	Saginaw
Sagawsouai	1822-C	Thames River
Shawanapenisse	1798-C	St. Joseph Island
Shawunepanasee	1836-A	Washington DC (No. MI-EUP cession)
Sawanabenase	1807-A	Detroit
Shawanipinissie	1827-C	Amherstburg
Shawshauwenaubais	1819-A	Saginaw
Shashawinibisie	1827-C	Amherstburg
Shashawaynaybeece	1855-A2	Detroit (Sault cession)
Shebense	1790-C	Detroit
Chebaas	1818-A1	St. Mary's, Ohio
Chebause	1832-A	Tippecanoe
Ghebause	1832-A	Tippecanoe (variant spelling?)
Shinguax	1817-A	Miami River, Ohio
Shingwalk	1819-A	Saginaw
"Augustin Bart"	1820-A	Sault Ste Marie
Shinguakouce	1850-C	Garden River
Shingwahcooce	1859-C	Garden River
"Shingwalk, jr."	1819-A	Saginaw

continued

Table 4. Anishnaabeg–Canadian–U.S. Treaty Signers (*cont.*)

Signer Name	Treaty	Treaty Signing Location and/or Comments
Ogista	1859-C	Garden River
Augustin	1867-C	Garden River
Augustin	1873-C	Garden River
Tegose	1855-A1	Detroit
Tagoush	1867-C	Garden River
Tegouche	1873-C	Garden River
Waubogee	1826-A	Fond du Lac
Waub Ogeeg	1836-A	Washington DC (No. MI-EUP cession)
Waubooge	1859-C1	Garden River
Wawbowjieg	1854-A	LaPointe
Waubojick	1855-A	Detroit
Wawbojieg	1855-A1	Sault Ste Marie
Wawbojieg	1855-A2	Detroit (Sault cession)
Wauweeyatam	1819 A	Saginaw
Wawiattin	1822-C	Thames River
Wacheness	1795-A	Greenville
Wittaness	1796-C	Thames River
Wetanis	1800-C	Windsor

1. Sturm, "Farewell to the Swan Creek Chippewa," 22.
2. Schmalz, *The Ojibwa of Southern Ontario*, 134.
3. Chute, "A Century of Native Leadership," 488n94.
4. Schmalz, *The Ojibwa of Southern Ontario*, 23, 114.

which can be translated as "son of Oshawano."[131] In addition to signing the American treaties listed, his name was added to the 1850 Robinson Treaty band rolls.[132] (Oshawano also plays a major role in events that will be presented later).

The third great Ojibway chief from the Sault area to appear in table 4 is Waubojeeg. He was signatory to several U.S. treaties from 1826 to 1855, and, like Oshawano, was placed on the 1850 Robinson rolls.[133] (This chief is not to be confused with Waubejejauk, who was also an influential area chief. Waubejejauk fell at the Battle of Thames in 1814 and his son, Nebenaigoching (of the 1850 Robinson treaty), was vested by the British in 1819 with the chiefdomship at Sault Ste. Marie.)[134]

Another set of names about which there is broad consensus pertain to the Odawa Jean Baptiste Assikinock, a British partisan in the War of 1812.[135] In the 1817 U.S. treaty, his name appears as "Sheganack, or Black Bird."[136] Assikinock signed several treaties in the United States but left for Canada during the Removal period where he was joined by a Canadian Ojibway chief, Aisance; together they established a power base at Penetanguishene.[137] J. B. Assikinock is listed as the interpreter for several of the northern Lake Huron Canadian treaties, including the 1850 Lake Huron Robinson Treaty, and was a signer of both the 1836 and the 1862 Manitoulin treaties. F. Assikinock, the son of J. B. Assikinock and also an interpreter for the Canadian government, was a participant as well in several treaty negotiations.[138]

The name J. B. Assikinock is also not be confused with that of Andrew J. Blackbird, another important northern Michigan chief and treaty signer whose name appears as Mukaday Benais in the 1836 Michigan land-cession treaty.[139] The same Andrew J. Blackbird, in his book *History of the Ottawa and Chippewa Indians of Michigan*, mentions that his uncle is named Ausegonock, clearly a reference to J. B. Assikinock.[140] Lastly, these men are not to be confused with another notable chief named "Mawcaw-day-pe-nay-se (Blackbird)," a treaty signer from the western Lake Superior region (see table 5).[141]

The inclusion of the entries for Kimewen and Kimmewun is supported by the reference to Kemewan's band as being among those emigrants to Canada struck from a payroll list.[142] In the 1817 U.S. treaty, the name Chemokcomon, found in table 4, is translated as the "American"[143]; in the 1820 entry, the listing is "Chemogueman, or Big Knife" ("Americans" and "Big Knives" were, at the time, regarded as synonymous by some Anishnaabeg).[144] Despite this and the many variations in spelling, the geographic and chronological unity of Chemokcomon's five entries leads to the conclusion that the entries represent the same person. There is no hard evidence that the other names listed in table 4 are those of the same person signing treaties on both sides of the border, but the arguments of geography and chronological unity, in addition to the similarity in names, supports their inclusion.

Table 5 presents the names of other individuals who, though not signatories to both a U.S. and a Canadian treaty, did sign at least one treaty with one of these countries, despite their connection to the country for which they had signed no treaty. The basis for an individual signer's connection to the other country, and therefore the basis for their inclusion on this list, is given in the "Comments" section of table 5.

While the information upon which individuals are included in table 5 is reliable, justifications for excluding certain names may be made. For example, Toposh, listed as a "Common Potawatomi Chief" at Port Sarnia, Ontario in 1845, was also a signatory to the Potawatomi–U.S. treaty of 1832. However, if Clifton's assertion[145] that no Potawatomis could claim historic residence in Canada is accepted, *any* Potawatomi who signed any one of the tribe's six treaties with the Canadian government could be listed in table 5, since all could be construed to be "American" Indians or their direct descendants. It was decided, however, that inclusion of the Potawatomis in table 5 required a more substantial U.S.–Canada link than this largely theoretical one.

The inclusion of Makitewaquit as an 1800 Canadian deed signer, and the names of Mukutay Oquot and Muckadaywacquot mentioned in the 1836 U.S. treaty, present a different problem. The 1836 treaty makes it very clear that Mukutay Oquot and Muckadaywacquot are two different people from two different places. It cannot be determined whether or not Makitewaquit of the 1800 deed is one or the other of these 1836 leaders, but given that this period is noted for the extensive movement

Table 5. Other Anishnaabeg–Canadian–U.S. Treaty Connections

Treaty Signer	Treaty	Comments (with treaty and tribal affiliation, when available)
Akosa	1836-A	Washington (Ottawa & Chippewa)
Aquasa	1850-V	On 1850 Robinson Treaty Voucher
Anewaba	1819-A	Saginaw (Chippewa)
Aneuwaybe	1850-V	On 1850 Robinson Treaty Voucher
Chingassamo	1836-A	Washington (Ottawa & Chippewa); moved from Cheboygan area to Canada; left power vacuum that Schoolcraft had to mediate.[1]
Kagegabe	1850-V	On 1850 Robinson Treaty Voucher
Kawgagawbwa	1855-A	Detroit (Ottawa & Chippewa)
Kawgayosh	1836-A	Washington (Ottawa & Chippewa); referred to by Schoolcraft as Gitshee Kawgaosh, a British chief.[2]
Kaybaynodin	1855-A	Detroit (Ottawa & Chippewa)
Kebaynodin		Signed Sault area petition to Canadian government[3]
Keneshteno	1847-A	Fond du Lac (Chippewa)
Kenishteno	1854-A	Moved to Canada[4]
Makitewaquit	1800-C	Signed Canadian Deed of Sale
Mukutay Oquot	1836-A	From Grand River, western MI.
Muckadaywacquot	1836-A	Washington (Ottawa & Chippewa); from SSM (see text)
Matwaash	1817-A	Miami River (Chippewa)
Matawaash	1850-V	On 1850 Robinson Treaty Voucher
Muckuday peenaas	1826-A	Fond du Lac (Chippewa)
Mawcawdaypenayse	1854-A	La Pointe (Chippewa); moved to Canada[5]
Mizi	1842-A	La Pointe (Chippewa)

continued

Table 5. Other Anishnaabeg–Canadian–U.S. Treaty Connections (*cont.*)

Treaty Signer	Treaty	Comments (with treaty and tribal affiliation, when available)
Mezye	1847-A	Fond du Lac (Chippewa); moved to Canada[6]
Nebenaigoching	1850-C	With Shingwauk, moved to Canada and became chief of "western" Sault area; other major signer of 1850 Robinson treaty
Ogemawpenasee	1839-S	On Ottawa and Chippewa Payroll of 1839 (U.S.)
Ogemahbenaissee	1859-C	Garden River (Ojibway)
Paybaumogeezhig	1826-A	Fond du Lac (Chippewa)
Pawpomekezick		Petitioned to move to Canada in 1850s[7]
Pasheskiskaquashcum	1815-A	Spring Wells (Chippewa)
Pazhekezkqueshcum		Moved to Walpole Island in 1820s[8]
Bauzhigiezhigwaeshikum		On Walpole Island, ca. 1845[9]
Pensweguesic	1817-A	Miami River (Chippewa)
Penaysewaykesek	1819-A	Saginaw (Chippewa)
Penasewegeeshig	1845	"Deserving Chippewa Warrior" at Port Sarnia in 1845[10]
Piawbedawsung	1855-A	Detroit (Ottawa & Chippewa)
Piawbedawsung	1855-A1	Sault Ste. Marie (Chippewa); Shingwauk's son-in-law; lived on Sugar Island; was also a signer of petition to Canadian government asking that Garden River be made a pan-Ojibway settlement[11]; referred to as the chief of the Garden River band[12]
Sabo	1819-A	Saginaw (Chippewa)
Saboo		Signed Sault area petition to Canadian government[13]
Shawanoe	1814-A	Greenville (either Miami or Odawa); moved to Walpole Island[14]

Treaty Signer	Treaty	Comments (with treaty and tribal affiliation, when available)
Shaniwaygwunabi	1836-A	Washington (Ottawa & Chippewa)
Shawunegonabe	1850-V	On 1850 Robinson Treaty Voucher
Tagawinini	1850-C	Sault Ste. Marie (Ojibway); lived at Saginaw; moved to Canada[15]
Toposh	1832-A	Tippecanoe River (Potawatomi)
Toposh	1845	"Common Potawatomi Chief" on Walpole Island in 1845[16]
Waanoos	1785-A	Fort MacIntosh (Chippewa)
Wawanosh		Early 1800s chief of the Canadian Saugeen Chippewa (St. Clair region);[17] "Deserving Chippewa Chief" on Walpole Island in 1845[18]

Note: See table 6 for treaty details.

1. Schoolcraft, *Personal Memoirs*, 658.
2. Schoolcraft, *Personal Memoirs*, 583.
3. Chute, "A Century of Native Leadership," 489n106.
4. Chute, "A Century of Native Leadership," 288.
5. Blackbird, "Petition to Canadian Government," 1845.
6. Chute, "A Century of Native Leadership," 110, 138.
7. Chute, "A Century of Native Leadership," 516n68.
8. Leighton, *Historical Development of the Walpole Island*.
9. Schmalz, *The Ojibwa of Southern Ontario*, 169.
10. Richardson, *Tecumseh and Richardson*, 101.
11. Chute, "A Century of Native Leadership," 118.
12. Pitezel, *Lights and Shades of Missionary Life*, 358.
13. Chute, "A Century of Native Leadership," 489n106.
14. Bauman, "The Migration of the Ottawa Indians," 109.
15. Chute, "A Century of Native Leadership," 153–54.
16. Richardson, *Tecumseh and Richardson*, 100.
17. Schmalz, *The Ojibwa of Southern Ontario*, 136.
18. Richardson, *Tecumseh and Richardson*, 101.

of Native people throughout the Lake Huron area, the possibility must be entertained.

On the other hand many of those who signed treaties with one country while also connected to the other are not included. For example, the name of "Paybahmesay" is found in the council proceedings of July 25, 1855, in Detroit, where he is identified as the "Grand River Chief."[146] This would place him in the west central area of Michigan's lower peninsula. In the proceedings, he argued for the right of Native people to remain on their lands and obtain a clear title to them. Four years later, "Babahmesay" appears as an 1859 treaty signer for the Thessalon River band located on the Georgian Bay North Channel.[147] Given that "P" and "B" are essentially interchangeable sounds in the common Anishnaabeg language, these names are no doubt the same. They were not included in table 5, however, because it seemed unlikely that, in 1855, Paybahmesay would argue for a permanent home in lower Michigan and then four years later (as Babahmesay) sign a treaty for a Canadian band. In the absence of adequate historical support, the mere similarity in the name in this and several other cases was insufficient evidence for inclusion in table 5.

An analogy to modern treaty-making may help to clarify the Anishnaabeg perspective shaping the selection of treaty signers whose names appear in tables 4 and 5. In negotiating the North American Free Trade agreements with the Canadian and Mexican governments, the United States, as a sovereign nation, did not feel obligated to send only "Canadian-Americans" to negotiate with Canadian representatives, nor did they appoint only "Mexican-Americans" to the negotiating team attempting to find common ground for agreement with the Mexican government. Similarly, the Anishnaabeg did not send only "American Indians" to treat with the agents of the U.S. government, just as it did not send only "Canadian Indians" to treat with Canadian (or British) negotiators.

In addition to these treaty-signings, examples proliferate of Anishnaabeg leaders on both sides of the border who acted independently of Canadian or U.S. forces. Clifton reports that following the signing of a land cession treaty by the Ojibway of Chenail Escarte (near present-day Wallaceberg, Ontario), many Ojibways from the American side of the border went to Canada to demand "their fair share" of the cession proceeds.[148] In another example from the early 1850s, Native leaders from the Sault area petitioned the Canadian government for title to (fur trader) Ermatinger's property on the Canadian side of the rapids. Of the many Native petitioners, only three were "Canadian" (Shingwauk, Mishkeash, and Nowquagabo); the rest were "American" and, as was previously pointed out, included chiefs who signed U.S. treaties.[149] Clearly, being Anishnaabe was the most important identifier for these people; being "American" or "Canadian" or "British" was decidedly of minor concern—if considered at all.

On the other hand, the border did not leave the Anishnaabeg unaffected, as the evidence has demonstrated. The wide interval of time between the first treaties (in the 1790s) analyzed in tables 4 and 5 and the last of them (in the 1870s) obviously contains several distinct historical periods covering many wars, including, among others, the Removal era, assimilation, religious denominationalism, and the Manitoulin Experiment. The treaties themselves cover a wide range of changing government and Native policies, first under the French and British regimes, later under U.S. and Canadian influence. The result of these "foreign" policies and treaties is that the Anishnaabeg—Ojibway/Chippewas, Ottawa/Odawas, and Potawatomis—did become, in one sense, a divided people, separated by an international border in the Lake Huron borderlands running from Walpole Island in the south to the area around the Sault in the north, with dozens of small reserves along the shores of Lake Huron in between.

Yet in another sense, the Anishnaabeg, in the face of and perhaps in spite of the differences being imposed upon them by outside governments, sought to maintain an identity — and their loyalties — first and foremost as Anishnaabeg. The last chapter of this study will examine contemporary Anishnaabeg in the Lake Huron borderlands and explore the extent of their success in maintaining their Anishnaabeg identity.

6

Twenty-First-Century Conditions, and Conclusion

The Rapids and the Lake Huron Borderlands
in Their Modern Context

Anishnaabeg oral tradition attributes the creation of the rapids at Sault Ste. Marie to a man who, wishing to trap beaver, built a great stone dam across the St. Mary's River and went off in search of his prey. While absent, he had his wife guard the dam. But it so happened that Manaboozho was chasing a deer in the area, and the deer jumped into the big pond behind the man's dam. Manaboozho begged the woman to help him catch this deer, a request the woman felt obliged to fulfill. With the dam unguarded, the beaver had a chance to escape, and, in the process, destroyed the dam. The stones fell into the river and created the rapids.

This retelling of the rapids creation story cannot match the drama and tragedy of the real life destruction of these same rapids. As we saw in the Introduction, the rapids of Bawating are the essential reason that the Anishnaabeg came to reside in the area and the reason for their centuries-old residence there. The natural resources that the rapids and surrounding area held led the Europeans to covet this area as well. But, the rapids' once-abundant whitefish resource — the resource that sustained the Anishnaabeg for centuries — was depleted after the area came under the control of the United States. That process of depletion, which began in 1820 with the land cession extracted from the Native people by Governor Cass, was essentially completed by the 1855 Detroit Treaty through which the United States wrested ultimate control of the rapids from the Ojibways. The 1855 treaty is barely a page in length, but it has resulted in a controversy that could fill many volumes, and has not been quieted by the passage of 150 years.

The land ceded by the 1855 Treaty with the Chippewas of Sault Ste. Marie is the same land that the Anishnaabeg retained in the 1820 cession, which states: "The United States will secure to the Indians a perpetual right of fishing at the Falls of St. Mary's, and also a place of encampment upon the tract hereby ceded, convenient to the fishing ground."[1] The "encampment," containing thirty-six acres, thus retained that most important resource—access to the rapids and its fish.[2] But the rapids became "an impediment to progress," as ships laden with the copper of Michigan's Upper Peninsula had to be unloaded above the falls and the cargo reloaded below the falls. Sometimes entire ships had to be portaged from Lake Superior to the St. Mary's River. A shipping lock was deemed essential. Work on the Sault's first lock (built by the State of Michigan) was begun in 1853 and was completed two months *before* the 1855 Detroit Treaty was signed.

The controversy centers on an allegation that the original 1855 treaty was replaced with a fraudulent one signed only a few days after the first. The following excerpt is from an affidavit signed and dated August 21, 1935, by Charlie Shawano (the grandson of Oshawano, whose name appears on the 1855 treaty). This affidavit sets out the controversy quite clearly:

> My Grandfather, O-shaw-waw-no-Ke-wan-ze, attended and aided in executing the treaty [in Detroit] on July 31, 1855. My said grandfather, together with nearly all of the Indians, returned to their homes on Lake Superior, and two days later, on August 2, 1855, the treaty was reenacted by two or three who had remained, and they signed the names without any authority, signing away the most valuable rights of the Indians of the Lake Superior country. The treaty of August 2nd, 1855, was a well-known fraud perpetrated upon the Indians, one of the greatest crimes ever committed upon the In-

dians, one of the great crimes ever committed under authority of a great nation . . . . I solemnly state upon my oath that my grandfather, the said O-shaw-waw-no-Ke-wan-ze, made a statement to me in the presence of my father, Ed Shawano, that he did not sign the treaty of August 2, 1855 . . . and that his signature was a forgery. . . . I heard my grandfather repeatedly saying that he never signed the treaty . . . and it was known at the time that some of these Indians [who signed the treaty] had been dead for some time when their names were attached to the second treaty.[3]

While it is a fact that anyone can draw up an affidavit to support their version of the "truth," the circumstances of the second Detroit Treaty lends credence to Charlie Shawano's version of events surrounding the destruction of the fishing grounds and the loss of the fishing resource belonging to the Anishnaabeg people.

The physical process of building the locks devastated much of the rapids, which were then further destroyed by the early twentieth-century construction of two hydroelectric power stations, both utilizing water diverted from the rapids. In addition to the construction of shipping canals and hydro-power canals on both the U.S. and Canadian sides of the rapids, "compensating gates" were built across the remaining rapids area. Every inch of the rapids is now under human control with the result that the rapids are reduced to a mere trickle; as a consequence, the fishery has been all but destroyed. (Recently, a low dam was built parallel to the rapids along its north edge to direct more water to Whitefish Island in order to create better conditions for spawning fish. This flooding has helped the sport fishery somewhat, but the fishery is still only a tiny fraction of what it was before 1855.)

The fishing resource of Bawating and the rapids themselves were not the only resources to fall prey to the advance of "progress." The upper Great Lakes were a virtual treasure trove of

Map 10. Lake Huron Borderlands in Modern Context

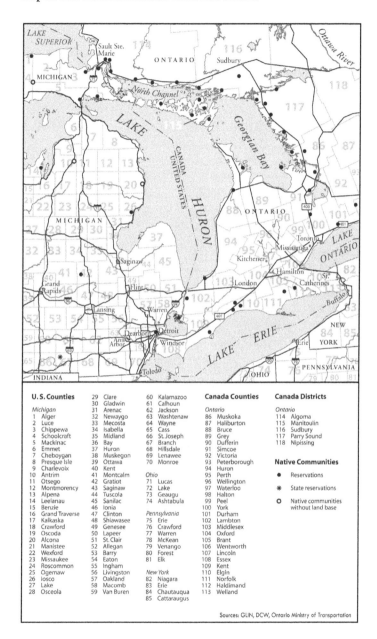

U.S. Counties				**Canada Counties**	**Canada Districts**
	29 Clare	60 Kalamazoo			
	30 Gladwin	61 Calhoun			
Michigan	31 Arenac	62 Jackson		*Ontario*	*Ontario*
1 Alger	32 Newaygo	63 Washtenaw		86 Muskoka	114 Algoma
2 Luce	33 Mecosta	64 Wayne		87 Haliburton	115 Manitoulin
3 Chippewa	34 Isabella	65 Cass		88 Bruce	116 Sudbury
4 Schoolcraft	35 Midland	66 St. Joseph		89 Grey	117 Parry Sound
5 Mackinac	36 Bay	67 Branch		90 Dufferin	118 Nipissing
6 Emmet	37 Huron	68 Hillsdale		91 Simcoe	
7 Cheboygan	38 Muskegon	69 Lenawee		92 Victoria	
8 Presque Isle	39 Ottawa	70 Monroe		93 Peterborough	**Native Communities**
9 Charlevoix	40 Kent			94 Huron	
10 Antrim	41 Montcalm	*Ohio*		95 Perth	● Reservations
11 Otsego	42 Gratiot	71 Lucas		96 Wellington	
12 Montmorency	43 Saginaw	72 Lake		97 Waterloo	✳ State reservations
13 Alpena	44 Tuscola	73 Geaugu		98 Halton	
14 Leelanau	45 Sanilac	74 Ashtabula		99 Peel	○ Native communities
15 Benzie	46 Ionia			100 York	without land base
16 Grand Traverse	47 Clinton	*Pennsylvania*		101 Durham	
17 Kalkaska	48 Shiawasee	75 Erie		102 Lambton	
18 Crawford	49 Genesee	76 Crawford		103 Middlesex	
19 Oscoda	50 Lapeer	77 Warren		104 Oxford	
20 Alcona	51 St. Clair	78 McKean		105 Brant	
21 Manistee	52 Allegan	79 Venango		106 Wentworth	
22 Wexford	53 Barry	80 Forest		107 Lincoln	
23 Missaukee	54 Eaton	81 Elk		108 Essex	
24 Roscommon	55 Ingham			109 Kent	
25 Ogemaw	56 Livingston	*New York*		110 Elgin	
26 Iosco	57 Oakland	82 Niagara		111 Norfolk	
27 Lake	58 Macomb	83 Erie		112 Haldimand	
28 Osceola	59 Van Buren	84 Chautauqua		113 Welland	
		85 Cattaraugus			

Sources: GLIN, DCW, Ontario Ministry of Transportation

natural resources: fur, fish, copper, iron ore, and lumber valued at several billions of dollars; few, if any of these resources remain.[4] For a map of the Lake Huron borderlands in their modern context, see map 10.

The Jay Treaty Revisited: Nation-Building

The building of the locks, begun in 1853, had so rapidly accelerated the exploitation of the area's natural resources that, after 1855, the Anishnaabeg's main struggle was simply to survive. But it was not only the depletion of the resources on which they depended for survival that was altering their way of life. The age-old solidarity of the Anishnaabeg people was also beginning to be eroded by the implementation of an official U.S.-Canada border through the middle of their homeland, as well as the passage of time. Yet a common language, a common history, and a common culture still serve to identify these people as one.

The most salient unifying force is the Jay Treaty of 1794. The passage of over two centuries has not diminished the relevance of this document to the Anishnaabeg of the Lake Huron borderlands. Although both the Canadian and the U.S. governments now refuse to recognize the provisions of the Jay Treaty, especially those that give Native people the right to "freely pass and re-pass" the border between the two countries exempt from custom duties, the Native people continue to claim that right. Indeed, the assertion of Jay Treaty rights continues to be one of the most visible exercises of Native sovereignty.

The Jay Treaty—made between the United States and Great Britain—mentions by name three distinct segments of the North American population: British subjects, citizens of the United States, and "Indians dwelling on either side of the said boundary line." It has been argued since at least 1795 that such recognition, when added to the volume of treaties signed by the Canadian and U.S. governments with Native nations, is tacit recognition of the sovereignty of Native peoples.[5]

Canada has long maintained that no right to free border-crossing exists, and the U.S. government, while admitting that the right of Native people to freely cross and recross the border does indeed exist, contends that there is no right to duty-free "importation" of goods by Native people.[6] Both governments contend that the provisions of the Jay Treaty were never implemented through specific enabling legislation, rendering its provisions moot. Both governments further contend that even if the Jay Treaty had been in effect in 1794, Native participation in the War of 1812, on behalf of the British, was a tacit abrogation of the Treaty. This abrogation is claimed despite the fact that the 1814 Treaty of Ghent, ending the War of 1812, specifically states that Native people are to have restored to them all of the rights that they held prior to the war. This would, presumably, include the provisions of the Jay Treaty.[7]

Despite the ambiguous international legal status of the Jay Treaty provisions, it is important to take a look at how Native people have exercised the rights granted to them under the Treaty, whether those rights are recognized by third-party governments or not. The obvious consequence of the assertion of Jay Treaty rights by Native people is a plethora of court cases in both the United States and Canada. A significant U.S. case occurred in 1930 when a Mohawk of St. Regis (also known as Akwesasne—a reservation that straddles the Canada-U.S. border) was denied the right to pass personal goods duty-free from one side of the reserve to the other—or, as the United States claims, from Canada into the United States. The duty-free right was denied by the courts based on the War of 1812 abrogation argument, despite the fact that the United States had included Jay Treaty language relative to Native rights into its various tariff acts for over a century. In fact, the Act of 1897 was the first U.S. tariff act *not* to include a Jay Treaty exemption for Native people.

In Canada the decisive court case was *Louis Francis v. the Queen.* In 1956 the Supreme Court of Canada ruled in *Francis* that there was no existing law or treaty that exempted Native people from the payment of duties on goods brought into Canada from the United States.[8] The official legal position of the two countries has not changed since these court cases.

Despite the outcomes of these legal proceedings, Native people from all areas of the U.S.-Canada border continued to forcefully assert their rights to duty-free crossing, again most notably at the St. Regis Reservation in 1968 when the Mohawk residents of the reserve mounted two blockades of the bridge crossing the St. Lawrence river.[9] The Anishnaabeg residing in Canada, with the full support of their "American" counterparts, continue to press for the recognition of those rights.[10] In August of 1992, Anishnaabeg from the area around Sault Ste. Marie and many more from other parts of Michigan, Ontario, Manitoba, and Wisconsin occupied the International Bridge between the two Saults to demonstrate their claim to rights granted by the Jay Treaty. As many as two thousand Native people participated in the protest, which included the "importation" into Canada of goods purchased on the American side without payment of Canadian customs duties.[11] In August of 1994, another commemoration took place at Sault Ste. Marie, one of a series of Jay Treaty right assertions planned by the Anishnaabeg of the upper Great Lakes that commemorated the one-hundredth anniversary of Jay's Treaty.

Anishnaabeg assertion of Jay Treaty rights is not, however, restricted to duty-free passage. In 1928 a Native of Walpole Island, claiming a right to pass freely across the border to seek employment in Algonac, Michigan, was denied entry on the grounds that he could neither read nor write. After a spirited protest to Washington, the U.S. government allowed his free passage.[12] In 1974 a federal district judge in Maine ruled that the Jay Treaty and that same 1928 immigration statute gave Native people born in Canada the right to live and work in the United States so as to "preserve the aboriginal right of American Indians to move freely throughout the territory originally occupied by them on either side of the U.S. and Canadian border."[13]

The non-Native population, however, does not always see the issue in the same light. William Johnson, in a *Montreal Gazette* editorial entitled "Historical Falsehoods," claims the Jay Treaty made an exception for Indians because they were considered too primitive to be bound by the rules of "civilized states."[14] Johnson goes on to reassert the (real) "historic falsehood" that the treaty was abrogated by the War of 1812. What apparently bothers many non-Natives is that Jay Treaty "protesters" seem to threaten the effectiveness of central control. In the words of Mike Waterman, a Seneca from New York who took part in a Jay Treaty protest at the Windsor–Detroit border: "We pay no taxes, we pay no duty, we pay no bridge toll."[15] The title of an article in the *Windsor Star* about that protest, "Indians Win Border Skirmish with Canada Customs," clearly points to the concern that the protests constitute a modern "frontier war," albeit, in this case, a peaceful one in the cause of Native sovereignty.[16] Not all of these Jay Treaty actions are peaceful, though. Along the international waterway that straddles the U.S.–Canada–Mohawk–New York–Ontario–Quebec border, a very lucrative "smuggling" trade — an estimated fifty thousand cartons of untaxed cigarettes crossing the border into Canada annually — has given rise to an increasingly violent cadre of "pirates."[17] In the face of this smuggling at the end of the twentieth century, the Canadian government lowered its cigarette tax in an attempt to stem the flow of tax-free cigarettes by essentially competing with the smugglers. Although the illegal smuggling of brand-name U.S. cigarettes seems to have abated, the "smuggling" is now of handmade cigarettes simply brought over in plastic bags, each containing two hundred cigarettes.[18]

Conclusion

John Price, in *Native Studies: American and Canadian Indians*, argues that forceful assertion of a Native right to unimpeded border-crossing "violates the values of both laws and nationalism of Americans and Canadians." But, he adds, "Their claim of a right to do this is one of the few things which sets Native people apart from all others. To Natives it is a symbolic act which validates their identity [and creates] a new proud ideology and social cohesiveness."[19] One might add that Great Lakes Native people appear to realize that the boundary of a country is only as viable as the people being separated allow it to be, though they are keenly aware that the central government's job is to attempt to maintain that division, unnatural as that may at times appear to them. Furthermore, to the Anishnaabeg at least, it seems the boundary "is far removed from the changing desires and aspirations of the inhabitants of the borderlands," and where culture and autonomy are involved, the border is very often ignored.[20] For example, the thrust toward greater Anishnaabeg cultural unity can be seen in the return of traditional societies throughout the borderlands area. The Three Fires Confederacy, active among the Anishnaabeg of Ontario, Manitoba, Michigan, Wisconsin, and Minnesota, are but one representation of this movement. Members of this reformed association are committed to the idea that to be Anishnaabeg requires a return to more traditional ways, preferably as followers of the teachings of the Midéwinin. One of the Midé prophetic beliefs is that "[i]n the time of the Seventh Fire a new people will emerge, to retrace their steps and history, to find what was left by the trail. . . . Their task is not easy. It will take time, hard work, perseverance, and faith. The new people must remain strong in their quest, but in time there will be a rebirth, and a rekindling of the sacred fire which will light the Eighth and Final Fire of eternal peace, understanding, and acceptance over the entire world."[21] According to this tradition, "the time of the Seventh Fire" is the present.

Although a return to these traditions can be found throughout the Lake Huron borderlands, many adherents to this Seventh Generation philosophy (in the spirit, it would seem, of the accepted right to individual autonomy) do not recognize the authority of these various Three Fires Societies, though they otherwise maintain their Anishnaabeg identity.[22]

The drive for unification is political as well as spiritual, with political unions fast becoming an Anishnaabeg hallmark. By 1986 forty-six Ojibway and Cree bands (including bands along the U.S.–Canada border) had formed the Nishnawbe-Aski Nation; nine Ojibway, Potawatomi, and Missisauga bands in Ontario's northern cottage country formed an alliance in 1989; seven Ojibway bands along the Georgian Bay North Channel formed the North Shore Tribal Council in 1991; and Ojibway bands on the Bruce Peninsula presented a united front in fishing rights confrontations in 1992.[23] In addition, the Inter-Tribal Council, headquartered in Sault Ste. Marie, Michigan, represents all of Michigan's recognized Native tribes. Cooperation among these organizations is high, and if, as in the past, the Native people of Canada under the authority of the North Shore Council organize a Jay Treaty border-crossing action, they can be assured of support from their fellow Anishnaabeg from the U.S. side of the border.[24]

Another political assertion of Anishnaabeg sovereignty occurred in the summer of 1993 when the Walpole Island First Nation — comprised of Ojibway, Odawa, and Potawatomi Indians — declared the imposition of a twenty-four dollar fishing fee on all Lake St. Clair anglers without regard to the international border, claiming that the entire area is unceded "Indian Territory" and consequently subject only to band sovereignty and regulation.[25] In implementing the fishing fee, the Walpole Island First Nation seems to have taken advantage of the fact that the land of the Walpole Island Indian Reserve (Canadian government Reserve No. 46) lies in Lake St. Clair waters that are claimed by both the United States and Canada.[26] Whatever the case, the unchallenged imposition of a fishing fee represents an assertion of Walpole Island as an independent Native Nation — a practical application of a right that any sovereign nation enjoys.

Additionally, and perhaps in response to the fact that Walpole Island lies in the territorial waters claimed by both Canada and the United States, cross-border "smuggling," not unlike that in the Akwesasne area along the St. Lawrence River, is prevalent in the area. Gerald Volgenau reported in the *Detroit Free Press* that a "smuggler's paradise" exists in the St. Clair River area north of, and bordering, Walpole Island.[27] Volgenau argues that the traffic goes both ways: cigarettes and whiskey are brought into Canada, while undocumented immigrants (mostly from the Caribbean and Asia) are brought into the United States. Arrest records, it is claimed, point to Walpole Island Native people as the most active players in this cross-border traffic.[28]

The question of sovereignty is a legal one invariably couched in terms of international law and precedent, and different, according to Michael Mason, for "American" Native people than for "Canadian" Native people. In North America, Indians possess what is described as "sovereignty-at-sufferance." This means, explains Mason, that "tribes have retained whatever degree of control over their people and territory Parliament or Congress permits." Mason maintains that through history and precedent, the Native people in Canada "have only the slightest residual governmental powers," while the Native people of the United States have "theoretical sovereignty and some self-governing powers."[29]

Mason's gloomy view of the political situation of Native people in Canada as they attempt to assert their sovereignty is belied at least in part by the creation of the fully self-governing Canadian province, Nunavut—a uniquely indigenous Canadian territory that enjoys an unprecedented measure of self-rule without colonial interference from Ottawa.[30] Nunavut (which means "Our Land" in the Inuit language of the Canadian far north) represents the "aspirations of [all] Native people in Canada [to ensure their respective tribes have] the status of *nations within*

Canada with an inherent right to self-determination through self-government."[31]

Nunavut's status is controversial, however, even among Native groups. Some Native leaders, including those of Nunavut, emphasize the necessity of pushing for Native sovereignty and self-government within the existing framework of the Canadian federal system. Others argue that sovereignty is not something that can be granted by, or negotiated with, a federal "visitor state" government. One Canadian Native rights group states the issue this way: "The First Nations will not allow the question of their self-determination to become a domestic issue for Canada to resolve, and they will not abandon or compromise their international standing."[32] The obvious implication of this position is that sovereignty exists outside the bounds of any strictly "Canadian" context.

While the same Native rights group cites as possible models the "mini-states" of Monaco and San Marino, few are willing to toy with the idea of complete independence and sovereignty outside of the framework of either the United States or Canadian federations. Mohawk writer and broadcaster Brian Maracle is an exception. He argues that the solution to the "problem" of Akwesasne — the Mohawk reserve at St. Regis that straddles the U.S.-Canada border and that has been the sight of gambling, cigarette smuggling, and Jay Treaty protests — is sovereignty for its Mohawk people. Maracle suggests that the Canadian border be drawn along the north of the reserve, and the U.S. border along the southern edge, in order to create a North American San Marino or Monaco-style mini-state complete with "tourism, the sale of postage stamps[,] . . . a duty free zone [and] a centre for international business and banking. . . . Anything else will guarantee only continued confrontation."[33] As this book is being written, the Mohawks of Akwesasne have forced the Canadian government to move their border station off Mohawk territory (the issue arose over Canada's insistence that its border guards be armed—the Mohawks simply refused to allow "foreign" agents to be armed on their territory).[34]

In the early sixteenth century, a Spanish theologian, Francisco de Vitoria, argued that occupation of a territory imputes to the occupants a right to that soil, and that there is an implicit right to sovereignty over the territory through that occupation. Scholars seem to agree that the legal rights of indigenous people to sovereignty and self-government as an inherent right derived from this principle of occupancy, which has remained remarkably intact since the sixteenth-century Vitoria opinion.[35] In fact the 1982 Canadian Constitution guarantees the "inherent rights" of Native people. In the United States it has been argued that it was the Supreme Court ruling in *McIntosh v. Johnson* that set the stage for the abrogation of Native rights to the soil (and the sovereignty implicit in that right). At issue in the case was ownership of land that had been granted to Johnson by the Cherokee in 1773 and 1775. The land was also claimed by McIntosh, who held a U.S. patent to it that was obtained after a Cherokee land cession.[36] In this landmark case, Chief Justice John Marshall ruled that Native people held an inherent right to the soil but that this right could only be extinguished by federal prerogative. In other words, Native people's rights to the soil could only be transferred to the federal government; they could not alienate that right to any individual or to any other entity.[37]

As Maureen Davies argues, in *Aspects of Aboriginal Rights in International Law*, the federal government's right to abrogate indigenous rights to the soil, as declared in the *McIntosh* decision, was based in large part on military conquest, not on the claimed European right to the soil by virtue of "discovery." These (U.S.) claims to Indian land, in Chief Justice Marshall's view, "have been maintained and established as far west as the river Mississippi, by the sword. . . . The title by conquest is acquired and maintained by force."[38] But, while an American assertion of military conquest may be a valid argument when applied to a British or French claim, it does not appear to be valid in the case of the Cherokees as was ruled, since they were not defeated in military battle.[39] A more liberal analysis of the *McIntosh* decision may very well lead to the conclusion that the Cherokees—and by extension, all Native peoples in the United States—never did lose their inherent rights to the soil (that is, their sovereignty) because they are not "conquered" people.

The notion that the Anishnaabeg lost their inherent sovereignty rights to the Canadian and U.S. governments through military defeat is also inaccurate, as the preceding chapters have shown. Following the defeat of the French by the British, the Ojibway chief Minnehaha provided a spirited summation of the situation: "Englishman, although you have conquered the French, you have not yet conquered us! We are not your slaves. These lakes, these woods and mountains, were left to us by our ancestors. They are our inheritance; and we will part with them to none."[40] The passage of time did not dampen this sentiment, which was reiterated after the defeat of the British by the Americans. Indeed, Canadian Native leader Elijah Harper was more recently quoted as saying: "We were never a conquered people. . . . We have never agreed to relinquish that right to govern ourselves. . . . [M]any Canadians are ignorant of that history."[41]

The 1831 U.S. Supreme Court case of *Cherokee Nation v. Georgia* contains an oft-quoted description of Indians as "domestic dependent nations," which some legal scholars construe as an argument for the *curtailment* of their rights. Others hold that it could just as easily be reinterpreted to allow a much greater measure of self-determination and self-government for Native people in the United States.[42] In Canada many have argued that the limited reaffirmation of the inherent Aboriginal right to access the area's resources found in the 1993 *Sparrow* decision could be extended to grant individual bands the inherent right to self-government.[43] In fact, across Canada, sovereignty in the form of self-government agreements is currently being sought by dozens of bands, including at least seventeen from the Lake Huron borderlands.[44]

These various Canadian court decisions form the basis for the concept of "nations within," relatively autonomous self-governing indigenous governments within the Canadian federation, of which Nunavut is an example. The same argument would apply to Native groups within the U.S. context, especially in the Anishnaabeg community, where there seems to be more support for the "Nunavut approach" and less for the "San Marino solution" to Native sovereignty. But the current Temagami land claim, the continued assertion of Jay Treaty rights, and the Walpole Island brand of sovereignty does typify the prevailing mood and thinking of the Anishnaabeg in their slow—one may even say *conservative*—push for unity, a national identity, and a measure of sovereignty and self-government.

The history of the Anishnaabeg is replete with references to their cultural unity. Edmund Danziger, in his essay "Canada's Urban Indians: The Detroit-Walpole Connection," states that during the 1900s thousands of Native people moved from Walpole Island to the Detroit area, bolstering the view that the Anishnaabeg felt not only comfortable on both sides of the international border but found a ready Native social structure to welcome them. For many, this social structure makes the cross-border transition as seamless as it was for Martin Kiyoshk, who, as Danziger points out, was born on Walpole Island; went to school at the Shingwauk boarding school in Sault Ste. Marie, Ontario; and lived most of his adult life in Detroit.[45]

Everett Claspy, in his book on the Potawatomi Indians of Southwestern Michigan, claims that late into the twentieth century these Native people maintained close ties with the Anishnaabeg of Walpole Island.[46] A resolution of the Chicago City Council adopted on July 31, 1990, supports the Illinois land claim of two to three thousand Potawatomi who fled to Canada after their refusal to sign a Removal treaty in 1833.[47] Only the continuing ties between the Potawatomis of Canada and the remnants of the Potawatomis in the Chicago area make this resolution explicable. It has been argued, relative to this same Potawatomi claim, which has been active in the courts and in Congress since at least 1864,[48] that the Potawatomis may have legal standing to sue the U.S. and Canadian governments under provisions of the International Joint Commission, which was established to "settle all questions [involving] the rights, obligations, or interests . . . of the inhabitants of the other [country], along their common border.[49] The persistence of the Potawatomi and the continuing support they receive from Anishnaabeg throughout the region speaks to the enduring unity of these people. And this persistence and unity have finally borne fruit; in 2000, the U.S. Federal government and the Potawatomi Nation of Canada came to an agreement to settle the "Canadian" Potawatomis' land claim for $1.83 million (USD).[50]

Courts are not the only places where the Anishnaabeg are engaged in the work of dissolving borders. At virtually all pow-wows held in the Great Lakes region, including areas well beyond the Lake Huron borderlands, the Grand Entry always includes veterans carrying the flags of both the United States and Canada.[51] These are not the "standard" flags of these countries, however. Known as "Indian" flags, they show an image of a Native warrior superimposed over the Stars and Stripes and the Maple Leaf.[52] These veterans and these flags are a vivid symbol of the commitment of the Anishnaabeg to protect and be loyal to their country, which, in this context, is a commitment to the country of the "United Anishnaabeg Nation" of the United States and Canada.[53]

In an impressive demonstration of the growing pan-tribal character of Great Lakes area pow-wows, Native people from over forty different nations, including Sioux, Delaware, Navajo, and Hopi, joined their Anishnaabeg relations at a pow-wow on Walpole Island in July of 1990.[54] Deepening the sense of pan-tribal solidarity at this Walpole Island pow-wow was the collection of money and petition signatures in support of Mohawks then in a standoff with the Canadian military at Oka, Quebec.[55]

The twenty-first century has also witnessed a flowering of "cross-border" activity. In addition to the ongoing claim of the Walpole Island First Nation to all of the "unceded" waters of Lake St. Clair, the Anishnaabeg at the northern end of our study area are exploring the "unceded Indian Territory" status of Sugar Island. As can be seen on map 8, the U.S.-Canada border at the southern end of Sugar Island is "undetermined." This indeterminate status was recognized by those surveying the border in 1828 when they simply couldn't agree which country would be "granted" Sugar Island. This "border anomaly" was in place in 1836 when the U.S. government signed a land cession treaty with the Anishnaabeg of the area; consequently, Sugar Island was not part of that cession treaty.

Eventually, through a provision of the Webster-Ashburton Treaty of 1842, it was determined that Sugar Island should lie within the boundaries of the United States. It should be noted that despite that agreement between the United States and Great Britain, all of "Sugar Island, with its islets," was still (in the language of the U.S. 1836 Treaty) "reserved for the use of the Chippewas" in 1842; in other words, it was "unceded Indian Territory." The Anishnaabeg of the area argue that despite the "land cession" nature of the 1836 Treaty, as far as Sugar Island is concerned, mention of "Sugar Island, with its islets," is more of a *land claim* by the United States, and not at all a *land cession* by the Anishnaabeg.[56] Furthermore, the "pre-federation" 1850 Huron-Robinson Treaty signed by the area Anishnaabeg with the British makes no mention of Sugar Island, due, no doubt, to the fact that the British had recognized Sugar Island as "part of the United States," since 1842. Moreover, as we have seen in tables 4 and 5, both the 1836 and the 1850 treaties were signed by individuals representing all of the Anishnaabeg of the upper Great

Lakes without regard to their "Canadian" or "American" Indian status. Furthermore, both visitor governments recognized the sovereignty of the "Anishnaabeg Nation" throughout the entire treaty-making era.

Another very significant twenty-first-century development at the northern terminus of the study area grew out of a serious e-coli contamination of the upper St. Mary's River in 2006. While undergoing an upgrade, the Sault, Ontario, sewage treatment plant apparently dumped raw sewage into the St. Mary's River on more than one occasion, and that raw sewage washed up on the shores of Sugar Island, on the U.S. side of the border. This created a serious problem of jurisdiction, with U.S. public health authorities unable to cross the border to investigate the presumably Canadian source of the contamination.

In response to the "international jurisdictional" issues borne of this environmental public health crisis, the Anishnaabeg of the area asserted their sovereignty over the river, forming the Anishnaabeg Joint Commission (AJC) to deal with the problem. For the Anishnaabeg have no "international jurisdictional" issues to contend with, while they do have the sovereign right—and the responsibility—to preserve the environmental integrity of their homeland "for the next seven generations."[57]

The Anishnaabeg Joint Commission is comprised of the leaders of the four area tribes: the Sault Ste. Marie Tribe of Chippewa Indians and the Bay Mills Indian Community on the southern side of the border, and the Batchewana and Garden River First Nations from the northern side. All have interests on Sugar Island: both the Sault Tribe and Bay Mills have reservation lands on the island, and Batchewana and Garden River territory lies directly across the St. Mary's River from Sugar Island. In fact, given the way the border was drawn, a small portion of the Garden River First Nation is part of "U.S. territory," and is registered as such with the Chippewa County register of deeds.[58]

In the most recent development at the northern terminus of

the study area, the four AJC tribes negotiated a Memorandum of Agreement (MOA) with the Customs and Border Protection Agency of the U.S. Department of Homeland Security. The issue under discussion was the requirement, effective June 1, 2009, under the Western Hemisphere Travel Initiative (WHTI) (2008) that all travelers entering the United States must possess a passport or other accepted document that establishes the bearer's identity and citizenship upon entering (or reentering) the United States.

Area tribes were adamant in their insistence that the "enhanced tribal identification card" required under the WHTI not declare the holder's citizenship to be "American Indian" or "Canadian Indian." In order to resolve this issue, the Batchewana and Garden River First Nations inserted the following language into the MOA: "In addition, the rights of both Batchewana First Nation and Garden River First Nation membership will be recognized according to the historical right as Indigenous Nations of North America." This is truly significant as it appears to be the first time in recorded history that the United States government recognized the sovereignty of these "Indigenous Nations of North America" without reference to their "Canadian" or "American" status.

Also of direct relevance to this study is the following language in the July, 2010 MOA: "The following is a listing of treaties and legislation that show the relationship between Batchewana First Nation, Garden River First Nation, Bay Mills Indian Community, and Sault Tribe as alliances, and as Indigenous Nations of North America." Included in that list of "treaties and legislation" are the 1820, 1836, and 1855 United States treaties, and the 1850 Huron-Robinson Canadian treaty. The basis for this statement in the MOA is that those who signed those treaties, as this study has shown, did not sign as "American Indians" or as "Canadian Indians" but as members of the "Anishnaabeg Nation," a fact now recognized by the U.S. government in the July, 2010 MOA.[59]

The numerous, ongoing pow-wows, the Jay Treaty protests, the formation of the AJC, the signing of the border-crossing MOA, the return of a strengthened Midéwiwin and Three Fires Societies, the strong ties of family and clan, and the continuous efforts to maintain their cherished language and culture demonstrate that the Anishnaabeg are emerging as a strong Lake Huron borderlands sovereign Nation with a profound sense of unity and a persistent cultural sense of being Anishnaabeg despite many centuries of assault. They may be divided by a line on a map, and they may be living in relatively isolated small communities throughout what was once a homeland belonging to no one but themselves, but, more importantly, they have never been divided, they have never been dispersed, and they have never been vanquished. They survive as the "Anishnaabeg of the Lake Huron Borderlands"—dispersed but not divided; separated by a border, but not defeated by it; outnumbered, but determined to be heard. We stand proud, strong, and united, for at least the next Seven Generations.

Appendix

Chronological Listing of Anishnaabeg Treaty-Signings

Table 6. Chronological Listing of Anishnaabeg Treaty-Signings

Date and Location	Tribes	Treaty Description	Signers
1785-A January 21 Fort MacIntosh	Wyandots Delawares Ottawas Chippewas	Attempt to fix line separating Indian nation from United States, with cession of some Native lands	Waanoos
1789-A January 9 Fort Harmar	Wyandots Delawares Ottawas Chippewas Potawatomis Sauks	Confirmation of 1785 Fort MacIntosh treaty with further cession of lands retained by Indians in that treaty	[C] Wetanasa
1790-C May 19 Detroit	Ottawas Chippewas Potawatomis Hurons	Cession of Essex County except Anderon Twp. and part of West Sandwich; Kent County except Zone Twp. and Gores of Chatham and Camden; Elgin County except Bayham Twp. and parts of South Dorchester and Malahide; in Middlesex County, Delaware and Westminster Twps. and part of North Dorchester	[C] Ouitanissa Wasson [P] Penash Keywaytenan Shebense

(continued)

Table 6. Chronological Listing of Anishnaabeg Treaty-Signings *(cont.)*

Date and Location	Tribes	Treaty Description	Signers
1795-A August 3 Greenville	Wyandots Delawares Shawnees Ottawas Chippewas Potawatomis Miamis Eel River Weas Kickapoos Piankashaws Kaskaskias	Establish peace between the government and the Indians of the western regions; establish an "Indian Territory"	[P] Wacheness [C] Nanguey Nemekass
1796-C September 7 River Thames	Chippewas	Cession of London Township and part of North Dorchester, Middlesex County; part of North Oxford Township, Oxford County	Nangee Peyshiky Negig Macounce Annamakance Wittaness Wasson
1798-C June 30 St. Joseph Island	Chippewas	Cession of St. Joseph, Cariboux, or Payentanassin Island, between Lake Huron and Lake Superior	Meatoosawkee Shawanapenisse
1800-C		Makitewaquit Nangy Wetanis[1]	
1805-A July 4 Fort Industry	Wyandots Ottawas Munsees and Delawares Shawnees Chippewas Potawatomis	Cession to United States for a Connecticut land company in northern Ohio	[O] Nekeik [C] Macquettoquet Little Bear

Date and Location	Tribes	Treaty Description	Signers
1807-A November 17 Detroit	Ottawas Chippewas Wyandots Potawatomis	To adjust Greenville treaty line separating "Indian territory" for the lands of the United States	[C] Sawanabenase Negig Macquettequet Nemekas
1814-A July 22 Greenville	Wyandots Delawares Shawnees Senecas Miamis Potawatomis Ottawas Kickapoos Eel River Weas	Peace treaty following War of 1812	[P] Penosh Shawanoe[2]
1815-A September 8 Spring Wells	Wyandots Delawares Senecas Shawnees Miamis Chippewas Ottawas Potawatomis	Following War of 1812, treaty establishes peace and affirms the 1795 Greenville Treaty	[C] Pasheskiska- quashcum Paanassee
1817-A September 29 On the Miami River, Ohio	Wyandots Senecas Delawares Shawnees Potawatomis Ottawas Chippewas	Cession of land in northern Ohio	[C] Shinguax Pensweguesic Chemokcomon Sheganack Matwaash
1818-A October 2 St. Mary's (N. Ohio)	Potawatomis	Cession of land in northern Ohio	Cheebaas

(continued)

Table 6. Chronological Listing of Anishnaabeg Treaty-Signings *(cont.)*

Date and Location	Tribes	Treaty Description	Signers
1819-A September 24 Saginaw	Chippewas	Cession of remaining portion of southeast Michigan	Wauweeyatam Sagunosh Sigonak Saugassauway Kewaytinam Penaysewaykesek Kitchmookman Shingwalk "Shingwalk, Jr" [Augustin] Shawshauwen- aubais Aneuwaybe
1820-A June 16 Sault Ste Marie, MI	Chippewas	Cession of 16 square miles at Sault Ste Marie to Governor Cass, for military fort	"Augustin Bart"[3]
1820-A1 July 6 L'Arbre Croche and Michilimackinac	Ottawas Chippewas	Cession of St. Martin Islands in the Straits of Mackinac area	Shawanoe Shaganash Chemogueman
1822-C July 8 River Thames	Chippewas	Cession of 580,000 acres on the north side of the River Thames in the London and Western districts of Ontario	Sagawsouai Wawiattin

Date and Location	Tribes	Treaty Description	Signers
1826-A August 5 Fond du Lac	Chippewas	The Chippewa recognize the authority and the jurisdiction of the U.S. government and agree to allow the United States to explore and mine any minerals in their country	Peeshickee Waubogee Muckuday Peenaas
1827-C July 10 Amherstburg	Chippewas	Cession of 10,280 acres, adjoining Lake Huron and the St. Clair River in the Gore and Home Districts of Ontario	Shashawinibisie Negig Shawanipinissie Saganash Animikince
1832-A October 27 Tippecanoe River	Potawatomis	Cession of Potawatomi lands in Indiana, Illinois, and Michigan south of the Grand River	Toposh Penashee Chebause Ghebause
1836-C August 9 Manitoulin Island	Ottawas Chippewas	Agree to set aside Manitoulin Island chain for use of all Indians who wish to reside there	Chigenaus Kitchemokman Assekinack Paimausegai Kimewen Mosuneko

(continued)

Table 6. Chronological Listing of Anishnaabeg Treaty-Signings *(cont.)*

Date and Location	Tribes	Treaty Description	Signers
1836-A Marchhington	Ottawas Chippewas	Cession of the northwest portion of Michigan's lower peninsula and the eastern half of the Upper Peninsula	Keezhigo Benais Waub Ogeeg Saganosh Chingassamo Kewayzi Shawano Mosaniko Pamossegay Gitchy Mocoman Maidosagee Kimmewun Shawunepanasee Kawgayosh Mukutay Oquot (from Grand River) Mukudaywac- quot (from Sault Ste Marie) Akosa Shaniwayg- wunabi
1839-S		Ottawa and Chip- pewa Payroll 1839 (from the Schoolcraft Papers)	Kemewan Ogemawpenasee
1842-A October 4 LaPointe	Chippewas	Cession of the western half of Michigan's Upper Peninsula and areas of northern Wis- consin	Mizi Penashi

Date and Location	Tribes	Treaty Description	Signers
1845 Walpole Island and Sarnia, Ontario	Chippewas Potawatomis	Mentioned in account of distribution of presents on Walpole Island and at Sarnia, Ontario; in 1844 all distribution of presents by Canadian government to "Visiting Indians" ceased; the 1845 list then implies that listed individuals are residents of Canada	[C] Penasewegeeshig [P] Toposh[4]
1847-A August 2 Fond du Lac	Chippewas	Cession of land in central Minnesota	Mezye Keneshteno
1850-C Sept. 7 & 9 Sault Ste Marie, Ontario	Ojibways	The "Robinson Treaties": two treaties that ceded the north shore of Lake Superior from the U.S./Canada border at Minnesota to Lake Huron and the Georgian Bay to Penetanguishene to the height of land which separates Ontario from the lands of the Hudson's Bay Company; the names listed are all from the Lake Huron portion of the treaty	Panaissy Oshawano Tagawinini Nebenaigoching Shinguakouce Assikinock[5]

(continued)

Table 6. Chronological Listing of Anishnaabeg Treaty-Signings *(cont.)*

Date and Location	Tribes	Treaty Description	Signers
1850-V September 7 Sault Ste Marie, Ontario	Ojibways	As part of the Robinson Treaty negotiations, payments were made that affected Native people whose names and amounts paid were entered on vouchers; voucher 2 lists Native people from Sault Ste Marie who were affected by the Robinson-Huron Treaty Voucher of 1850	Anewaba Kagegabe Aquasa Shawunegonabe Matawaash
1854-A September 30 La Pointe	Chippewas	Cession of land in the far northeast of Minnesota	Mawcawday- penayse Wawbowjieg Kenishteno
1855-A July 31 Detroit	Ottawas Chippewas	Eliminated the threat of removal for the remaining Ottawa and Chippewa people of Michigan and granted them allotments of land within the areas they already held by virtue of the 1836 treaty; also contained a clause that expressly included the members of the Garden River band (Canadian residents who may have been signatories to the 1836 treaty)	Oshawano Tegose Piawbedawsung Nawogezhick Kawgagawbwa Waubojieg[6]

Date and Location	Tribes	Treaty Description	Signers
1855-A1 June 27, 1856 Sault Ste Marie, Michigan	Chippewas	Local ratification of the 1855 Treaty of Detroit	Wawbojick Nawwegezhick Piawbedawsung Tegose
1855-A2 August 2 Detroit	Chippewas	Ceded to the United States the right of fishing and encampment granted to the Chippewa in the 1820 treaty	Shashawaynay- beece Nawwegezhick Oshawwawno Wawbojieg
1859-C June 10 Garden River	Ojibways	Cession of Laird, Macdonald, and Meredith Twps. and land on Echo Lake and Garden River; also Squirrel Island in Lake George	Shingwahcooce Nahwegezhig Ogemahbenais- see Ogista
1859-C1 July 29 Gros Cap near the Sault	Batchewana and Goulais bands of Ojibway	Cession of reserves set aside in the 1850 Robinson Treaty with the exception of Whitefish Island in the Rapids, which was used as a fishing station	Waubooge
1859-C2 June 11 Bruce Mines	Ojibways	Cession of land at Thessalon and agreement to move to Garden River	Penashe Nahwegezhig Ogemahbenais- see
1862-C October 6 Manitoulin Island	Ottawas Chippewas ("and other occupants")	Cession of Manitoulin Island except for certain reserves; also Barrie and Cockburn Islands	Assiginack[7] Keghikgodoness

(continued)

Table 6. Chronological Listing of Anishnaabeg Treaty-Signings *(cont.)*

Date and Location	Tribes	Treaty Description	Signers
1867-C July 9 Garden River	Ojibways	Cession of a block of land on Peltier River, near Garden River, for grist mill	Augustin Naway Kesick Tagoush
1873-C May 20 Garden River	Ojibways	Cession of land for erection of church	Augustin Tegouche

Note: Names of signers are preceded by a [C] for Chippewa or Ojibway, [O] for Odawa, and [P] for Potawatomi, only if explicitly denominated within the treaty or document. In places where no tribe reference is given with a name and only one tribe is listed as treaty signer, it can be assumed that all signers are members of that listed tribe. In some cases tribal affiliation is not given in the treaty itself and was determined using other sources.

Source: Unless otherwise noted, all U.S. treaty data is taken from Kappler, *Indian Treaties: 1778–1883*, and all Canadian treaty data is taken from Canada Government, *Indian Treaties and Surrenders*.

1. Huron Church Reserve, Hiram Walker Papers.
2. Listed as Miami but Robert Bauman claims he was Odawa. Bauman, "The Migration of the Ottawa Indians," 109.
3. The Ojibway chief Shingwauk signed under his French pseudonym, "Augustin Bart."
4. Richardson, *Tecumseh and Richardson*.
5. Assikinock is listed as interpreter.
6. Waubojieg is also shown as "Waubojick."
7. Assiginack is not shown as interpreter.

Notes

Introduction

1. Erdrich and Dorris, "Manitoulin Island," 383.
2. Wesley, "Frontier Defense," 126.
3. Turner, *Significance of the Frontier in American History*, 3.
4. Limerick, "Adventures of the Frontier in the Twentieth Century," 72–75.
5. Turner, *Significance of the Frontier in American History*, 3.
6. Turner, *Significance of the Frontier in American History*, 3.
7. Lamb, "Sino-Indian and Sino-Russian Borders," 147.
8. Kristof, "Nature of Frontiers and Boundaries," 273.
9. Thelen, "Of Audiences, Borderlands, and Comparisons," 438.
10. Kristof, "Nature of Frontiers and Boundaries," 271–72.
11. Baker, *True Stories of New England Captives*.
12. Howard, *Saga of Chief Joseph*.
13. Henderson, *Mexican Exiles in the Borderlands*.
14. Sealey and Lussier, *The Métis*.
15. House, *Frontier on the Rio Grande*, 55.
16. McKinsey and Konrad, *Borderlands Reflections*, 6.
17. McKinsey and Konrad, *Borderlands Reflections*, 7.
18. McKinsey and Konrad, *Borderlands Reflections*, 13.
19. McKinsey and Konrad, *Borderlands Reflections*, 8.
20. McGee, "Four Centuries of Borderland Interaction," 141.
21. Samek, *The Blackfoot Confederacy*, 181.
22. McGee, "Four Centuries of Borderland Interaction," 147.
23. House, *Frontier on the Rio Grande*, 95.
24. Quimby, "Archeology of the Upper Great Lakes Area," 52.
25. Chapman and Putnam, *Physiography of Southern Ontario*, 150; Dickinson, *To Build a Canal*, 3.
26. Quimby, "Archeology of the Upper Great Lakes Area," 38.

27. Quimby, "Archeology of the Upper Great Lakes Area," 6–7; Taylor and Meighan, *Chronologies in New World Archeology*.

28. Griffin and Quimby, "Prehistoric Copper Pits on the Eastern Side of Lake Superior," 81; Quimby, "Archeology of the Upper Great Lakes Area," 62.

29. Whittlesy, "Ancient Miners of Lake Superior," 49.

30. Dixon, "Early Migrations of the Indians of New England and the Maritime Provinces," 74.

31. Quimby, "Archeology of the Upper Great Lakes Area," 106.

32. Brose, "Late Prehistory of the Upper Great Lakes Area," 570–71.

33. Kidd, "Radiocarbon Date on a Midéwiwin Scroll from Burntside Lake, Ontario," 41.

34. Gerald Vizenor, in his book *Summer in the Spring*, claims that the Anishnaabeg followed a miigis shell westward. The miigis shell is said to resemble the cowrie and is the symbol of midéwiwin spirit power. See Vizenor, *Summer in the Spring*, 142.

35. Mallery, *Picture Writing of the American Indians*, 566.

36. Dewdney, *Sacred Scrolls of the Southern Ojibway*, 9.

37. Cartwright, *Disease and History*, 32; Warren, *History of the Ojibway Nation*.

38. See: Bolton, *Terra Nova*, 60; Cartwright, *Disease and History*, 32; Clifton et al., *People of the Three Fires*, 76.

1. A Historical Accounting of the Anishnaabeg People

1. The following four examples are from Schmalz, *Ojibwa of Southern Ontario*: Quoting Champlain: "We met with three hundred men of a tribe named by us the *Cheveux Releves* or "High Hairs [Ojibwa]," p. 14. Quoting Nicholas Perrot: "I have learned from the lips of the old men among the Ottawa tribes," 21; Schmalz then gives this explanatory note: "Ottawa" is the term used here, but it is safe to assume that these were mainly Ojibwa," 271n10. "Sachems of the Ottawa [mainly Ojibwa] nation," 31. "Ottawa Sinago [Ojibwa] chief," 274n24.

2. References to tribes of the Nicolet journey from: Butterfield, *History of the Discovery of the North West*, 48–65; and Le Jeune, "Relation," 413–14.

3. Historical references to the tribes mentioned in the Nicolet accounts taken from Hodge, *Handbook of American Indians North of Mexico*.

4. Hodge, *Handbook of American Indians North of Mexico*, 1: 909.

5. Clifton, *Prairie People*, 10.

6. Butterfield, *History of the Discovery of the North West*, 48–65.

7. Clifton, *Prairie People*, 14.

8. Clifton, *Prairie People*, 15.

9. Winsor, "Pageant of Saint Lusson," 9.

10. Thwaites, "Saint-Lusson's Process Verbal," 26–29.

11. Thwaites, "Saint-Lusson's Process Verbal," 26–29; Perrot, "Memoir on the Manners, Customs, and Religion of the Savages of North America," 223.

12. Dablon, "Jesuit Relation."

13. Dablon, "Jesuit Relation."

14. The disclaimer reads as follows: "This map is a diagrammatic guide to the coverage of this volume rather than an authoritative depiction of tribal ranges. Sharp boundaries have been drawn and no territory is unassigned. Tribal units are sometimes arbitrarily defined, subdivisions are not mapped, no joint or disputed occupations are shown, and different kinds of land use are not distinguished. Since the map depicts the situation at the earliest periods for which evidence is available, the ranges mapped for different tribes often refer to quite different periods, and there may have been many intervening movements, extinctions, and changes in range. *Boundaries in the western half of the area are especially tentative for these early dates.*" Trigger, "Early Iroquoian Contacts with Europeans," viii; emphasis added. The western half of the map is the portion adapted for use in this study.

15. Hodge, *Handbook of American Indians North of Mexico*, 2: 74, 755–56.

16. Hodge, *Handbook of American Indians North of Mexico*, 2: 755–56.

17. Skinner, *Mascoutens or Prairie Potawatomi Indians*, 9.

18. Clifton, *Prairie People*, 19.

19. Hodge, *Handbook of American Indians North of Mexico*, 1: 810–12.

20. Tanner, *Atlas of Great Lakes Indian History*, 30.

21. Hodge, *Handbook of American Indians North of Mexico*, 1: 584–91.

22. Smith, "The Wyandot Indians."

23. Hodge, *Handbook of American Indians North of Mexico*, 1: 684–85.

24. Unless otherwise noted, the discussion of tribal names and meanings is taken from my book, *Indians and Other Misnomers* (Golden CO: Fulcrum, 2001).

25. Feest and Feest, "Ottawa," 774.

26. McClurken, "We Wish to Be Civilized," 3.

27. Clifton, *Prairie People*, 12, 17.

28. Baraga, *Dictionary of the Ojibway Language*.

29. Capp, *Story of Bawating*, 9.

30. Warren, *History of the Ojibway Nation*, 36, 37.

31. Rogers, "Southeastern Ojibwa," 769.

32. Jenness, *Indians of Canada*, 279.

33. McLean, "Letter to Ottawa"; Swanton, *Indian Tribes of North America*, 260.

34. Neill, "History of the Ojibways," 399.

35. Neill, "History of the Ojibways," 399.

36. Schoolcraft, *Historical and Statistical Information*, 483n1.

37. Hickerson, *Chippewa and Their Neighbors*, 44.

38. Danziger, "Canada's Urban Indians," 6.

39. Tanner, *Atlas of Great Lakes Indian History*, 4.

40. Jenness, *Indians of Canada*, 1.

41. Vizenor, *Summer in the Spring*, 136.

42. Lajeunesse, *Windsor Border Region*, xlv. Harry Brockel takes this "jump" translation to a loftier, more ludicrous plane. He says: "What we call the falls or rapids of the St. Mary's River the French identified as 'Sault Ste. Marie.' The literal translation of the French word *sault* is *jump*; thus did the French fur-traders identify the need for their early flotillas of canoes or bateaux to make the 'jump' up and over (or down and over) the [rapids]." From Brockel, foreword of *To Build a Canal*, xi–xii.

43. Greenberg and Morrison, "Group Identities in the Boreal Forest."

44. The interested reader will find several volumes on the Ojibways, Odawas, and Potawatomis in virtually any library. For a fine introduction to these Nations, refer to *People of the Three Fires* by James Clifton, et al.

45. Axtell, *Indian Peoples of Eastern America*, 106.

46. Jenness, *Indians of Canada*, 125.

2. The French Period: The 1600s to 1763

1. The Ojibways called the Iroquois to the east the Nadowes — the Rattlesnakes (literally, like unto the adders); adding the diminutive "-siw" gives the term for the Sioux, Nadowesiw — the Little Rattlesnakes. In the French spelling this *siw* becomes Sioux (Warren, *History of the Ojibway Nation*, 83).

2. Cadillac, "Necessity of a Post at Detroit," 42–44.

3. Perrot, "Memoir on the Manners, Customs, and Religion of the Savages of North America," 270.

4. Dubuisson, "Report of Sr. Dubuisson to M. de Vaudreuil," 541.

5. Dubuisson, "Report of Sr. Dubuisson to M. de Vaudreuil," 549.

6. Stone and Chaput, "History of the Upper Great Lakes Area," 605.

7. L'Arbre Croche is now called Cross Village.

8. White, *Middle Ground*, 259.

9. White, *Middle Ground*, 265.

10. White, *Middle Ground*, 288.

11. White, *Middle Ground*, 288.

12. Thelen, "Of Audiences, Borderlands, and Comparisons," 437.

13. Owsley, *Struggle for the Gulf Borderlands*.

14. House, *Frontier on the Rio Grande*, 55.

3. The British Period: 1763 to 1795

1. Jameson, *Winter Studies and Summer Rambles in Canada*, 206.

2. White, *Middle Ground*, 367.

3. Schoolcraft, *Historical and Statistical Information*.

4. White, *Middle Ground*, 404.

5. De Peyster, "Letter to Capt. Alexander McKee, Detroit, Jan 24, 1783."

6. De Peyster, "Letter to Capt Alexander McKee, Detroit, Jan 24, 1783"; De Peyster, "Letter to Gen. Fred Haldimand, Detroit, Jan 7, 1783."

7. Robertson, "Captain Robertson to Captain Brehm," 361.

8. Indian Council, "In Council, Detroit, 28 June 1783."

9. Robertson, "Captain Robertson to Captain Brehm," 361.

10. Dorchester, "Letter to Col. A. McKee," 116.

11. McKee, "Letter to Sir John Johnson."

12. Committee of Merchants, "Memorandum No. 4."

13. This treaty is given the designation "#1" in the 3-volume set of treaties printed by the Canadian government; see Canada, *Indian Treaties and Surrenders*, 1.

14. Taylor, *Northwest Ordinance 1787*, 61–62.

15. Clayton, " Northwest Ordinance," 3.

16. Rakove, "Ambiguous Achievement," 17.

17. Taylor, *The Northwest Ordinance 1787*, 62.

18. Indian Speech, "Indian Speech to the Congress of the U.S."; White, *Middle Ground*, 440.

19. White, *Middle Ground*, 446.

20. White, *Middle Ground*, 404.

21. Wise, "Indian Diplomacy of John Graves Simcoe," 43.

22. Edmunds, *Potawatomi*, 130.

4. The United States and the Division of the Anishnaabeg Homeland

1. NAC, "List of Nations Who Received Presents at Swan Creek."

2. Wise, "Indian Diplomacy of John Graves Simcoe," 38.

3. Atcheson, "A Compressed View of the Points to be Discussed," 1815.

4. Committee on Indian Affairs, "Report of the Committee on Indian Affairs," 12.

5. Committee on Indian Affairs, "Report of the Committee on Indian Affairs," 3.

6. Cruikshank, "Employment of Indians in the War 1812," 327.

7. Waubojeeg's daughter, Oshawuscodawaqua, married Irish fur-trader John Johnston. Their eldest daughter, Obabahonwahgezhegoqua (The Sound Which Stars Make Rushing Through The Sky), who became Schoolcraft's wife in 1823, was also known as Jane (Paterson, "Life of Schoolcraft," 32, 39).

8. MacDonald, "Commerce, Civility, and Old Sault Ste. Marie," 23; McDonald, *Fur Trade Letters*, 30.

9. Cruikshank, "Employment of Indians in the War 1812," 1896.

10. Schoolcraft, *Historical and Statistical Information*, 119.

11. McDonald, *Fur Trade Letters*, 272–73.

12. McDonald, *Fur Trade Letters*, 274.

13. McKay, "Speech to Representatives of the Western Indians."

14. Black Hawk, "Reply to Lt. Col McKay."

15. Cass, "Governor Cass to Secretary of War, near Zaneville, Ohio, February 17, 1815." 508.

16. Cook, *Drummond Island*, 35.

17. Cook, *Drummond Island*, 36.

18. JLC, *Journal of the Legislative Council of the Province of Canada*; Ocaita, "Speech to the British."

19. Minutes, "Minutes of a Council Held at Michilimackinac."

20. Claus, "Number of Indians Receiving Presents at Fort George," 249.

21. NAC, "Accounting of Indians Provisioned at Grand River, Ontario, June 7, 1814."

22. NAC, "Accounting of Indians Provisioned at Grand River, Ontario, Nov. 1, 1814."

23. McClurken, "We Wish to Be Civilized," 241.

24. Johnston, "Reminiscences by George Johnston," 606.

25. Johnston, "Reminiscences by George Johnston," 607.

26. Johnston, "Reminiscence #2," 608.

27. Schoolcraft, *Historical and Statistical Information*, 398.

28. Cass, "Governor Cass to Secretary of War, Detroit, November 21, 1819."

29. Cass, "Governor Cass to Secretary of War, Sault Ste. Marie, June 17, 1820," 36.

30. Cass, "Governor Cass to Secretary of War, Sault Ste. Marie, June 17, 1820," 37.

31. Cass, "Governor Cass to Secretary of War, Sault Ste. Marie, June 17, 1820," 36.

32. Much of the discussion of Shinwaukonce / Shingwauk comes from Chute, "A Century of Native Leadership."

33. Kappler, *Indian Treaties*, 187.

34. Schoolcraft, *Historical and Statistical Information*, 248; Petrone, *First People*.

35. MacDonald, "Commerce, Civility, and Old Sault Ste. Marie," 53; Chute, "Century of Native Leadership," 99; Canada, *Indian Treaties and Surrenders*, 261, 301, 140.

36. McKay, "Report from the Indian Department."

37. Cass, "Governor Cass to Secretary of War, Sault Ste. Marie, June 17, 1820," 37.

38. Cass, "Governor Cass to the President, Detroit, March 20, 1825."

39. Cass, "Governor Cass to Secretary of War, Detroit, March 21, 1825," 663.

40. Claus, "Cass to Secretary of War, Detroit, March 20, 1825," 665.

41. Cass, "Governor Cass to Secretary of War, Detroit, March 20, 1825," 664.

42. Cass, "Governor Cass to Secretary of War, Detroit, March 20, 1825," 664–65.

43. Cass, "Governor Cass to Secretary of War, Detroit, April 25, 1822," 236.

44. Chute, "Century of Native Leadership," 30.

45. Moore, *History and Digest*, 170.

46. Shouapaw, "Indian Council," 484.

47. Kappler, *Indian Treaties*, 113.

48. McCall, "Peace of Michilimackinac," 380.

49. Schoolcraft, *Historical and Statistical Information*, 117.

50. Kappler, *Indian Treaties*, 454.

51. Schoolcraft, *Historical and Statistical Information*, 110.

52. William Warren, in his *History of the Ojibway Nation,* lists twenty-one clans, some of only remote importance. Warren gives a short account of how the five clans as listed in the Sault Tribe account came into being, but lists six major clans (which he claims make up eighty percent of the total), adding the Wolf clan to the original five (Warren, *History of the Ojibway Nation*, 45).

53. Sault Tribe, "Sault Ste. Marie Tribe of Chippewa Indians Annual Report," 11.

54. Chute, "Century of Native Leadership," 231.

55. Fraser, *Walking the Line*, 112.

56. Colton, *Tour of the American Lakes*, 69.

57. Colton claims in his book, *Tour of the American Lakes*, that the question of Drummond settled the boundary between Great Britain and the United States in this region. This, of course, is not true. The disposition of Sugar Island was not settled until 1842. See map 8.

58. Schoolcraft, *Historical and Statistical Information*, 249.

59. Cook, *Drummond Island*.

60. Catlin, *Letters and Notes*, 161.

61. Schoolcraft, *Historical and Statistical Information*, 407.

62. Frideres, *Native People in Canada*, 57.

63. JLA, *Journal of Legislative Assembly*.

64. JLC, *Journal of Legislative Council of Province of Canada*.

65. Jenness, *Indians of Canada*, 6.

66. Clifton, *Place of Refuge for All Time*; Matheson, "Potawatomi claim on Walpole Island."

67. Wightman, *Forever on the Fringe*, 10.

68. Clifton, "Visiting Indians in Canada," 6.

69. Clifton, "Visiting Indians in Canada," 25.

70. NAC, "Number of Native People Receiving Presents at Manitowaning, August 20, 1838," 7.

71. Head, "Memorandum to Lord Glenelg, November 20, 1836," 90.

72. JLA, *Journal of the Legislative Assembly*.

73. Schoolcraft, *Historical and Statistical Information*, 249.

5. Anishnaabeg Treaty-Making and the Removal Period

1. Kappler, *Indian Treaties*, 8.

2. Tanner, *Atlas of Great Lakes Indian History*, 155.

3. Canada, *Indian Treaties and Surrenders*.

4. Canada, *Indian Treaties and Surrenders*, 1.

5. Canada, *Indian Treaties and Surrenders*, 27.

6. Kappler, *Indian Treaties*, 117.

7. Dickason, *Canada's First Nations*, 238.

8. Dickason, *Canada's First Nations*, 236.

9. Schmalz, *Ojibwa of Southern Ontario*, 139.

10. Kappler, *Indian Treaties*, 450.

11. Schoolcraft, *Historical and Statistical Information*, 533.

12. Schoolcraft, *Historical and Statistical Information*, 533.

13. Canada, *Indian Treaties and Surrenders*, 112.

14. Dickason, *Canada's First Nations*, 237.

15. Ellwood, "Robinson Treaties of 1850."

16. Chute, "Century of Native Leadership," 230; Strachan, "Letter From Anderson to Strachan."

17. Petrone, *First People*, 59–60.

18. Koennecke, "History of Parry Island"; Elgin, "Disturbance at Lake Superior," 1485–86.

19. Brown et al., *Dictionary of Canadian Biography*, 407; Cook, *Drummond Island*, 121.

20. Canada, *Indian Treaties and Surrenders*, 149.

21. Darcy Henton, "Indian Band Seeks Control of Temagami," *Toronto Star*, February 11, 1992, A8; and "Court Rebuff on Temagami Won't End Fight, Indians Say," *Toronto Star*, August 16, 1991, 12A.

22. Indian and Northern Affairs, "Indian Treaties."

23. Ontario, *Akwesasne to Wunnumin Lake*, 269.

24. Tanner, *Atlas of Great Lakes Indian History*, 57 (map 30).

25. Canada, *Indian Treaties and Surrenders*, 149.

26. Barnes, *Temagami*.

27. Temagami Band, "Temagami Band Loses Claim," *(Toronto) Globe and Mail*, August 16, 1991, A1.

28. Canada, *Indian Treaties and Surrenders*, 235.

29. Canada, *Indian Treaties and Surrenders*, 112.

30. Canada, *Indian Treaties and Surrenders*, 112.

31. Canada, *Indian Treaties and Surrenders*, 235.

32. Kappler, *Indian Treaties*, 454.

33. Canada, *Indian Treaties and Surrenders*, 149.

34. Schoolcraft, *Historical and Statistical Information*, 407.

35. Burns et al., *Rebellion in the Canadas*, 9, 11.

36. Clench, "D 86: J. B. Clench to S. P. Jarvis," 326.

37. Wawanosh et al., "D-87," 326–27.

38. Clench, "D 86: J. B. Clench to S. P. Jarvis," 326.

39. Read and Stagg, *Rebellion of 1837 in Upper Canada*, lxxx.

40. Burns et al., *Rebellion in the Canadas*, 13.

41. Fryer, *Volunteers, Redcoats, Rebels, and Raiders*, 23, 46, 67, 89; Anderson, "B-68: T. G Anderson to S. P. Jarvis," 189.

42. Read, *Rising in Western Upper Canada*, 19, 105.

43. Read, *Rising in Western Upper Canada*, 105.

44. Anderson, "B-68: T. G Anderson to S. P. Jarvis," 189; Read and Stagg, *Rebellion of 1837 in Upper Canada*, lxxx.

45. Fryer, *Volunteers, Redcoats, Rebels, and Raiders*, 74.

46. Read, *Rising in Western Upper Canada*, 147.

47. Clifton et al., *People of the Three Fires*, 64.

48. Clifton, *A Place of Refuge for All Time*, 34.

49. McKee, "Letter to Sir John Johnson."

50. Richardson, *Tecumseh and Richardson*, 108.

51. Jenness, *Indians of Canada*, 1.

52. JLC, appendix EEE.

53. Copway, *Traditional History*, 191.

54. McClurken, "We Wish to Be Civilized," 206.

55. Jarvis, "Letter to George Ironsides," 101.

56. Bauman, "Migration of the Ottawa Indians," 105.

57. Jacobs, "Land claims research paper."

58. Bauman, "Migration of the Ottawa Indians," 109.

59. JLC, appendix 21.

60. McClurken, "We Wish to Be Civilized," 21.

61. Sturm, "Farewell to Swan Creek Chippewa," 22.

62. Copway, *Traditional History*, 183.

63. Sturm, "Farewell to Swan Creek Chippewa," 22; Schoolcraft, *Historical and Statistical Information*, 658.

64. Kappler, *Indian Treaties*, 451.

65. Kappler, *Indian Treaties*, 453.

66. McClurken, "We Wish to Be Civilized," 211.

67. Neumeyer, "Michigan Indians Battle Against Removal," 278.

68. Sturm, "Farewell to Swan Creek Chippewa," 22.

69. Neumeyer, "Michigan Indians Battle Against Removal," 280.

70. Head, "Appendix A," 8.

71. Head, "Appendix A," 12.

72. Head, "Memorandum to Lord Glenelg, November 20, 1836," 92.

73. Head, "Letter to Lord Glenelg, January 29, 1838," 180.

74. Head, "Appendix A," 12–13.

75. McClurken, "We Wish to Be Civilized," 206.

76. Schoolcraft, *Historical and Statistical Information*, 463.

77. Bleasdale, "Manitowaning," 149.

78. Coleman, "Evidence of the Rev. James Coleman," 10.

79. Jameson, *Winter Studies and Summer Rambles in Canada*, 246.

80. Chute, "Century of Native Leadership," 160.

81. McClurken, "We Wish to Be Civilized," 25–27.

82. Indian Affairs Branch, *Indians of Ontario*.

83. Bleasdale, "Manitowaning," 147; Indian Affairs Branch, *Indians of Ontario*.

84. Copway, *Traditional History*, 178.

85. Hedley, "Native Peoples in Canada."

86. McClurken, "We Wish to Be Civilized," 327, 338–39, 345.

87. Blackbird, *History of Ottawa and Chippewa Indians of Michigan*, 64.

88. Bleasdale, "Manitowaning," 156.

89. JLA, *Journal of the Legislative Assembly*.

90. Copway, *Traditional History*, 202.

91. O'Meara, *Report of a Mission*, 30.

92. Chute, "Century of Native Leadership," 149.

93. Wightman, *Forever on the Fringe*, 10.

94. Bleasdale, "Manitowaning," 147.

95. Brown et al., *Dictionary of Canadian Biography*, 9–10.

96. Schoolcraft, *Historical and Statistical Information*, 658.

97. Magnaghi, *Guide to the Indians of Michigan's Upper Peninsula*, 50.

98. Bruce, "Letter to Indian Department."

99. Ironsides, "Reply to Bruce."

100. Chute, "Century of Native Leadership," 526; note 48.

101. Bleasdale, "Manitowaning," 155.

102. Bleasdale, "Manitowaning," 155–56.

103. Brown et al., *Dictionary of Canadian Biography*, 407–8.

104. Bleasdale, "Manitowaning," 156.

105. Ontario, *Akwesasne to Wunnumin Lake*, 258; Erdrich and Dorris, "Manitoulin Island," 383.

106. Bleasdale, "Manitowaning," 149.

107. Clifton, "Visiting Indians in Canada," 44.

108. Bleasdale, "Manitowaning," 155.

109. Head, "Memorandum to Lord Glenelg, November 20, 1836," 91.

110. JLC, appendix 21.

111. Bleasdale, "Manitowaning," 152.

112. Indian Affairs Branch, *Indians of Ontario*, 20.

113. Indian Affairs Branch, *Indians of Ontario*, 28.

114. Smith, "Letter from Smith to Peter Russell."

115. JLA, *Journal of the Legislative Assembly*.

116. Blackbird and Neokema, "Petition to Canadian Government."

117. Anderson, "B-68: T. G Anderson to S. P. Jarvis"; Clifton, "Visiting Indians in Canada," 40.

118. "Council Report, July 5, 1847," 6193.

119. American Indians, "Petition from American Indians."

120. Chute, "Century of Native Leadership," 518, note 84.

121. Neumeyer, "Michigan Indians Battle against Removal," 285, 287.

122. Canada, *Indian Treaties and Surrenders*, 227–29.

123. Department of Indian Affairs.

124. United States, "Proceedings of a Council," 15.

125. United States, "Proceedings of a Council," 17–18.

126. Kappler, *Indian Treaties*, 727.

127. Potawatomi treaty years in parentheses taken from Kappler, *Indian Treaties*.

128. Kappler, *Indian Treaties*, 410.

129. Kappler, *Indian Treaties*, 187.

130. Chute, "Century of Native Leadership," 66.

131. Tanner, *United States of America v. State of Michigan*, 16, note 40; Chute, "Century of Native Leadership," 273; Schoolcraft, *Historical and Statistical Information*, 249.

132. Chute, "Century of Native Leadership," 273.

133. Chute, "Century of Native Leadership."

134. Chute, "Century of Native Leadership," 100.

135. Brown et al., *Dictionary of Canadian Biography*, 9.

136. Kappler, *Indian Treaties*, 151.

137. Chute, "Century of Native Leadership," 153.

138. Brown et al., *Dictionary of Canadian Biography*, 1976: 9–10; Canada, *Indian Treaties and Surrenders*, 228, 230, 231.

139. Kappler, *Indian Treaties*.

140. Blackbird, *History of Ottawa and Chippewa Indians of Michigan*.

141. Kappler, *Indian Treaties*, 651.

142. McClurken, "We Wish to Be Civilized," 224.

143. Kappler, *Indian Treaties*, 151.

144. Kappler, *Indian Treaties*, 188.

145. Clifton, *Place of Refuge for All Time*.

146. United States, "Proceedings of a Council," 2.

147. Canada, *Indian Treaties and Surrenders*, 231.

148. Clifton, "Visiting Indians in Canada," 26.

149. Chute, "Century of Native Leadership," 489, note 106.

6. Twenty-First-Century Conditions, and Conclusion

1. Kappler, *Indian Treaties*, 188.

2. Warner and Groesbeck, "Historical Report," 329.

3. Shawano, "In the Matter of the Treaty."

4. Bellfy, "Michigan's Upper Peninsula."

5. AIM, "Brief to the Committee on Indian Affairs," 18.

6. McCandles, "McCandles, Commissioner of Immigration v. United States ex rel. Diabo," App. 6.

7. AIM, "Brief to the Committee on Indian Affairs," 11; and Sampat-

Mehta, *The Jay Treaty*, 12–14; for the official Canadian position see THRC, "Treaty of Amity."

8. Slattery and Stelck, *Canadian Native Law Cases*, 150–82; THRC, "Treaty of Amity," 14.

9. AIM, "Brief to the Committee on Indian Affairs," 17, App. 9.

10. Jack Storey, "Protest by Shopping," *The (Sault Ste. Marie) Evening News*, July, 19, 1993, A1.

11. U.S. and Canada, "U.S. and Canadian Tribes," 1.

12. Chauvin, "Walpole Island Is Home of a Thousand Indians."

13. *Indian News*, 1.

14. William Johnson, "Historical Falsehoods," *The Montreal Gazette*, May 7, 1993, B3.

15. Mike Waterman, quoted in Brian Cross, "Indians Win Border Skirmish with Canada Customs," *Windsor Star*, June 7, 1993, A3–4.

16. Brian Cross, "Indians Win Border Skirmish with Canada Customs," *Windsor Star*, June 7, 1993, A8.

17. Clyde Farnsworth, "Shootouts," *New York Times*, January 1, 1994, 1–4.

18. Brennan, Richard. "RCMP plays cat-and-mouse game with cigarette smugglers." TheStar.com (Toronto), November 14, 2009 (www.thestar .com/news/ontario).

19. Price, *Native Studies*, 227.

20. Kristof, "Nature of Frontiers and Boundaries," 272.

21. Smith, *Seventh Fire*, 6–7.

22. Smith, *Seventh Fire*, 176.

23. Smith, *Seventh Fire*, 103, 125, 136.

24. Jack Storey, "Protest by Shopping," *The (Sault Ste. Marie) Evening News*, July, 19, 1993, A1.

25. Gene Schabath, "Tribe Says It Will Charge to Fish Lake St. Clair," *Detroit News*, June 27, 1993, C1.

26. St. Clair Flats, Mich.–Ont. Map, 1968.

27. Gerald Volgenau, "In Michigan, the Action Is on the Water," *Detroit Free Press*, December 1, 1993, A12.

28. Gerald Volgenau, "In Michigan, the Action Is on the Water," *Detroit Free Press*, December 1, 1993, A12.

29. Mason, "Canadian and United States Approaches to Indian Sovereignty," 423–24.

30. Robertson, "Land Deal Sets Stage for New Canadian Territory"; Kadlum, "The TFN Perspective."

31. Fleras and Elliot, *Nations Within*, 21.

32. Fleras and Elliot, *Nations Within*, 25.

33. Brian Maracle, "Sovereignty Is Solution to Strife at Akwesasne," *Toronto Star*, May 7, 1990, A17.

34. For background on the situation see Mohawk Council of Akwesasne "Daily Briefing," June 3, 2009, www.akwesasne.ca/news.

35. Davies, "Aspects of Aboriginal Rights," 20.

36. Shattuck and Norgren, *Partial Justice*, 34.

37. Wilkinson, *American Indians*, 39–40.

38. Prucha, *Documents of United States Indian Policy*, 36.

39. Davies, "Aspects of Aboriginal Rights," 39–40.

40. Henry, *Travels and Adventures in Canada*, 44.

41. Karina Bynre, "Harper Sees Self-rule Irony: Aboriginals Never Conquered." *Winnipeg Free Press*, March 26, 1994, A3.

42. Fleras and Elliot, *Nations Within*, 169.

43. Smith, *Seventh Fire*, 128.

44. Smith, *Seventh Fire*, 24, 47, 103.

45. Danziger, "Canada's Urban Indians."

46. Claspy, *Potawatomi Indians of Southwestern Michigan*, 13.

47. "Resolution Adopted by the City Council of Chicago."

48. Johnson, "Potawatomi Nation Treaty Entitlement Claim."

49. Baca, "Legal Memorandum Concerning Potawatomies," 23.

50. For an example of U.S. support, see National Congress of American Indians Resolution #SAC-06–003, http://www.ncai.org/index.

51. The discussion of pow-wows that follows is based in large part on the personal experiences of this author and other first-hand accounts related to him.

52. A photograph by Alan R. Kamunda (1995) with an "American" Indian flag can be seen on the front page of the *Detroit Free Press*, March 27, 1995, accompanying an article that outlines the economic wealth of the Sault Ste. Marie Tribe of Chippewa Indians. The flag is in the background of a picture of the Sault Tribe chairman at the time, Bernard Bouschor.

53. Julie Gravelle, "Indians Use Powwows to Help Share Culture," *Detroit Free Press*, August 6, 1991, 4A.

54. Dozier, Marian. "Powwow Participants Show Solidarity; Some Collect Money for Tribe in Quebec." *Detroit Free Press*, July 23, 1990, 8F.

55. Dozier, Marian. "Powwow Participants Show Solidarity; Some Collect Money for Tribe in Quebec." *Detroit Free Press*, July 23, 1990, 8F.

56. I have been actively involved with the "Un-ceded Indian Territory" status of Sugar Island, and the information presented here stems from that personal involvement (which grew directly out of the research conducted for this book).

57. See Sault Tribe, "Local Tribes Sign Water Treaty," November 9, 2006, Press release: www.saulttribe.com/index. The Anishnaabeg Joint Commission's St. Mary's River action got me involved with that emerging organization. I now serve as the AJC's university liaison, and, given that role, the events that I relate in this section are based in part on my personal experience.

58. In my role as Anishnaabeg Joint Commission university liaison, this information was related to me by Lyle Sayers, the chairman of the Garden River First Nation, in the summer of 2008. Maps of this section of the border show this "border anomaly" quite clearly.

59. I received an undated draft copy of this Memorandum of Agreement from Blaine Belleau, Garden River Councilor, on July 6, 2010. "Memorandum of Agreement," 1, 3.

Bibliography

Abbreviations

AAO   Archives of Ontario (Toronto)
MG   Manuscript group
MPHC   Michigan Pioneer and Historical Collections
NAC   National Archives of Canada (Ottawa)
RG   Record group

Unpublished Works

American Indian Movement (AIM). "Brief to the Committee on Indian Affairs and Northern Development of the House of Commons (Canada)." Manuscript, University of Regina, Saskatchewan, ca. 1973.

American Indians. "Petition from American Indians . . . who wish to seek asylum in Canada, August 27, 1852." NAC, RG10, vol. 198, pt. 1, no. 6101–6200 (Reel C-11517), 116288–6289.

Anderson, Thomas G. "Reply to Chiefs Blackbird and Neokema; August 1, 1845." NAC, RG10, vol. 150 (Reel C-11494), 87003–7004.

Blackbird and Neokema (Ojibway chiefs). "Petition to Canadian Government, June 24, 1845." NAC, RG10, vol. 150 (Reel C-11494), 87003–4.

Black Hawk (Sauk Chief). "Reply to Lt. Col. McKay, August 3, 1817." NAC, MG19-F29.

Bruce, Robert. "Letter to Indian Department, April 25, 1850." NAC, RG10, vol. 612 (Reel C-13386), 787.

Cadillac, Antoine de la Mothe. "The Necessity of a Post at Detroit; n.d., ca. 1701." MPHC vol.33 (1903), 42–44.

———. "Report of Detroit in 1703, August 31, 1703," MPHC vol. 33 (1903), 161–81.

Cass, Lewis. "Governor Cass to the Secretary of War, near Zaneville, Ohio, February 17, 1815." In Clarence Edwin Carter, ed., *The Territorial Papers of the United States, Vol. 10: The Territory of Michigan, 1805–1820.* Washington: GPO, 1942. 507–12.

———. "Governor Cass to the Secretary of War, Detroit, November 21, 1819." Carter 10, 872–73.

———. "Governor Cass to the Secretary of War, Sault Ste. Marie, June 17, 1820." In Clarence Edwin Carter, ed., *The Territorial Papers of the United States, Vol. 11: 1820–1829.* Washington: GPO, 1943. 36–37.

———. "Governor Cass to the Secretary of War, Detroit, April 25, 1822." Carter 11, 236–37.

———. "Governor Cass to the Secretary of War, Detroit, March 20, 1825." Carter 11, 663–66.

———. "Governor Cass to the President, Detroit, March 20, 1825." Carter 11, 660–62.

———. "Governor Cass to the Secretary of War, Detroit, March 21, 1825." Carter 11, 662–63.

Canadian Government. "List of Nations Who Received Presents at Swan Creek, December 4, 1794." NAC, MG19-FI, vol. 6 (Claus Papers), 289–91.

———. "Accounting of Indians Provisioned at Grand River, Ontario, June 7, 1814." RG10, vol. 28 (reel C-11008), 16994–95.

———. "Accounting of Indians Provisioned at Grand River, Ontario, November 1, 1814." RG10, vol. 29 (reel C-11008), 17460–61.

———. "Number of Native People Receiving Presents at Manitowaning, August 20, 1838." RG10, vol. 124, 69777; and RG10, vol. 10017 (Reel 11177), 7.

Claus, Daniel. "Number of Indians Receiving Presents at Fort George, 1808." NAC, MG19-FI (Claus Papers), vol. 9 (Reel C-1480), 249.

Clifton, James A. "Visiting Indians in Canada." Manuscript prepared for the Fort Malden National Historical Park, Parks, Canada, 1979.

Committee of Merchants. "Memorandum No. 4 to Sir John Johnson, April 13, 1786." *MPHC* vol. 11 (1887), 485–88.

Committee on Indian Affairs. "Report of the Committee on Indian Affairs, relative to excitements, on the part of British subjects, of the Indians, to commit hostility against the United States, and to the evidence of such hostility prior to the late campaign on the Wabash." Washington DC, 1812.

"Council Report, July 5, 1847." RG10, vol. 123 (reel C-11481), 6190–98.

Danziger, Edmund Jefferson, Jr. "Canada's Urban Indians: The Detroit–Walpole Island Connection." Unpublished Essay. Nin.da.waab.jig/Walpole Island Heritage Center, May 1984.

Department of Indian Affairs. Records relating to Whitefish Island, Sault Ste Marie. NAC, RG10, vol. 2824, file 168, 291–1 (Reel C-11283), 1906.

Department of Indian Affairs and Northern Development. "The Treaty of Amity, Commerce and Navigation, 1794–1796; Jay Treaty." Manuscript. Ottawa: Treaties and Historical Research Centre, 1979.

De Peyster, Maj. A. S. "Letter to Captain Alexander McKee, Detroit, January 24, 1783." MPHC vol. 11 (1887), 340–41.

———. "Letter to Gen. Fred Haldimand, Detroit, January 7, 1783." MPHC vol. 11 (1887), 335–36.

———. "Letter to Gen. Fred Haldimand, Detroit, June 28, 1783." MPHC vol. 11 (1887), 372.

Dorchester, Lord. "Letter to Col. A. McKee, April 23, 1796." MPHC vol. 25 (1896), 116.

Dubuisson, Charles R. "Report of Sr. Dubuisson to M. de Vaudreuil, June 15, 1712." MPHC, vol. 33 (1903), 537–52.

Head, Sir Francis B. "Memorandum to Lord Glenelg, November 20, 1836." NAC, RG10, vol. 10026 (Reel C-11060), 90–92.

———. "Letter to Lord Glenelg, January 29, 1838." *Journals of the House Assembly of Upper Canada: 1839.* Appendix, 180–84.

Huron Church Reserve. Deed of Sale, September 11, 1800. AO. Hiram Walker Papers, 20–299.

Indian and Northern Affairs. "Indian Treaties." Map no. MCR 15. (revised 1977), 1970.

———. *Indian News* Vol. 16 (12) (July–September 1974), 1+.

Indian Council. "In Council, Detroit, June 28, 1783," vol. 11 (1887), 370–71.

"Indian Speech to the Congress of the U.S., December 18, 1786." MPHC, vol. 11 (1887), 467–70.

Ironsides, George. "Reply to Bruce, June 3, 1850." NAC, RG10, vol. 612 (Reel C-13386), 834.

Jacobs, Dean M. "Land Claims Research Paper: Walpole Island Indian Reserve." Association of Iroquois and Allied Indians, nd.

Jarvis, S. P. "Letter to George Ironsides, August 24, 1837." NAC, RG10, vol. 10028 (Reel 11060), 101.

JLA-*Journal of the Legislative Assembly.* Sixth Parliament 1st Sess. vol. 16. Appendix 21, part 2. AO. B41-Reel 36, 1858.

Journal of the Legislative Council of the Province of Canada (JLC). Appendix T, June 24, 1847. Canada National Archives, Ottawa.

———. Appendix EEE, vol. 4, appendix 2, 1844–45. Canada National Archives, Ottawa.

———. Appendix 21, 1858. Canada National Archives, Ottawa.

Johnson, I. V. B. "The Potawatomi Nation Treaty Entitlement Claim: Background Information and Statement of Claim." Metier, Ontario: Potawatomi Nation in Canada, Moose Deer Point. Manuscript. Nin. da.waab.jig/Walpole Island Heritage Center, May 1989.

Johnston, George. "Reminiscences by George Johnston, of Sault Ste. Marys, 1815. No. 1." MPHC vol. 12 (1888), 605–7.

———. "Reminiscence No. 2 1816." MPHC vol. 12 (1888), 607–8.

———. "Reminiscence No. 3 1820." MPHC vol. 12 (1888), 608–11.

Matheson, G. M. "Potawatomi Claim on Walpole Island." NAC, RG10, vol. 10028, February 14, 1931.

McCandles, [name]. "McCandles, Commissioner of Immigration, v. United States ex rel. Diabo." Circuit Court of Appeals, Third Circuit. March 9, 1928, no. 3672. AIM, 1973.

McDonald, Lieutenant Colonel. "Speech Delivered to Assembled Chiefs at Mackinac, June 5, 1814." NAC, RG8-C257 (Reel C-2852), 272–74.

McKay, Lieutenant Colonel. "Speech to Representatives of the Western Indians; August 3, 1817." NAC, MG 19-F29.

McKay, William. "Report from the Indian Department, Drummond Island, July 24, 1822." NAC, RG10, vol. 40 (reel C-11012), 22043.

McKee, Alexander. "Letter to Sir John Johnson, Detroit, June 2, 1785." MPHC 11 (1887), 457–58.

———. "Letter of October 24, 1795." NAC, RG10, vol. 10028 (Reel C-11060), 81F-G.

McLean, J. D. "Letter to Ottawa, September 5, 1916." NAC, RG10, vol. 10030 (reel 11060), 113.

"Memorandum of Agreement between Batchewana First Nation, Garden River First Nation, and United States Customs and Border Protection." Undated draft copy. Circa July 2010.

"Minutes of a Council Held at Michilimackinac, June 3, 1818." Capt. T. G. Anderson Papers. AO, MS23(1).

Miscouaky (chief). "Speech of Miscouaky, Chief of the Outaouas, to Marquis de Vaudreuil, September 26, 1706." MPHC vol. 33 (1903), 288–94.

———. "Resolution Adopted by the City Council of Chicago, July 31, 1990."

Ocaita (Odawa chief). "Speech to the British, Drummond Island, July 7, 1818." NAC, MG19–F29.

Ontario Native Affairs Secretariat. *Akwesasne to Wunnumin Lake: Profiles of Aboriginal Communities in Ontario.* Toronto, 1991.

Robertson, Capt. Daniel. "Captain Robertson to Captain Brehm, Michilimackinac, July 6, 1783." MPHC vol. 11 (1887), 373–74.

Sabrevois, Jacques-Charles de. "Extract from the Letter of M. de Sabrevois to the Marquis de Vaudreuil, April 8, 1717." MPHC 33 (1903), 582–84.

Sault Tribe. "Sault Ste. Marie Tribe of Chippewa Indians Annual Report." Sault Ste. Marie: n.p., 1993.

Schoolcraft, Henry Rowe. *Historical and Statistical Information Respecting the History, Condition and Prospects of the Indian Tribes of the United States: Collected and Prepared under the Direction of the Bureau of Indian Affairs per act of Congress of March 3rd 1847.* 6 vols. Philadelphia, 1851–1857.

———. *Personal Memoirs of a Residence of Thirty Years with the Indian Tribes on the American Frontiers: With Brief Notices of Passing Events, Facts, and Opinions, AD 1812 to AD 1842.* Philadelphia, 1851.

Shouapaw. "Indian Council, June 29, 1816." MPHC vol. 16 (1890), 479–87.

Shawano, Charlie. "In the Matter of the Treaty between the United States of America and the Chippewa and Ottawa Indians of the Sault Ste. Marie band, held in the City of Detroit, Michigan, July 31st and August 2nd, 1855." Affidavit sworn before Judge Charles H. Chapman, Probate Court, Chippewa County, Sault Ste. Marie MI, August 21, 1935.

Smith, D. W. "Letter from Smith to Peter Russell, February 20, 1799." Russell Papers. AO 75(5) [reel 7–444]

Smith, Robert Emmett, Jr. "The Wyandot Indians." PhD dissertation, Oklahoma State University, 1973.

St. Clair Flats, Michigan–Ontario. N4230-w8237.5/7.5. AMS 4469 II SW. Map. Series v862. Washington DC: U.S. Geological Survey, 1968.

Strachan Papers. "Letter from Anderson to Strachan, Coldwater, July 18, 1835." AO, M535(3) (reel 7–419).

Tanner, Helen Hornbeck. Unpublished court document supporting claim to fishing rights of the Bay Mills Indian Community in the Case: *United States of America v. State of Michigan*, No. M 26–73C.A., U.S.D.C., Western District of Michigan, Northern Division, 1974.

U.S. Government. "Proceedings of a Council with the Chippeways and

Ottawas of Michigan Held at the City of Detroit, by the Hon. George W. Manypenny and Henry C. Gilbert, Commissioners of the United States: July 25, 1855." Transcript (microfilm FM-140). National Archives, Washington DC.

Vaudreuil, Pierre de Rigaud. "Words of the Marquis de Vaudreuil to the Savages Who Came Down from the Upper Country, Montreal, c1711." *MPHC* vol. 33 (1903), 503–6.

———. "Reply of the Marquis de Vaudreuil to the Words of the Ottawa, June 24, 1717." *MPHC* vol. 33 (1903), 584–86.

Voucher #2, Sault Ste Marie, September 7, 1850." JLC, Sessional Papers, 1851, Appendix 2, AO, F1027–1–2.

Published Works

Anderson, Thomas G. "B-68: T. G. Anderson to S. P. Jarvis, New Market, December 10, 1837." In Colin Read and Ronald J. Stagg, *The Rebellion of 1837 in Upper Canada: A Collection of Documents*, 189–90. Ottawa: Carleton University Press, 1985.

Anonymous. "No. 135: My Love Has Departed." Densmore, Francis. *Chippewa Music*. Smithsonian Institute Bureau of American Ethnology Bulletin 45, 150–51. Washington DC: GPO, 1910.

Atcheson, Nathaniel. "A Compressed View of the Points to Be Discussed in Treating with the U.S.ofA." *The Pamphleteer* 9.5 (1815): 105–40.

Axtell, James. *The Indian Peoples of Eastern America: A Documentary History of the Sexes*. New York: Oxford University Press, 1981.

Baca, A. Baltazar. "Legal Memorandum Concerning Canadian Potawatomies," from his law office in Washington DC. Nin.da.waab.jig/Walpole Island Heritage Center, April 21, 1986.

Baker, Charlotte Alice. *True Stories of New England Captives Carried to Canada During the Old French and Indian Wars*. Cambridge MA: np, 1897.

Baraga, Frederic. *A Dictionary of the Otchibwe Language*. Montreal: Beauchemin and Valois, 1878, 1880. Reprinted in 1992 by the Minnesota Historical Society as *A Dictionary of the Ojibway Language*.

Barnes, Michael. *Temagami*. Toronto: Stoddart, 1992.

Bauman. Robert F. "The Migration of the Ottawa Indians from the Maumee Valley to Walpole Island." *Northwest Ohio Quarterly* 21.3 (1949): 86–112.

———. "Kansas, Canada, or Starvation." *Michigan History* 36.3 (September 1952): 287–99.

Bellfy, Philip C. *Indians and Other Misnomers.* Golden CO: Fulcrum, 2001.

———. "Michigan's Upper Peninsula, an Internal Colony: The Sault Ste. Marie Experience." Master's thesis, Michigan State University, 1981.

Blackbird, Andrew J. *History of the Ottawa and Chippewa Indians of Michigan.* Ypsilanti MI: The Ypsilanti Job Printing House, nd.

Bleasdale, Ruth. "Manitowaning: An Experiment in Indian Settlement." *Ontario History* 66 (1974): 147–57.

Bolton, Charles Knowles. *Terra Nova: The Northeast Coast of America before 1602.* Boston: Faxon, 1935.

Brockel, Harry C. "Foreword." In John N. Dickinson, *To Build a Canal: Sault Ste Marie, 1853–1854 and After.* Columbus: Ohio State University Press, 1981.

Brose, David S. "Late Prehistory of the Upper Great Lakes Area." In *Handbook of North American Indians, Vol. 15: Northeast,* edited by Bruce Trigger, 569–82. Washington DC: Smithsonian Institution, 1978.

Brown, George W., David Hayne, and Francess G. Halpenny, eds. *Dictionary of Canadian Biography, vol. 9 (1861–70).* Toronto: University of Toronto Press, 1976.

Burns, Robert J., Marianne McLean, and Susan Porters. *Rebellion in the Canadas, 1837–38.* Traveling exhibit catalog. Ottawa: National Archives of Canada, 1987.

Butterfield, C. W. *History of the Discovery of the North West by John Nicolet in 1634 with a Sketch of His Life.* Cincinnati: Robert Clarke, 1881.

Canada Government. *Indian Treaties and Surrenders,* vol. 1. Ottawa: C. H. Parmelee, 1973.

Capp, Edward, H. *The Story of Bawating: Being the Annals of Sault Ste. Marie.* Sault Ste. Marie, Ontario: np, 1904.

Cartwright, Frederick F. *Disease and History.* London: Rupert Hart-Davis, 1972.

Catlin, George. *Letters and Notes on the Manners, Customs, and Conditions of the North American Indians, vol. 2.* Minneapolis: Ross and Haines, 1965 (first published in London in 1844).

Chapman, L. J., and D. F. Putnam. *The Physiography of Southern Ontario.* Toronto: Ontario Ministry of Natural Resources, 1984.

Chauvin, Francis X. "Walpole Island Is Home of a Thousand Indians." *Border Cities Star* (Windsor, Ontario), August 7, 1929. AO, Mss. Misc. Coll. #13, MU2133.

Chute, Janet. "A Century of Native Leadership: Shingwaukonse and His Heirs." PhD Dissertation, McMaster University (Canada), 1986.

Claspy, Everett. *The Potawatomi Indians of Southwestern Michigan*. Dowagiac MI: np, 1966.

Clayton, Andrew R. L. "The Northwest Ordinance from the Perspective of the Frontier." *Northwest Ordinance* (1989): 1–23.

Clench, J. B. "D 86: J. B. Clench to S. P. Jarvis, Colborne on Thames, December 18, 1837." In Colin Read and Ronald J. Stagg, *The Rebellion of 1837 in Upper Canada: A Collection of Documents*, 326. Ottawa: Carleton University Press, 1985.

Clifton, James A. *A Place of Refuge for All Time: The Migration of the American Potawatomi into Upper Canada, 1830 to 1850*. Paper #26. Ottawa: National Museums of Canada, Canadian Ethnology Service, 1975.

———. *The Prairie People: Change and Continuity in Potawatomi Indian Culture, 1665–1965*. Lawrence: Regents Press of Kansas, 1977.

Clifton, James A., George L. Cornell, and James M. McClurken. *People of the Three Fires*. Grand Rapids: Michigan Indian Press, 1986.

Coleman, James. "Evidence of the Rev. James Coleman, Respecting the Indians of Walpole Island, and the Mississaugas of the Credit." From *Reports of the Missionaries on Sarnia and Walpole Island Reserves as reported in Appendix T of Journals of Legislative Assembly 1847*. Sarnia Indian Series #7. Brights Grove, Ontario: George Smith, 1977.

Colton, Calvin. *Tour of the American Lakes, and Among the Indians of the Northwest Territory, in 1830: Disclosing the Character and Prospects of the Indian Race, vol. 1*. Port Washington NY: Kennikat Press, 1972 (first published in London in 1833).

Cook, Samuel F. *Drummond Island: The Story of British Occupation: 1815–1828*. Lansing MI: np, 1896.

Copway, George (Kah-ge-ga-gah-bowh). *The Traditional History and Characteristic Sketches of the Ojibway Nation*. Toronto: Coles, 1972.

Cruikshank, E. "The Employment of Indians in the War 1812." *The Annual Report of the American Historical Association for the Year 1895*, 321–38. Washington DC: GPO, 1896.

Dablon, Father. "Jesuit Relation . . . years 1669–1670: Of the Nature and Some Peculiarities of the Sault, and of the Nations Which are Accustomed to Repair Thither." In *The Indians of North America*, edited by Edna Kenton, 195–97. New York: Harcourt, 1927.

Danziger, Edmund Jefferson Jr. *The Chippewas of Lake Superior*. Norman: University of Oklahoma Press, 1979.

Davies, Maureen. "Aspects of Aboriginal Rights in International Law." In *Aboriginal Peoples and the Law: Indian, Métis, and Inuit Rights in Canada*, edited by Bradford W. Morse. Ottawa: Carleton University Press, 1991.

Dewdney, Selwyn. *The Sacred Scrolls of the Southern Ojibway*. Toronto: University of Toronto Press, 1975.

Dickason, Olive Patricia. *Canada's First Nations: A History of Founding Peoples from Earliest Times*. Toronto: McClelland and Stewart, 1992.

Dickinson, John N. *To Build a Canal: Sault Ste. Marie, 1853–1854 and After*. Columbus: Ohio State University Press, 1981.

Dixon, Roland Burrage. "The Early Migrations of the Indians of New England and the Maritime Provinces." *American Antiquarian Society Proceedings*, vol. 24 (1914): 65–76.

Edmunds, R. David. *The Potawatomi: Keepers of the Fire*. Norman: University of Oklahoma Press, 1978.

Elgin, Lord (James Bruce). "Disturbance at Lake Superior: Letter to Lord Grey (Henry George), no. 118 (November 23, 1849), Toronto (Appendix XVII)." In *The Elgin-Grey Papers* vol. 1, edited by Arthur G. Doughty, 1485–486. Ottawa: J. O. Patenaude, 1937.

Ellwood, E. M. "The Robinson Treaties of 1850." Master's thesis, Wilfred Laurier University, 1977.

Erdrich, Louise, and Michael Dorris. "Manitoulin Island." *Antaeus* 64–65 (1990): 381–89.

Feest, Johanna, and Christian F. Feest. "Ottawa." In *Handbook of North American Indians, Vol. 15: Northeast*, edited by Bruce Trigger, 772–86. Washington DC: Smithsonian Institution, 1978.

Ferrie, Colin C. "D 92: Colin C. Ferrie to W. H. Draper, Hamilton, 22 December 1837." In Colin Read and Ronald J. Stagg, *The Rebellion of 1837 in Upper Canada: A Collection of Documents*, 333–34. Ottawa: Carleton University Press, 1985.

Fleras, Augie, and Jean Leonard Elliot. *The Nations Within: Aboriginal-State Relations in Canada, the United States, and New Zealand*. Toronto: Oxford Press, 1992.

Foreman, Grant. *Indian Removal: The Emigration of the Five Civilized Tribes of Indians*. Norman: University of Oklahoma Press, 1972.

Fraser, Marian Botsford. *Walking the Line*. San Francisco: Sierra Club, 1989.

Frideres, James. *Native People in Canada: Contemporary Conflicts*. Scarborough, Ontario: Prentice, 1984.

Fryer, Mary Beacock. *Volunteers, Redcoats, Rebels, and Raiders: A Military History of the Rebellion in Upper Canada*. National Museums of Canada: Canada War Museum Historical Publication #23. Toronto: Dundurn, 1987.

Goodman, Anthony. "Introduction." In *War and Border Societies in the Middle Ages*, edited by Anthony Goodman and Anthony Tuck. London: Routledge, 1992.

Greenberg, Adolph, and James Morrison. "Group Identities in the Boreal Forest: The Origin of the Northern Ojibwa." *Ethnohistory* 29.2 (1982): 75–102.

Griffin, J. B., and G. I. Quimby. "Prehistoric Copper Pits on the Eastern Side of Lake Superior." In *Lake Superior Copper and the Indians: Miscellaneous Studies of Great Lakes Prehistory*, 77–82. Museum of Anthropology of the University of Michigan, Anthropological Paper No. 17. Ann Arbor: University of Michigan Press, 1961.

Head, Sir Francis B. "Appendix A: Memorandum on the Aborigines of North America." From *A Narrative*. London: John Murray, 1839.

Hedley, Max J. "Native Peoples in Canada." In *Profiles of Canada*, edited by Kenneth G. Pryke and Walter C. Soderlund. Toronto: Copp, 1992.

Henderson, Peter V. N. *Mexican Exiles in the Borderlands: 1910–13*. El Paso: Texas Western Press, 1979.

Henry, Alexander. *Travels and Adventures in Canada and the Indian Territories Between the Years 1760 and 1776*. Toronto: Morang, 1901.

Hickerson, Harold. *The Chippewa and Their Neighbors: A Study in Ethnohistory*. New York: Holt, Rinehart, and Winston, 1970.

Hodge, Frederick Webb. *Handbook of American Indians North of Mexico*. Smithsonian Institution Bureau of Ethnology Bulletin 30. New York: Pageant Books, 1959.

House, John W. *Frontier on the Rio Grande: A Political Geography of Development and Social Deprivation*. New York: Oxford University Press, 1982.

Howard, Helen Addison. *Saga of Chief Joseph*. Lincoln: University of Nebraska Press, 1978.

Indian Affairs Branch. *Indians of Ontario: An Historical Review*. Ottawa, 1966.

Jameson. Anna. *Winter Studies and Summer Rambles in Canada.* Toronto: Thorn, 1943.

Jenness, Diamond. *The Indians of Canada.* Canada Department of Mines, National Museum of Canada, Bulletin #65. Ottawa, 1932.

———. *The Ojibwa Indians of Parry Island: Their Social and Religious Life.* Canada Department of Mines, National Museum of Canada, Bulletin #78. Ottawa, 1935.

Kadlum, Bob. "The Tungavik Federation of Nunavut Perspective." *Northern Perspectives* 18.4 (November–December 1990): 1.

Kappler, Charles J., ed. *Indian Treaties: 1778–1883.* New York: Interland, 1972.

Kidd, Kenneth E. "A Radiocarbon Date on a Midéwiwin Scroll From Burntside Lake, Ontario." *Ontario Archeology* 35 (1981): 41–43.

Koennecke, Franz M. "The History of Parry Island: An Anishnabwe Community in the Georgian Bay: 1850–1920." Master's thesis, University of Waterloo, 1984.

Kristof, Ladis K. D. "The Nature of Frontiers and Boundaries," *Annals of the Association of American Geographers* 49.1 (March 1959): 269–82.

Lajeunesse, Ernest J. *The Windsor Border Region: Canada's Southernmost Frontier.* Toronto: University of Toronto Press, 1960.

Lamb, Alastair. "The Sino-Indian and Sino-Russian Borders: Some Comparisons and Contrasts." In *Studies in the Social History of China and Southeast Asia,* edited by Jerome Ch'en and Nicholas Tarling. London: Cambridge University Press, 1970.

Leighton, Douglas. *The Historical Development of the Walpole Island Community.* Occasional Paper #22. Wallaceburg, Ontario: Walpole Island Research Centre, 1986.

Le Jeune, Paul. "Relation of what occurred in New France in the Year 1640," vol. 1. In *The Indians of North America,* 2 vols., edited by Edna Kenton, 411–16. New York: Harcourt, 1927.

Limerick, Patricia Nelson. "The Adventures of the Frontier in the Twentieth Century." In *The Frontier in American Culture,* edited by Richard White and James R. Grossman. Berkeley: University of California Press, 1994.

MacDonald, Graham A. "Commerce, Civility and Old Sault Ste. Marie." *Beaver* 312.2 (1981): 9–25, and 312.3 (1981): 52–59.Magnaghi, Russell M.

A Guide to the Indians of Michigan's Upper Peninsula: 1621–1900. Marquette MI: Belle Fontaine Press, 1984.

Mallery, Garrick. Picture Writing of the American Indians, vol. 2. New York: Dover, 1972.

Mason, Michael D. "Canadian and United States Approaches to Indian Sovereignty." Osgoode Hall Law Journal 21.3 (1983): 422–74.

McCall, Clayton W. "The Peace of Michilimackinac." Michigan History 28 (1944): 367–83.McDonald, Lois Halliday. Fur Trade Letters of Francis Ermatinger, Written to His Brother Edward During His Service with the Hudson's Bay Company: 1818–1853. Glendale CA: Arthur H. Clark, 1980.

McClurken, James. "We Wish to Be Civilized: Ottawa–American Political Contests on the Michigan Frontier." PhD dissertation, Michigan State University, 1988.

McGee, Harold. "Four Centuries of Borderland Interaction: It Depends Upon Who Draws the Line and When?" In The Northeastern Borderlands: Four Centuries of Interaction, edited by Stephen J. Hornsby, Victor A. Konrad, and James J. Herlan. Fredericton, New Brunswick, Canada: Acadiensis, 1989.

McKinsey, Lauren, and Victor Konrad. Borderlands Reflections: The United States and Canada. Borderlands Monograph Series #1. Orono: Canadian–American Center, University of Maine, 1989.

Moore, John Bassett. History and Digest of the International Arbitrations to Which the United States Has Been a Party. . . 1.6 (Maps) 53rd Cong., 2nd sess. Misc. H. Doc. 212. Washington: GPO, 1898.

Neill, Edward D. "History of the Ojibways, and Their Connection with Fur Traders, Based upon Official and Other Records." Collections of the Minnesota Historical Society 5 (1885): 395–510.

Neumeyer, Elizabeth. "The Michigan Indians Battle Against Removal." Michigan History 55 (1971): 275–88.

O'Meara, Rev. F. Report of a Mission to the Ottahwahs and Ojibwas on Lake Huron. London: Printed for the Society for the Propagation of the Gospel, 1846.

Owsley, Frank Lawrence, Jr. The Struggle for the Gulf Borderlands: The Creek War and the Battle of New Orleans, 1812–1815. Gainsville: University Presses of Florida, 1981.

Paterson, Fraser Clan. "The Life of Henry Rowe Schoolcraft." Master's thesis, Michigan State College (University), 1936.

Perrot, Nicolas. "Memoir on the Manners, Customs, and Religion of the Savages of North America." Blair. vol. I: 1911. 25–274.

Petrone, Penny. *First People: First Voices*. Toronto: University of Toronto Press, 1983.

Pitezel, John H. *Lights and Shades of Missionary Life*. Cincinnati: Walden and Stowe, 1857.

Price, John. *Native Studies: American and Canadian Indians*. Toronto: McGraw-Hill, 1978.

Prucha, Francis Paul, ed. "#32: Johnson and Graham's Lessee v. William McIntosh, 1823." *Documents of United States Indian Policy*. Lincoln: University of Nebraska Press, 1975.

Quimby, George Irving. "The Archeology of the Upper Great Lakes Area." In *Archeology of the Eastern United States*, edited by James B. Griffin. Chicago: University of Chicago Press, 1952.

——. *Indian Life in the Upper Great Lakes: 11,000 BC to AD 1800*. Chicago: University of Chicago Press, 1960.

Rakove, Jack N. "Ambiguous Achievement: The Northwest Ordinance." In *The Northwest Ordinance*, edited by Frederick D. Williams, 1–20. Lansing: University of Michigan Press, 1989.

Read, Colin. *The Rising in Western Upper Canada, 1837–38: The Duncombe Revolt and After*. Toronto: University of Toronto Press, 1982.

Read, Colin, and Ronald J. Stagg. *The Rebellion of 1837 in Upper Canada: A Collection of Documents*. Ottawa: Carleton University Press, 1985.

Richardson, Maj. John. *Tecumseh and Richardson: The Story of a Trip to Walpole Island and Port Sarnia*. Toronto: Ontario Book Company, 1924.

Robertson, David. "Land Deal Sets Stage for New Canadian Territory." *The Northern Miner* 77.42 (December 23, 1991): 1–2.

Rogers, E. S. "Southeastern Ojibwa." In *Handbook of North American Indians, Vol. 15: Northeast*, edited by Bruce Trigger, 760–71. Washington DC: Smithsonian Institution, 1978.

Sampat-Mehta, R. *The Jay Treaty as It Affects North American Indians*. Ottawa: Beauregard Press, 1972.

Salway, Peter. *The Frontier People of Roman Britain*. London: Cambridge University Press, 1965.

Samek, Hana. *The Blackfoot Confederacy, 1880–1920: A Comparative Study of Canadian and U.S. Indian Policy*. Albuquerque: University of New Mexico Press, 1978.

Sault Ste. Marie Tribe of Chippewa Indians. "U.S. and Canadian Tribes Block International Bridge." *Win Awenen Nisitotung: He Who Understands* 14.4 (September 1992): 1.

Schmalz, Peter S. *The Ojibwa of Southern Ontario*. Toronto: University of Toronto Press, 1991.

Sealey, D. Bruce, and Antoine S. Lussier. *The Métis: Canada's Forgotten People*. Winnipeg: Pemmican, 1975.

Shattuck, Petra T., and Jill Norgren. *Partial Justice: Federal Indian Law in a Liberal Constitutional System*. New York: Berg, 1991.

Skinner, Alanson. *The Mascoutens or Prairie Potawatomi Indians*. Vol. 6. Bulletin of the Public Museum of the City of Milwaukee, 1924.

Slattery, Brian, and Sheila E. Stelck. *Canadian Native Law Cases*. Saskatoon: University of Saskatchewan Native Law Centre, 1987. In Dan Smith, *The Seventh Fire: The Struggle for Aboriginal Government*. Toronto: Key Porter, 1993.

Stone, Lyle M., and Donald Chaput. "History of the Upper Great Lakes Area." In *Handbook of North American Indians, Vol. 15: Northeast*, edited by Bruce Trigger, 602–9. Washington DC: Smithsonian Institution, 1978.

Sturm, John. "Farewell to the Swan Creek Chippewa." *Chronicle: The Quarterly Magazine of the Historical Society of Michigan* 21.2 (1985): 20–25.

Swanton, John R. *The Indian Tribes of North America*. Smithsonian Institution Bureau of Ethnology Bulletin #45. Washington DC: GPO, 1952.

Tanner, Helen Hornbeck, ed. *Atlas of Great Lakes Indian History*. Norman: University of Oklahoma Press, 1987.

Taylor, R. E., and Clement W. Meighan. *Chronologies in New World Archeology*. New York: Academic Press, 1978.

Taylor, Robert M., Jr., ed. *The Northwest Ordinance 1787: A Bicentennial Handbook*. Indianapolis: Indiana Historical Society, 1987.

Thelen, David. "Of Audiences, Borderlands, and Comparisons: Toward the Internationalization of American History." *Journal of American History* 79.2 (September 1992): 432–62.

Thwaites, Reuben, ed. "Saint-Lusson's Process Verbal." In *Collections of the State Historical Society of Wisconsin* 11 (1883): 26–29.

Trigger, Bruce. "Early Iroquoian Contacts with Europeans." In *Handbook of North American Indians, Vol. 15: Northeast*, edited by Bruce Trigger, 344–56. Washington DC: Smithsonian Institution, 1978.

Trigger, Bruce, ed. *Handbook of North American Indians, volume 15: North-east.* Washington DC: Smithsonian Institution, 1978.

Turner, Frederick Jackson. *The Significance of the Frontier in American History.* A paper read at the meeting of the American Historical Association in Chicago, July 12, 1893. Printed in the *Proceedings of the State Historical Society of Wisconsin.* Madison, 1893.

U.S. Census Bureau. *1990 Census of Population: General Population Characteristics: Michigan.* Washington DC: GPO, 1992.

Vizenor, Gerald, ed. *Summer in the Spring: Anishinaabe Lyric Poems and Stories.* Norman: University of Oklahoma Press, 1993.

Warner, Robert M., and Lois J. Grossbeck. "Historical report on the Sault Ste. Marie area." Indian Claims Commission Docket no. 18-F and 18-R, Plaintiff's exhibit v-42." In *American Indian Ethnohistory,* edited by David Agee Horr. New York: Garland, 1974.

Warren, William. *History of the Ojibway Nation.* Minneapolis: Ross and Haines, 1957.

Wawanosh, et. al. "D87: Joshua Wawanosh, Edward Ogeebegun, and Gordon Megezeez to Kanoodung, Maushkenoozha, Wannedegoosh, and John Kiya Ryley, St. Clair Mission, December 14, 1837." In Colin Read and Ronald J. Stagg, *The Rebellion of 1837 in Upper Canada: A Collection of Documents,* 326–27. Ottawa: Carleton University Press, 1985.

Wesley, Edgar B. "Frontier Defense." In the *Dictionary of American History, vol. 3.* New York: Charles Scribner's Sons, 1996.

White, Richard. "Frederick Jackson Turner and Buffalo Bill." In *The Frontier in American Culture,* edited by Richard White and James R. Grossman. Berkeley: University of California Press, 1994.

———. *The Middle Ground: Indians, Empires, and Republics in the Great Lakes Region, 1650–1815.* New York: Cambridge University Press, 1991.

Whittlesy, Charles. "The Ancient Miners of Lake Superior." In Roy W. Drier and Octave J. DuTemple, *Prehistoric Copper Mining in the Lake Superior Region: A Collection of Reference Articles* (paper 5). Calumet MI: privately printed, 1961.

Wightman, W. R. *Forever on the Fringe: Six Studies in the Development of Manitoulin Island.* Toronto: University of Toronto Press, 1982.

Wilkinson, Charles F. *American Indians, Time, and the Law: Native Societies in a Modern Constitutional Democracy.* New Haven: Yale University Press, 1987.

Winsor, Justin. "The Pageant of Saint Lusson, Sault Ste. Marie, 1671: A Commencement Address at the University of Michigan, June 30, 1892." Cambridge: John Wilson and Son University Press, 1892.

Wise, S. F. "The Indian Diplomacy of John Graves Simcoe." *Canadian Historical Association: Report of the Annual Meeting* (1953): 36–44.

Index

Fort Stanwix, Treaty of (1768), 42, 83

Fox War of 1712, 27

French and Indian Wars, 38, 39, 42. *See also* European-Native relations (British); European-Native relations (French); Paris, Treaty of (1763)

French-Native relations. *See* European-Native relations (French)

frontier, xviii–xxii; and borders, xx; and boundaries, xx–xxi; as "Divided Cultural Enclave," xxii–xxiv; as "empty areas" cultural landscape, xxii–xxiii, xxiv; population density of, xix, xx; and regional borderlands cultures, xxii. *See also* borderlands

Fryer, Mary, 96

fur trade, 4–5, 17–19; and effect on Native life, 17–18, 22–23, 29, 34; economic and social constraints on French, 22; and British presence in Great Lakes, 22, 64; as British revenue source, 42; Native people's continued control of, 34. *See also* European-Native relations (British); European-Native relations (French)

Garden River: as pan-Ojibway settlement, 105, 112–16; as partly U.S. territory, 148

Georgian Bay area, 84; Odawa migration to, 100

Ghent, Treaty of (1814), x, 61, 62; and U.S.-Canada border, 70, 136

gifts. *See* presents allotment (American); presents allotment (British-Canadian); presents allotment (French)

Gitshee Kawgaosh, 86

Goodman, Anthony, xxii

Greenberg, Adolph, 14

Greenville, Treaty of (1795), xvii, 51, 84; and conflict with Jay's Treaty, 56

Harmar, General, 49–50

Harper, Elijah, 144

Head, Sir Francis Bond, 87, 91; and Canadian residency requirement, 80–81; and elimination of presents allotment, 103; and end of Manitoulin Experiment, 111; and Manitoulin Island "removal" plan, 94, 96, 103–4; role of in 1837–38 rebellions, 94, 96

Hickerson, Harold, 12

History and Digest (Moore), 70

History of the Ojibway (Neill), 11

History of the Ojibway Nation (Warren), xxxv, 10–11

History of the Ottawa and Chippewa (Blackbird), 123

Hodge, Frederick Webb, 7

House, John, xxii

immigration. *See* migration (Anishnaabeg); migration to Canada

Indian Buffer State proposal, 54–55, M7

Indian Council of June (1816), 72

The Indians of Canada (Jenness), 10

Indian treaties, 90. *See also* treaties; treaty signatories; treaty signings; *and specific treaty by title*

Inter-Tribal Council, 140

Ironsides, George, 89; and Manitoulin Island, 108

Iroquois: conflict with French, 18–19;

land claims and territorial control
(*continued*)
  Northwest Ordinance; presents
    allotment (American); presents
    allotment (British-Canadian);
    presents allotment (French);
    Revolutionary War; *and individual*
    treaties by title
land tenure, 39–41
La Pointe, Treaty of (1854), 113
Limerick, Patricia, xix–xx
Little Crow (Sioux), 72–73
locations of tribes at contact, M5
locks (at Sault Ste. Marie), 133, 135
Louis Francis v. the Queen, 136–37
Lusson, Daumont de Saint, 4–5

Mackinac, Fort. *See* Fort Mackinac
Mackinac (Michilimackinac) Island:
  American threats to Native people
    passing, 68; British abandonment
    of, 61; British cession of, 63; as
    British post, 60–61; as French post,
    22, 26, 28; objections to American
    withdrawal from, 69; Ojibway land
    cession of, 83. *See also* fur trade
Maidysage, 73
Manitoulin Experiment, 94;
  "civilizing" effects of, 104–5; end
    of, 109–11; and removal policy, 102,
    103–5; Schoolcraft's view of, 104. *See*
    also Manitoulin Island
Manitoulin Island, 3, 108–11; 1838
  presents distribution at, 79, 80;
    "American" vs. "British" Indians
    on, 108–9; unceded territory of,
    110; as important Anishnaabeg
    center, 105; Native retention of
    east end of, 92; and Odawas, 2,
    8, 41, 77, 108; and Ojibways, 101,

108, 110; and Potawatomis, 110;
    religious denominationalism on,
    106–8; set aside for Native use,
    87; and Shingwauk's alliances, 74;
    Shingwauk's refusal to move to,
    105; and Treaty of 1836, 86–87, 91,
    101; and Treaty of 1862, 91. *See also*
    Manitoulin Experiment
Manitowaning (Manitoulin Island
  outpost), 108–9, 110; presents at, T2.
    See also Manitoulin Island
Maracle, Brian, 142
Marest, Father, 25
Marshall, Chief Justice John, 143
Mason, Michael, 141
Matchedash Bay, 84
McClurken, James, 100, 107
McComb, General, 65
McDonald, Lt. Col., 59, 60, 62
McGee, Harold, xxiv
McIntosh v. Johnson, 143
McKee, Superintendent-General
  Alexander, 97
McKinsey, Lauren, xxii–xxiv
Methodists, 106; on Manitoulin,
  107; at Garden River, 108. *See also*
    religious factionalism
Mica Bay, miners driven from, 88
Michigan land cession treaty (1836),
  73. *See also* Washington, Treaty of
    (1836)
Midé religion, xxxv
Midéwinin (Midé) teachings, 139–40
migration (Anishnaabeg), xxxiv–
  xxxvii, 101–8; scrolls, xxxv–xxxvi;
    Anishnaabeg record of, F1, 1, 12; in
    Upper Great Lakes during removal
    era, 101–8; from Canada to U.S.,
    111–12

migration to Canada, 111; before Monroe removal policy, 77; by Potawatomis, 97–99; by Odawas, 99–100; Anishnaabeg petitions for, 113

Minnehaha, Chief, 144

Miscouaky, 24–25

Mohawk reserve at St. Regis. *See* Akwesasne (Mohawk reserve)

Monroe, James, and 1825 removal policy, 77, 93

Moore, John Bassett, 70

Moravian Indians, 111

Morrison, James, 14

Native sovereignty, 141–44; in Canada, 141–42, 143, 144–45; and abrogation of indigenous rights, 143–45; and the "mini-state" model, 142; in Nunavut, 141–42; and principle of occupancy, 143; and self-rule, 142, 144–45; in United States, 141. *See also* Anishnaabeg, sovereignty; Jay('s) Treaty (1794); Native sovereignty

Native Studies (Price), 138

Nebenaigoching, 87, 89, 123

Nebenegwune, 89–90

Neill, Edward, 11

Neokema, 112

Nicolet, Jean, 2, 3–4, 7

Nishnawbe-Aski Nation, 140

North Shore Tribal Council, 140

Northwest Ordinance, 46–48; and Native opposition to U.S. expansion, 47–48; and policy of western development, 104

Ocaita, 62

Odawas, 9. *See also* Anishnaabeg

Ogista (Shingwalk, jun.), 67–68; as treaties signatory, 118

The Ojibwa of Southern Ontario (Schmalz), 2

Ojibways (Ojibwes), 10–13. *See also* Anishnaabeg

Old Copper cultural mosaic, xxxiii

Oshawano, as treaties signatory, 118–22

Ossagon, 115

Ottawas. *See* Odawas

Pageant of St. Lusson, 5

Papineau, Denis-Benjamin, 87

Paris, Second Treaty of (1783), 45–46; treatment of Native land in, 45; Native view of, 45, 46, 53; omission of "Indian Territory" in, 54

Paris, Treaty of (1763): and effects of French land cessions to British, 34

Parry Island, and Potawatomi immigrants, 98–99

Peace of 1667, 21

Peau de Chat, 159, 87, 89

Penetanguishene: and impetus for emigration to Canada, 77; and Anishnaabeg majority, 78–79

Perrot, Nicholas, 5

Perrot, Nicolas, 25

Pontiac, x, xvii, 37–38. *See also* Pontiac's "Conspiracy"

Pontiac's "Conspiracy," x, xvii, 37; lack of Native consensus for, 33; and French failure to support siege, 33; as final stage of "Beaver War," 34–35; continued resistance following end of, 37. *See also* Pontiac

Pontiac's rebellion. *See* Pontiac's "Conspiracy"

111; migration to U.S. from, 111
Saugeen Tract, land cession, 85
Sault Ste. Marie area, 21, 64–72;
    destruction of fishing resources
    at, 131, 133; as Great Lakes trading
    center, 21; indigenous loyalties
    in, 73; and land cession of 1820,
    85; and land cession of 1855, 132,
    133; land seizures in, 62; pressure
    on French fort at, 22; as site of
    Pageant of Saint Lusson, 21; U.S.-
    Native relations in, 71–72. See also
    fur trade
Schmalz, Peter, 2
Schoolcraft, Henry Rowe, 12, 43,
    108; and admonishment of Native
    travelers to Canada, 76; and
    fostering of U.S.-Native relations,
    70, 71; and presents distribution, 73;
    and revision of 1836 treaty, 100; and
    view of Manitoulin Experiment, 104
Schoolcraft, James, 86
self-government / self-determination.
    See Native sovereignty
Sessaba, 66
settlement patterns in the mid-
    1700s, 39–41, 146
Seventh Fire philosophy, 139. See also
    Midéwinin (Midé) teachings
Severn River, 84
Shawano, Charlie, 132–33
Shawano, Ed, 133
The Shawnee Prophet. See
    Tenskwatawa
Shewbeketone, 73
Shingabawassin, 73
Shingwalk, jun. See Ogista
Shingwauk (Shingwalk,
    Shingwaukonce), 59, 67, 68, 87,

89; absence from first American
    presents distribution, 73; as
    "Canadian" petition signer, 120;
    and cession of 1820, 73; and Garden
    River settlement plan, 105, 112,
    113; importance as Native leader,
    73, 106; and petition for U.S.
    Anishnaabeg to move to Canada,
    112; and religious sectarianism at
    Garden River, 108; residency of, 74;
    as treaties signatory, 118. See also
    Garden River
Shingwaukonce. See Shingwauk
    (Shingwalk, Shingwaukonce)
Shouapaw, 72
Sikassige, xxxiv–xxxv
Simcoe, John Graves, 54
Simcoe, Lake, 84
Skinner, Alonson, 7
smallpox, 31
smuggling. See border (Canada-U.S.)
sovereignty. See Native sovereignty
sovereignty-at-sufferance, 141
Sparrow (supreme court decision), 144
St. Clair, General, 50
St. George's Island. See Sugar Island
St. Joseph Island, 58, 60; land cession
    at, 84
St. Martin Islands, land cession of, 85
St. Mary's River: and boundary
    dispute, 70–71, 148, 86; destruction
    of fishing resources of, 131, 133;
    islands of, 144
St. Regis Reserve. See Akwesasne
    (Mohawk reserve)
Sugar Island: and boundary dispute,
    70–71, 86; as unceded Indian
    Territory, 147
Summer in the Spring (Vizenor), 13

Winners of the North American Indian Prose Award

Three Fires Unity: The Anishnaabeg of
the Lake Huron Borderlands
Phil Bellfy

Boarding School Seasons:
American Indian Families, 1900–1940
Brenda J. Child

Listening to Our Grandmothers' Stories:
The Bloomfield Academy for Chickasaw Females, 1852–1949
Amanda J. Cobb

Northern Athabascan Survival:
Women, Community, and the Future
Phyllis Ann Fast

Claiming Breath
Diane Glancy

Choctaw Nation: A Story of American Indian Resurgence
Valerie Lambert

They Called It Prairie Light:
The Story of Chilocco Indian School
K. Tsianina Lomawaima

Son of Two Bloods
Vincent L. Mendoza

All My Sins Are Relatives
W. S. Penn

Completing the Circle
Virginia Driving Hawk Sneve

Year in Nam: A Native American Soldier's Story
Leroy TeCube

To order or obtain more information on these or other
University of Nebraska Press titles, visit www.nebraskapress.unl.edu.

CPSIA information can be obtained
at www.ICGtesting.com
Printed in the USA
LVHW041706150819
627784LV00001B/50/P